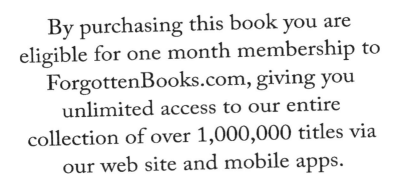

ISBN 978-0-260-05349-7
PIBN 10924710

Annual Report

of the
Librarian of Congress

*for the Fiscal Year
Ending June 30, 1973*

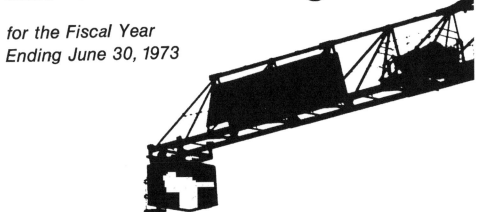

Library of Congress
Washington
1974

Library of Congress Catalog Card Number 6-6273

ISSN 0083-1565 *Key title:* Annual report of the Librarian of Congress

Illustrations on cover and throughout the report depict cranes on the construction site of the Library of Congress James Madison Memorial Building.

CONTENTS

Joint Committee on the Library, 93d Congress, 1st Session

Representative Lucien N. Nedzi, *Chairman*

Senator Howard W. Cannon, *Vice Chairman*

Members of the Committee: Senators Claiborne Pell, Harrison A. Williams, Jr., Marlow W. Cook, and Mark O. Hatfield; Representatives Samuel L. Devine, Wayne L. Hays, John Brademas and Orval Hansen. *Chief Clerk:* John L. Boos.

Library of Congress Trust Fund Board

An act of Congress, approved March 3, 1925, as amended, created the Library of Congress Trust Fund Board, a quasi-corporation with perpetual succession and all the usual powers of a trustee, including the power to "invest, reinvest, or retain investments" and, specifically, the authority "to accept, receive, hold, and administer such gifts, bequests, or devises of property for the benefit of, or in connection with, the Library, its collections, or its services, as may be approved by the Board and by the Joint Committee on the Library." (U.S.C. 2: 154-163)

A notable provision of the act (Section 2, last paragraph) permits endowment funds, up to a total limit of $10,000,000, to be treated as a perpetual loan to the United States Treasury, at an assured interest of four percent per annum.

Members of the Board on June 30, 1973: George P. Shultz, Secretary of the Treasury, *Chairman;* Representative Lucien N. Nedzi, Chairman of the Joint Committee on the Library; L. Quincy Mumford, Librarian of Congress, *Secretary;* and Mrs. Charles William Engelhard, Jr. *(term expires March 8, 1975).* Walter S. Gubelmann was appointed to the Board in October 1973. Mr. Gubelmann's term will expire on March 9, 1978.

Forms of Gifts or Bequests to the Library of Congress

OF MATERIAL

"To the United States of America, to be placed in the Library of Congress and administered therein by the authorities thereof."

OF MONEY FOR IMMEDIATE APPLICATION

General Gift: "To the United States of America, to be deposited with the Treasurer of the United States to the credit of the Library of Congress, subject to disbursement by the Librarian of Congress."

Specific Gift: "To the United States of America, to be deposited with the Treasurer of the United States to the credit of the Library of Congress, subject to disbursement by the Librarian of Congress in furtherance of [describe purpose which may be any specific purpose consistent with the general program of the Library of Congress]."

Example: Gift or bequest to the Library facsimile program—"To the United States of America, to be deposited with the Treasurer of the United States to the credit of the Library of Congress, subject to disbursement by the Librarian of Congress in furtherance of the Library facsimile program."

OF ENDOWMENTS OF MONEY, SECURITIES, OR OTHER PROPERTY

'To the Library of Congress Trust Fund Board, to be administered for the benefit of, or in connection with the Library of Congress, its collections, or its service."

NOTE.—Subject to Federal statutes and regulations, gifts, bequests, or devises to the United States for the benefit of the Library of Congress, including those to the Trust Fund Board, and any income therefrom, generally are exempt from Federal and District of Columbia taxes.

vi

OFFICERS OF THE LIBRARY

As of October 1, 1973

L. Quincy Mumford, Librarian of Congress
John G. Lorenz, Deputy Librarian of Congress
Elizabeth Hamer Kegan, Assistant Librarian of Congress

OFFICE OF THE LIBRARIAN

Jean Allaway, Administrative Officer, Permanent Committee for the Oliver Wendell Holmes Devise
Ernest C. Barker, Chief Internal Auditor
James H. Hutson, Coordinator, American Revolution Bicentennial Program
Thomas C. Brackeen, Coordinator, Equal Opportunity Office
Marlene D. Morrisey, Executive Assistant to the Librarian
(Vacant), Executive Secretary, Federal Library Committee, and Chairman, U.S. National Libraries Task Force on Automation and Other Cooperative Services
Herbert J. Sanborn, Exhibits Officer
John J. Kominski, General Counsel
Mary C. Lethbridge, Information Officer
Helen-Anne Hilker, Interpretive Projects Officer
Adoreen M. McCormick, Legislative Liaison Officer
Paul Vassallo, Director, National Serials Data Program
Sarah L. Wallace, Publications Officer
Gladys O. Fields, Special Assistant to the Librarian

ADMINISTRATIVE DEPARTMENT

Fred E. Croxton, Director
Howard A. Blancheri, Executive Officer
Frazer G. Poole, Coordinator of Building Planning
Paul R. Reimers, Coordinator of Information Systems
William R. Nugent, Assistant Coordinator of Information Systems
    Charlene A. Woody, Chief, Computer Applications Office
    Martin V. Hughes, Chief, Computer Service Center
    Theodore E. Leach, Chief, Systems Development and Standards Office
Charles G. LaHood, Jr., Chief, Photoduplication Service

Management Services

Arthur Yabroff, Assistant Director for Management Services

Buildings Management Office

Gerald T. Garvey, Chief

Central Services Division

Ida F. Wilson, Chief

Financial Management Office

Donald C. Curran, Chief
William C. Myers, Accounting Officer
John O. Hemperley, Budget Officer
Edwin M. Krintz, Disbursing Officer

Procurement and Supply Division

Floyd D. Hedrick, Chief

Personnel

Robert W. Hutchison, Assistant Director for Personnel
Eugene C. Powell, Jr., Assistant Personnel Director
Eugene Walton, Assistant Personnel Director for Equality Programs
Elizabeth W. Ridley, Employee Relations Officer
Hamilton B. Webb, Health Services Officer
Leon W. Seidner, Personnel Operations Officer
George E. Stringer, Personnel Security Officer
Robert L. Kuntzelman, Placement and Classification Officer
Harvey H. Joiner, Jr., Training Officer

Preservation

Frazer G. Poole, Assistant Director for Preservation
Matt T. Roberts, Binding Officer
Emmett G. Trainor, Collections Maintenance Officer
Lawrence S. Robinson, Preservation Microfilming Officer
John C. Williams, Research Officer
Peter Waters, Restoration Officer

CONGRESSIONAL RESEARCH SERVICE

Lester S. Jayson, Director
Norman Beckman, Deputy Director
Walter Kravitz, Acting Assistant Director
Charles A. Goodrum, Assistant Director
Basil T. Owens, Executive Officer
James W. Robinson, Coordinator of Research

American Law Division

Joseph E. Ross, Chief
Elizabeth Yadlosky, Assistant Chief
(Vacant), Assistant Chief

Congressional Reference Division

Elizabeth F. Stroup, Chief

Economics Division

John B. Henderson, Chief
Douglas N. Jones, Assistant Chief

Education and Public Welfare Division

William H. Robinson, Acting Chief

Environmental Policy Division

Wallace D. Bowman, Chief
Robert Wolf, Assistant Chief

Foreign Affairs Division

Charles R. Gellner, Chief
Warren R. Johnston, Assistant Chief

Government and General Research Division

Frederick L. Scott, Acting Chief

Library Services Division

Merwin C. Phelps, Chief
Frederick J. Rosenthal, Assistant Chief

Science Policy Research Division

Charles S. Sheldon II, Chief
Walter A. Hahn, Assistant Chief

Senior Specialists Division

Lester S. Jayson, Chief

COPYRIGHT OFFICE

Abe A. Goldman, Acting Register of Copyrights
(Vacant), Deputy Register of Copyrights
L. Clark Hamilton, Assistant Register of Copyrights
Abe A. Goldman, General Counsel
Rose V. Lembo, Administrative Officer

Cataloging Division

Leo J. Cooney, Chief
Adelia O. Heller, Assistant Chief

Examining Division

Richard E. Glasgow, Chief
Dorothy M. Schrader, Assistant Chief

Reference Division

Waldo H. Moore, Chief
Mark A. Lillis, Assistant Chief

Service Division

Cicily P. Osteen, Chief
(Vacant), Assistant Chief

LAW LIBRARY

Carleton W. Kenyon, Law Librarian
(Vacant), Associate Law Librarian

American-British Law Division

Marlene C. McGuirl, Chief
Robert L. Nay, Assistant Chief
Loretta A. Norris, Librarian, Anglo-American Law Reading Room

European Law Division

Edmund C. Jann, Chief
Ivan Sipkov, Assistant Chief

Far Eastern Law Division

Tao-tai Hsia, Chief

Hispanic Law Division

Rubens Medina, Chief

Near Eastern and African Law Division

Zuhair E. Jwaideh, Chief

PROCESSING DEPARTMENT

William J. Welsh, Director
Glen A. Zimmerman, Executive Officer
Thomas R. Barcus, Technical Officer
Grace E. Hall, Office Manager

MARC Development Office

Henriette D. Avram, Chief
Lucia J. Rather, Assistant Chief

National Union Catalog Publication Project

Johannes L. Dewton, Head
David A. Smith, Assistant Head

Technical Processes Research Office

(Vacant), Chief
John C. Rather, Specialist in Technical Processes Research

Office of the Assistant Director (Acquisitions and Overseas Operations)

Edmond L. Applebaum, Assistant Director
Mary Berghaus, Assistant to the Assistant Director

Exchange and Gift Division

Nathan R. Einhorn, Chief
Peter H. Bridge, Assistant Chief

Order Division

Robert C. Sullivan, Chief
Jennifer V. Magnus, Assistant Chief
Shirley B. Lebo, Principal Evaluations Officer

Overseas Operations Division

Frank M. McGowan, Chief
Peter J. de la Garza, Assistant to the Chief
Rodney G. Sarle, Field Director, Brazil
Alvin Moore, Jr., Field Director, East Africa
Eunice S. Gupta, Field Director, India
John C. Crawford, Field Director, Indonesia
Mary J. Marton, Field Director, Spain
Marion Schild, Field Director, Italy
Hisao Matsumoto, Field Director, Japan
Jerry R. James, Field Director, Pakistan, and Acting Field Director, Arab Republic of Egypt
Arnold J. Jacobius, Field Director, German Federal Republic

Selection Office

Jean B. Metz, Selection Officer
Donald W. Woolery, Assistant Selection Officer

Office of the Assistant Director (Cataloging)

C. Sumner Spalding, Assistant Director
Robert M. Hiatt, Staff Assistant to the Assistant Director

Cataloging Instruction Office

Edith Scott, Chief Instructor
Susan Aramayo, Deputy Chief Instructor

Decimal Classification Division

Benjamin A. Custer, Chief and Editor, *Dewey Decimal Classification*
Edna E. Van Syoc, Assistant Chief

Descriptive Cataloging Division

Elizabeth L. Tate, Chief
William R. Huntley, Assistant Chief
Paul W. Winkler, Principal Descriptive Cataloger
William A. Gosling, Project Manager, Cataloging in Publication

MARC Editorial Division

Barbara J. Roland, Chief
Margaret M. Patterson, Assistant Chief

Shared Cataloging Division

Nathalie P. Delougaz, Chief
Hugo W. Christiansen, Assistant Chief

Subject Cataloging Division

Edward J. Blume, Chief
David G. Remington, Assistant Chief
Eugene T. Frosio, Principal Subject Cataloger

Office of the Assistant Director (Processing Services)

Robert R. Holmes, Assistant Director
Paul M. Hibschman, Staff Assistant to the Assistant Director

Card Division

Paul E. Edlund, Chief
John J. Pizzo, Assistant Chief for Management
James L. Stevens, Assistant Chief for Operations
Constance Stevens, Head, Customer Services Section
Natalie Wells, Head, Publishers Liaison Section

Catalog Management Division

Barbara M. Westby, Chief
Patricia S. Hines, Assistant Chief

Catalog Publication Division

Gloria H. Hsia, Chief
Kay F. Wexler, Assistant Chief
Patrick S. Bérnard, Principal Editor

Serial Record Division

Joseph H. Howard, Chief
Robert D. Desmond, Assistant Chief

REFERENCE DEPARTMENT

Paul L. Berry, Director
Robert H. Land, Assistant Director for Bibiliographic and Reference Services
John Charles Finzi, Assistant Director for Library Resources
Edward A. D'Alessandro, Special Assistant for Planning Management
Jack McDonald, Jr., Administrative Officer

Division for the Blind and Physically Handicapped

Frank Kurt Cylke, Chief
Charles Gallozzi, Assistant Chief
Mary Jack Wintle, Assistant Chief for Acquisitions
James M. Hahn, Assistant Chief for Reader Services

Federal Research Division

William R. Dodge, Chief

General Reference and Bibliography Division

Robert H. Land, Chief
Edward N. MacConomy, Jr., Assistant Chief
Julian W. Witherell, Head, African Section
Ruth S. Freitag, Head, Bibliography and Reference Correspondence Section

Virginia Haviland, Head, Children's Book Section
George H. Caldwell, Head, Public Reference Section
Robert W. Schaaf, Head, Union Catalog and International Organizations Reference Section

Geography and Map Division

Walter W. Ristow, Chief
John A. Wolter, Assistant Chief
Donald A. Wise, Head, Acquisitions Section
David K. Carrington, Head, Processing Section
Richard W. Stephenson, Head, Reference and Bibliography Section

Latin American, Portuguese, and Spanish Division

Mary Ellis Kahler, Chief
Earl J. Pariseau, Assistant Chief
Donald E. J. Stewart, Editor, *Handbook of Latin American Studies*

Loan Division

Legare H. B. Obear, Chief
(Vacant), Assistant Chief
Thomas E. Gwinn, Head, Library Station in the Capitol

Manuscript Division

Roy P. Basler, Chief
John C. Broderick, Assistant Chief
John D. Knowlton, Head, Preparation Section, and Technical Officer
Carolyn H. Sung, Head, Reader Service Section

Music Division

Edward N. Waters, Chief
Donald L. Leavitt, Assistant Chief
Alan Jabbour, Head, Archive of Folk Song
(Vacant), Head, Recorded Sound Section
Robert B. Carneal, Chief Engineer, Recording Laboratory
William J. Lichtenwanger, Head, Reference Section

Orientalia Division

Warren M. Tsuneishi, Chief
Edwin G. Beal, Jr., Assistant Chief
K. T. Wu, Head, Chinese and Korean Section
Lawrence Marwick, Head, Hebraic Section
Andrew Y. Kuroda, Head, Japanese Section
George N. Atiyeh, Head, Near East Section
Louis A. Jacob, Head, Southern Asia Section

CONSULTANTS OF THE LIBRARY

CONSULTANT IN POETRY IN ENGLISH

Josephine Jacobsen (through June 15, 1973)
Daniel Hoffman (from September 10, 1973)

HONORARY CONSULTANTS

Aeronautics

Charles A. Lindbergh

American Cultural History

Arna Bontemps (died June 4, 1973)
Margaret Mead
Henry Nash Smith

American History

Julian P. Boyd
Henry S. Commager
Benjamin A. Quarles

American Letters

Gwendolyn Brooks
James Dickey
Josephine Jacobsen
Clare Booth Luce
Bernard Malamud
James A. Michener
William Jay Smith
William Stafford
Wallace Stegner
William Styron
John Updike

Domestic and International Copyright Affairs

Abraham L. Kaminstein

Early Printed Books

Frederick R. Goff

English Bibliography

Arthur A. Houghton, Jr.

Government Document Bibliography

James B. Childs

Graphic Arts and Cinema

Edgar Breitenbach

History of Canon Law and Roman Law

Stephan George Kuttner

Humanities

David C. Mearns

Journalism and Communications

William I. Nichols

Musicology

Harold Spivacke

Near Eastern Bibliography

Robert F. Ogden

Reference and Bibliography

John L. Nolan

Slavic Studies

Sergius Yakobson

Southeast Asian Bibliography

Cecil Hobbs

Walt Whitman Studies

Charles E. Feinberg

xii

LETTER OF TRANSMITTAL

The President of the Senate
The Speaker of the House of Representatives

SIRS:

As required by law, I have the honor to submit this report on the Library of Congress, including the Copyright Office, for the fiscal year ending June 30, 1973. It is accompanied by four issues of its supplement—the *Quarterly Journal of the Library of Congress*—and a copy of the annual report of the Library of Congress Trust Fund Board.

L. Quincy Mumford
Librarian of Congress

LIBRARY OF CONGRESS
Washington, D.C.

ORGANIZATION CHART

As of October 1, 1973

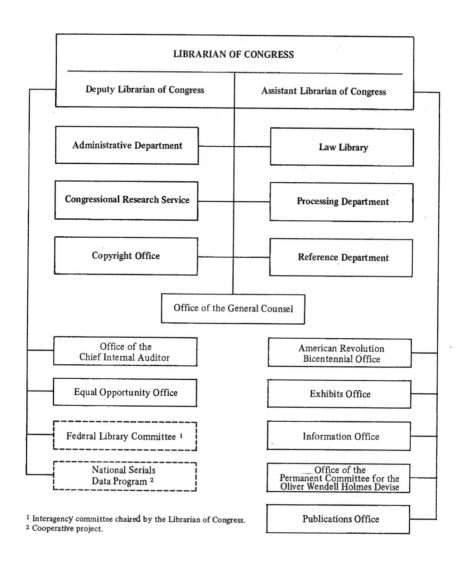

LIBRARIAN OF CONGRESS

Deputy Librarian of Congress | Assistant Librarian of Congress

Administrative Department | Law Library

Congressional Research Service | Processing Department

Copyright Office | Reference Department

Office of the General Counsel

Office of the Chief Internal Auditor | American Revolution Bicentennial Office

Equal Opportunity Office | Exhibits Office

Federal Library Committee [1] | Information Office

National Serials Data Program [2] | Office of the Permanent Committee for the Oliver Wendell Holmes Devise

Publications Office

[1] Interagency committee chaired by the Librarian of Congress.
[2] Cooperative project.

ADMINISTRATIVE DEPARTMENT

Office of the Director
Building Planning Office
Information Systems Office
Photoduplication Service

Assistant Director for Management Services
Buildings Management Office
Central Services Division
Financial Management Office
Procurement and Supply Division

Assistant Director for Personnel
Employee Relations Office
Health Services Office
Personnel Operations Office
Personnel Security Office
Placement and Classification Office
Training Office

Assistant Director for Preservation
Binding Office
Collections Maintenance Office
Preservation Microfilming Office
Preservation Research and Testing Office
Restoration Office

CONGRESSIONAL RESEARCH SERVICE

Office of the Director
American Law Division
Congressional Reference Division
Economics Division
Education and Public Welfare Division
Environmental Policy Division
Foreign Affairs Division
Government and General Research Division
Library Services Division
Science Policy Research Division
Senior Specialists Division

COPYRIGHT OFFICE

Office of the Register
Cataloging Division
Examining Division
Reference Division
Service Division

LAW LIBRARY

Office of the Law Librarian
American-British Law Division
European Law Division
Far Eastern Law Division
Hispanic Law Division
Near Eastern and African Law Division

PROCESSING DEPARTMENT

Office of the Director
MARC Development Office
National Union Catalog Publication Project
Technical Processes Research Office

Office of the Assistant Director (Acquisitions and Overseas Operations)
Exchange and Gift Division
Order Division
Overseas Operations Division
Selection Office

Office of the Assistant Director (Cataloging)
Cataloging Instruction Office
Decimal Classification Division
Descriptive Cataloging Division
MARC Editorial Division
Shared Cataloging Division
Subject Cataloging Division

Office of the Assistant Director (Processing Services)
Card Division
Catalog Management Division
Catalog Publication Division
Serial Record Division

REFERENCE DEPARTMENT

Office of the Director
Division for the Blind and Physically Handicapped
Federal Research Division
General Reference and Bibliography Division
Geography and Map Division
Latin American, Portuguese, and Spanish Division
Loan Division
Manuscript Division
Music Division
Orientalia Division
Prints and Photographs Division
Rare Book Division
Science and Technology Division
    National Referral Center for Science and Technology
Serial Division
Slavic and Central European Division
Stack and Reader Division

Early in calendar 1973, four cranes appeared on square 732, the plot of land south of the Library's Main Building, east of the Cannon House Office Building, and bounded by Independence Avenue, First, Second, and C Streets SE. They were joined a few months later by two taller brothers. Since then, the six have circled in a giant mechanical ballet, as the Library of Congress James Madison Memorial Building gradually forms around them.

Although dictionaries vary in their definition of a crane, they agree it is a device or machine for raising and lowering heavy weights and for transporting them horizontally for a limited distance. One definition is more specific, describing the device as having two motions, "one a direct lift and the other a horizontal movement . . . ."

Cranes are essential to the construction of the Library's third building. But different kinds of cranes are needed to build the *library*—the staff, the collections, the service—that the building will house. Obviously, the spate of materials pouring into the Library of Congress requires tremendous forces to direct it into proper channels for evaluation, processing, shelving, and transmittal to the waiting users. And the men and women who perform these many tasks also need the "direct lift" and the "horizontal movement," if they are to realize their potential, if they are to understand and communicate with their fellow workers and the publics that the Library serves. Unfortunately, there are no cranes of metal and pulleys and chains to direct the raw materials that make a library a purposeful, functional organization. But there are people, at all levels and in all divisions, who are supplying the needed physical force, the spiritual lift, and the horizontal flow of open communication. No sidewalk superintendents marvel at their performance, but some of their accomplishments are detailed in the chapters of this report.

In contemplating the gigantic tasks confronting the Library of Congress, the general tendency is to think of the number of acquisitions from all over the world coming daily to its doors. When one considers the people and processes involved in the operation, it is staggering and somewhat sobering to record the additions to the collection in a single year. In fiscal 1973, they totaled close to 1.8 million, bringing the Library's collections to 72.5 million pieces. Included in this figure were 16.5 million volumes and pamphlets, 31 million manuscripts, 3.5 million maps, 3.4 million volumes and pieces of music, 8.5 million photographic negatives, prints, and slides, 2.8 million talking books on discs, 1.2 million books in raised characters, and over a quarter million talking books on tape. The number of microforms is steadily growing; at the close of the fiscal year, the Library holdings had reached some 260,000 reels of newspapers on microfilm, 650,000 reels and strips of other materials on microfilm, 400,000 micro-opaques, and 900,000 microfiches. **Size of the collections**

Materials in the collections come to the Library from many sources. A noteworthy purchase of the past year, made possible by money contributed by an anonymous donor, was the collection of over 220 letters and cards written by **Gifts**

1

Sigmund Freud to Karl Abraham during the period from 1907 through 1926. All the Freud letters published in *A Psycho-Analytic Dialogue,* edited by Hilda Abraham and Ernest Freud (New York: Basic Books, 1965), are included, as well as some that have never been published.

Other generous donors helped to build the collections of the national library by presentations of materials. Gifts and deposits included additions to the papers of Senator Robert A. Taft, Branch Rickey, Ogden and Whitelaw Reid, Marcia Davenport, Ludwig Mies van der Rohe, and former Senator Clinton Anderson; to the NAACP papers; to the music manuscripts of Gene Gutché, Arne Oldberg, George Gershwin, Ernest Bloch, Victor Babin, and George Antheil. Other additions to existing collections included drawings by Howard Brodie of the court martial of Lt. William L. Calley, Jr., and a group of motion pictures produced between 1916 and 1934, presented by Paul Killiam.

New to the collections were the papers of Helen Traubel, Justice John M. Harlan (the first of that name), Edoardo Weiss, Herman Hollerith, Agnes E. Meyer, Goodman Ace, and Alma Gluck, as well as records of the proprietors of the locks and canals on the Connecticut River. Other welcome gifts were photographs by Arthur Rothstein, a 17th-century antiphonary, and a wood block and proof of an engraving by Leonard Baskin after an original work by Ben Shahn.

Exchanges
The Library also received a gift of 39 volumes covering various cultural topics from the National Library of Peking and reciprocated with a similar gift of 52 books and pamphlets. This exchange was significant because it was the first direct dealing by the Library with any Mainland Chinese institution since the United States severed diplomatic relations more than two decades ago. Later in the fiscal year, the Library received from the National Library of Peking a shipment of 237 items in 27 titles, including 202 volumes of a 1961 reprint of the extant volumes of the 15th-century compendium *Yung-lo ta tien* as well as a number of other scholarly works, some not yet available for purchase. The *Yung-lo ta tien* is a monumental encyclopedic dictionary that was compiled between 1403 and 1409 by order of Ch'eng-tsu, third emperor of the Ming Dynasty, who reigned under the title Yung-lo. From the State Public Library, Ulan-Bator, Mongolia, monographs and two serial publications were received; from the Library of Social Sciences in Hanoi, 161 monographs and monographic series plus 81 serial publications; and from the State Central Library, Pyongyang, North Korea, 33 monographs and 36 serial issues, printed in English.

National Program for Acquisitions and Cataloging
Other institutions as well as the Library benefit from the National Program for Acquisitions and Cataloging, which acquires publications of scholarly value on a worldwide basis and promptly distributes the cataloging data to other libraries. The fiscal 1973 appropriation for NPAC was $7,667,138, an increase of $385,138 over fiscal 1972. Although the increase covered the full-year costs of the statutory pay raise and provided some additional funds to cope with inflation and devaluation, it did not permit any expansion of the program. The funds were appropriated directly to the Library of Congress instead of being transferred from the Office of Education as in previous years.

The Library submitted the first annual evaluative report on NPAC to the appropriate congressional committees in accordance with section 232 of Public Law 92-318, the education amendments for 1972. This report was included in the transcript of hearings before the House Subcommittee on Legislative Branch Appropriations.

3

Before the demise of the Latin American Cooperative Acquisitions Program
(LACAP) early in 1973, the Library began efforts to ensure the uninterrupted   **Latin American**
acquisition of materials from this area. The end of LACAP will not affect the   **Cooperative**
present intensive NPAC regional acquisitions program in Brazil, which will continue   **Acquisitions Program**
to operate as it has for the past seven years.

From January 1, 1962, through June 30, 1973, the Library of Congress Special
Currency Program, known familiarly as the P.L. 480 Program, acquired over 17.3   **Public Law 480**
million items for American libraries. Within the first six months of calendar 1973,   **Program**
however, the Office of Management and Budget informed the Library that excess
currencies available for funding the programs in Sri Lanka, Israel, and Yugoslavia
were running out. Accordingly, the Tel Aviv office was closed in May 1973 and the
issue of the *Accessions List: Israel*, covering the month of April, was the final
number in this serial of 10 years' standing. From March 1964 through May 1973
the Public Law 480 office in Tel Aviv acquired and shipped more than 1.6 million
items to American research libraries, and an additional 46,000 monographs and
serials were distributed to the 300 participants in the English-language program
between 1965 and 1969. The Library will continue to process Israeli acquisitions.

To continue acquisitions of current Yugoslavian materials, the Library selected a
blanket-order and subscription agent who planned significant expansion of his
activities.

The program in Sri Lanka was terminated on June 30, 1973, but Public Law 480
coverage was succeeded in July by a cooperative acquisitions program supported by
17 libraries—California at Berkeley, Chicago, Cornell, Duke, Harvard, Illinois,
Michigan, Michigan State, Minnesota, Pennsylvania, Syracuse, Texas, Virginia,
Washington, Wisconsin, and Yale Universities and the Center for Research Libraries.
Participation in the program is open to any American library prepared to contribute
$500 annually for English-language publications only, $700 for English and Tamil
publications, or $2,000 for publications in English, Tamil, and Sinhalese. The New
Delhi office will continue to issue and distribute the *Accessions List: Sri Lanka*.

All libraries share with the Library of Congress the concern for cataloging and
processing incoming materials as rapidly as possible to make the information in
them available to users. Cataloging and the distribution of the resulting data
through publications, printed cards, and magnetic tape go on apace in the many
divisions of the Processing Department. But other avenues for distribution have
been opened and old methods improved. One of these is Cataloging in Publication.
Over 400 publishers were participating in this program at the close of fiscal 1973,   **Cataloging**
and between the inception of the program in July 1971 and the end of June 1973   **in Publication**
more than 18,000 titles had been processed. This figure included 850 titles coopera-
tively cataloged by the Library of Congress and the National Library of Medicine.
Weekly receipts averaged about 300 titles, representing approximately 55 percent
of the U.S. book trade production. This figure should increase to approximately 75
percent with the addition late in fiscal 1973 of many of the larger publishers. Funds
for CIP in the 1974 appropriations will allow expansion of the program to selected
government documents that are widely acquired and cataloged by libraries. This
action would in no way diminish the continuing emphasis on enlisting the remaining trade book publishers in the program.

Computers have long held the promise of answers to many library problems
concerning the organization, processing, storage, manipulation, and retrieval of
information. An early step in this direction was the development at the Library of

Congress of the MARC format. Future automation projects in technical processing depend on the implementation of the Multiple-Use MARC System (MUMS), which consists of three major components: task control, message control, and data management. At the close of the fiscal year, the final version of task control was operational, online terminal support had been completed, and implementation of batch support had begun. The first version of the data management programs for the storage and retrieval of bibliographic records by LC card number was operational and plans were under way for its integration with the rest of MUMS. Redesign of the MARC input system at the Library was the first application scheduled to function under MUMS in fiscal 1974.

Multiple-Use MARC System

Growth of the MARC data base has been creditable. At the end of fiscal 1973 it contained records for approximately 354,000 monograph titles, 11,000 films, and 22,000 single-sheet maps. Since February 1, 1973, serials in the roman alphabet that are cataloged for printed cards have also been input to the MARC system.

MARC data base

Use of the MARC data bases in various Library operations expanded. For example, the CIP Office was provided with a monthly listing of all CIP titles not yet converted to full cataloging. Other monthly searches were made for listings of titles on Central and Eastern Europe and on the People's Republic of China. One-time searches were made for children's literature translated from the Danish or Japanese, telecommunications, environmental economics, politics, economics, and foreign relations in the Caribbean area, and atlases published in 1972. The Reference Department handled the details of many of these runs.

The Card Division in September 1972 began the sale and distribution of MARC tapes for films and filmstrips cataloged by the Library and in June 1973 of tapes for French-language monographs and maps. In May, the division completed the computer programs necessary to print cards from the MARC-Map records. About 4,900 maps in this category are cataloged annually by the Library, and in fiscal 1973 the cataloging was available for the first time in both machine-readable and card form.

MARC tapes

On September 30, 1972, approximately 49,000 retrospective catalog records for 1968 were made available on tape for sale by the Card Division. Produced during the RECON Pilot Project, these records, with those issued through the MARC Distribution Service since its inception in April 1969, represent, in machine-readable form, the Library's English-language cataloging of monographs from 1968 to date.

Retrospective catalog records

Reports for the past several years have detailed progress in the mechanization of the Card Division. Since September 27, 1971, when the printing, slitting, and collating portion of the project became operational, more than 39 million catalog cards have been photocomposed, printed, and cut for distribution to subscribers and for LC use.

Automated card production

In the project to automate Order Division activities, two of the four tasks have been completed: the collection and printing of data for regular and new subscription orders and the creation of a permanent machine-readable file of these orders and use of the collected data for management information. The third task was in progress at the close of fiscal 1973. It will bring under control all records pertaining to purchase subscriptions. At its completion work will begin on the fourth and final task, fiscal control.

Automation of the Order Division

In applying computer aids to LC operations, effort was concentrated on increasing the capabilities of existing systems and implementing a number of systems using generalized online software. For the Congressional Research Service, new programs provided computerized page makeup of the subject index to the *Digest of Public General Bills and Resolutions*, a set of management information reports was developed to help in controlling the load of congressional inquiries, and a file of bibliographic citations to literature on current events was programed for display on video screens.

Computer-aided projects

For the Reference Department, an experimental book paging system was tested on one deck and, at the close of the fiscal year, was under evaluation for possible extension to other decks. Testing also began on a system developed to provide online input and retrieval of information regarding the status of materials being manufactured for blind and physically handicapped readers.

A system for the generation of catalog cards for copyright Class N (Sound Recordings), featuring online data collection and weekly production of new cards for the copyright card catalog, was implemented. This phase will make it possible in the future to prepare the *Catalog of Copyright Entries* in microform.

The generalized bibliographic system (BIBSYS) was used in preparing a bibliography of the Arab world and the Antarctic bibliography, as well as in the processing and publishing of current titles for the National Serials Data Program. A capability was developed for computer production of microfiche using standard LC print tapes as the source from which hard copy and microfiche could be produced simultaneously.

BIBSYS

Further expansion of the range of data sources available to CRS came in June 1973 when the Service began use of the *New York Times* Information Bank, a computerized index that provides immediate access to abstracts of all important articles appearing since 1970 in the *New York Times* and some 30 other publications. Retrieved by keywords from computerized records, the data is displayed on a CRT screen and can be reproduced in hard copy through an attached printer.

In addition to the direct support of LC and congressional activities, the Information Systems Office was actively engaged in planning the computer complex for the James Madison Memorial Building.

Behind all this activity to collect and to process is service to the scholar, to the researcher, to the reader. In the chapter on the Law Library it is pointed out that vast resources in the collections are of little avail if they are not accessible and that, frequently, the staff member must compile his own finding aids before he can pursue a problem. These aids are also made available to others. During the past fiscal year, the staffs of the Reference Department, including the Division for the Blind and Physically Handicapped, and the Law Library prepared some 133,000 bibliographic entries and compiled 238 bibliographies.

Reference and reader services

Readers used almost 2.25 million items from the collections in the Library and another quarter million were borrowed by Members of Congress, agencies of the government, libraries beyond the Washington area, and other authorized borrowers. Loans indicated that the subject of greatest concern to borrowers was social sciences, followed by language and literature, fiction, science, and history—in that order. Topping the congressional waiting list in number of requests was Halberstam's *The Best and the Brightest*, dealing with President John F. Kennedy and the individuals in his administration. Other popular nonfiction titles were *Dr. Atkins' Diet Revolution* and *The President and Congress*, by Fisher. In the fiction category, the leading titles dealt with politics, war, international intrigue, and an adventurous bird with the unlikely name of Jonathan Livingston Seagull.

Interlibrary loans

Libraries outside the Washington area received almost 31,000 items on interlibrary loan, requests coming from all 50 states, the Canal Zone, Puerto Rico, Guam, and the Virgin Islands. More and more foreign libraries used the American Library Association's interlibrary loan request form and gave evidence of having verified citations in locally owned sets of the *National Union Catalog: Pre-1956 Imprints*. Foreign libraries making the heaviest use of this service were located, in order, in Canada, West Germany, England, and Denmark, but requests were received from 41 countries. Use of the teletype in loan transactions is growing rapidly, almost doubling in four years.

For many years December was the busiest month of the year in the Library reading rooms, hosts of readers forsaking holly and mistletoe for reference and research in the LC collections. In 1972, however, it dropped to fourth place, and in 1973 to ninth. March, November, and April moved to the head of the list in number of call slips submitted, followed by October. June took last place.

Reader interests

Interests of the Library's users were as wide ranging as its collections. One does not have to seek far to discover the causes prompting queries on unconventional sources of energy, American Indians, women's rights, the origin of the word *watergate*, or presidential impeachment and resignation. The widespread participation in plans for observance of the Bicentennial of the nation's independence was the basis for a growing number of inquiries relating to the American Revolution—French participation in the war, the winter at Valley Forge, the origin of the name of the *Gaspee*, and Washington's Canadian spies are examples.

Individual studies, interests, and research lie behind such other questions as the kinds of wild animals found in the woods of England in the 15th century, representations of Hercules on Etruscan vases, the annual suicide rate in Italy and Paris from 1880 to 1905, the whereabouts of the manuscript of Napoleon's first abdication, women among the pioneer conservationists, rainfall patterns in Missouri, the earliest map naming the United States, Soviet publications on American Indians, the great Moscow fire of 1571, and Romanian attitudes toward minorities before and after World War II. Readers pursuing these subjects and many others submitted close to 1.2 million questions to various Library divisions in person, by letter, or by telephone. The telephone service area, incidentally, is widening, the General Reference and Bibliography Division reporting calls from Thailand and Australia during the year. The total figure for research and reference inquiries does not include the

Congressional inquiries

requests submitted to CRS, which handled over 181,000 inquiries from Members and committees of Congress.

Service to blind and physically handicapped readers

The number of blind and physically handicapped readers continued to grow, approaching 400,000 at the end of fiscal 1973. To help alleviate the staff and space demands upon regional libraries as the number of readers increased across the country, more states established subregional libraries. The total number of cooperating libraries reached approximately 125, of which 51 are regional libraries.

Since January 1973 all disc talking books have been recorded at 8 1/3 rpm and all cassette talking books ordered after June 30, 1973, will be recorded at 15/16 ips. The slower recording speeds allow twice as much material to be accommodated on each disc or cassette, making it possible, without additional funds, to increase the number of copies issued for each title selected. —

Chosen for an experimental test for the benefit of readers with sufficient vision to enjoy the illustrations, *Jonathan Livingston Seagull* was issued in a book-record combination, proving so popular that librarians have requested a reissue to enable them to meet demands. Ten titles were selected for testing prototypes of the new projected-book machines designed for persons with no manual dexterity but who do have eyesight. The titles included both fiction and nonfiction and were aimed specifically at veterans. The prototypes utilize a 16-mm film cassette with automatic advance and rewind and were evaluated for cost, ease of use, and design changes.

A cassette tape duplication workshop was held at the Division for the Blind and Physically Handicapped in January 1973. For the first time, regional and subregional librarians were instructed on the duplication of cassette books and the handling of master tapes from the selection of the book to the final copy and distribution.

In April 1973, service to talking-book readers in the District of Columbia was transferred from the division to the newly established Regional Library at the Martin Luther King Memorial Library of the District of Columbia.

Because it is the Library of Congress, an important LC function is to meet and to anticipate, if possible, the manifold needs of Members and committees of Congress for current information on a constantly expanding number of questions.

Beginning in January 1973, CRS provided each of the 46 congressional committees with a list of subjects and policy areas that the committee might want to pursue in depth during the 93d Congress and a list of programs and activities within the committee's jurisdiction that are scheduled to expire during the period. In addition, CRS was prepared to supply, upon request, a statement of the purpose and effect of any legislative proposal scheduled for committee hearings.

The Legislative Reorganization Act gave renewed emphasis to the need of committees for indepth analysis of legislative issues. Although CRS has always provided this type of assistance to Members and committees, since the enactment of the 1970 act it has allocated additional resources and developed new procedures to facilitate these requests.

In its seminars on public policy issues CRS held seven programs for Members and three programs for congressional staff. In January 1973 the Service officially opened its second reference center in a congressional office building. The new center—in the Russell Senate Office Building—answered more than 3,000 inquiries in its first six months.

Librarians are sometimes credited with an almost fanatical obsession for the care of the materials in their custody. What is not always understood is that their solicitude arises from a concern for the needs of the reader. In other words, to make them useful to many generations, books and other materials must be preserved and protected. This activity has been of paramount concern to many librarians, scholars, and researchers during the past year.

When Hurricane Agnes stormed through eastern United States in June 1972, she left behind a sorry trail of sodden, mud-laden libraries, historical societies, and similar organizations. She also left painful evidence of the need for coordinating the technical aspects of treating flood-damaged library materials. Accordingly, with the assistance of a grant from the National Endowment for the Arts, the Preservation Office sponsored a meeting of conservators and scientists at the Library of Congress on August 3, 1972, to plan a research program aimed at some of the problems involved in the salvage of such materials. As an outgrowth of this meeting, the Preservation Research and Testing Office began an investigation of various methods for drying water-damaged items and the identification of optimum techniques for

Service to
Congress

Preservation
of
library materials

Studies on
salvage of
water-damaged items

8 REPORT OF THE LIBRARIAN OF CONGRESS, 1973

their salvage. The laboratory has also been involved in a long-range full-scale evaluation of currently used or proposed deacidification techniques.

In a search for improved means of protecting or supporting fragile documents without resorting to lamination, the Restoration Office undertook investigations with a variety of plastic films. Several promising new techniques were developed and are in the process of evaluation and testing. During the last half of the fiscal year, the Restoration Office inaugurated a series of indepth surveys aimed at identifying materials in the Library's special collections that need conservation treatment. The surveys will result in a series of comprehensive reports listing the various segments or special groups and an estimate of the staff and funds needed to accomplish the task.

Throughout this report the reader will come upon evidences of increased concentration on establishing opportunities for training and for advancement, on better communication. These activities are part of the direct lift and the horizontal movement that are as important in molding a staff as in erecting a building.

Allegations of racial discrimination

Charges of alleged racial discrimination made against the Library by a personal member of the American Library Association at its annual conference in Dallas in June 1971 and the association's subsequent acceptance at the 1972 midwinter meeting of the statement of an ALA factfinding team have been recounted in previous reports. In accepting the statement, the association asked for a further study of action on the team's recommendations, the findings to be presented at the 1973 midwinter meeting at the latest. Accordingly, when the group met in Washington, January 28-February 3, 1973, Robert Wedgeworth, ALA executive director, listing progress on each recommendation and concluding that the group assigned to this task considered "its responsibilities for the original complaint relieved . . . ," requested that the file be closed. On motion from the floor, the association asked that more information be obtained about the Library's affirmative action programs. Accordingly, five members of the American Library Association, accompanied by Mr. Wedgeworth, visited the Library on June 5, 6, and 7, 1973, to be briefed on developments in this area. Their report, however, was deferred by the ALA conference in June at Las Vegas.

Affirmative action

On February 23, 1973, with my approval of the Equal Employment Opportunity Plan of Affirmative Action for fiscal year 1973, the Library's affirmative action programs were launched. Developed in cooperation with the Equal Opportunity Office and staff groups, the plan outlined action in 13 categories of personnel administration, training, counseling, recruitment, communication, complaints, incentive awards, and similar areas. Responsibility for action on individual items was assigned to specific offices or officers.

Equality programs

With funds provided in the Supplemental Appropriations Act for fiscal 1973, the position of assistant director of personnel for equality programs was established and assigned primary responsibility for developing and coordinating affirmative action programs. Eugene Walton was appointed to this position on April 23. The Equal Employment Opportunity Act of 1972, under which the Library's program operates, requires the development of an annual Affirmative Action Plan and semiannual reports on its progress. Among continuing functions that must support the plan are training and education for upward mobility of employees, establishment and maintenance of effective communication between managers, supervisors, and employees, employee counseling, creation of career ladders, and review and improvement of testing procedures.

The supplemental appropriation of $150,000 to the Library to implement pro-
visions of the Equal Employment Opportunity Act of 1972 aided the expansion of   Equal opportunity
training, recruitment, and counseling programs, and at the same time established a
core of permanent full-time positions to staff the Equal Opportunity Office. The
primary aim of the expanded counseling and training programs has been the creation of additional opportunities for staff members to develop their capabilities and,
as a result, advance in grade, responsibility, and achievement. Of the 73 complaints
resolved during the fiscal year, all but four were resolved by a counselor, an officer,
or the coordinator. In fact, three-fourths were settled satisfactorily at the first level.
    After the selection of officers and counselors, the first objective of the program
was their training in equal opportunity activities. In addition, the staff of the Equal
Opportunity Office took courses in such subjects as personnel management for
EEO specialists, advanced EEO counseling, affirmative action plans, upward
mobility programs, and women's programs.
    Just before the close of fiscal year 1972, I issued a Special Announcement asking
departments and divisions to work with me in establishing ad hoc Human Relations   Human relations
Committees in each of the six departments and the Office of the Librarian. Each
committee was asked to send a delegate to the Human Relations Council, which
would be representative of the entire Library and which would consider topics of
general staff concern. By the close of fiscal 1973 committees had been established
in each department, the council was formed, and the various groups have considered a variety of problems in this formative year, among them training, promotions, career development with emphasis on upward mobility, and improvement of
communication channels.
    The users of any library will demand growing collections, want new services and
programs, require more staff to satisfy their requests; the inevitable concomitant of
a successful library, therefore, is the need for additional space. The effort to
balance requirements with available space has furrowed many a brow at the Library
while anxious eyes watch the progress of construction across the street.
    Despite the adverse weather conditions and strikes that slowed the work on the
James Madison Memorial Building during the first half of the fiscal year, good   Third building
progress was made in the overall planning. In January 1973, Phase I—the foundation work—had been completed. The contract for Phase II, quarrying and fabrication of the exterior marble and granite, was awarded in December 1971 and over
50 percent of the stone had been delivered to a Washington storage yard by the
close of fiscal 1973. Phase III covers construction of the shell of the building and
placement of the exterior marble. The contract was awarded in December 1972 but
work did not begin until January 1973. Meanwhile, the task of checking the
drawings and specifications for the final phase was under way. The Building Planning Office developed final furniture layouts and installed model offices and
reading rooms in a test area at the Library's Pickett Street Annex in Virginia, where
two 24-foot long, double-faced ranges of compact bookstacks were also installed
for testing. The design of the stacks, developed by the Building Planning staff,
incorporates some features not available in existing models.
    Of as great importance to libraries as buildings is the money on which to operate.
Public Law 92-342, which made appropriations to the legislative branch for fiscal   Appropriations,
1973, allowed $78,291,450 in direct appropriations to the Library of Congress. The   fiscal 1973
act provided 32 additional positions in the Administrative, Processing, and Reference Departments and the Law Library, 18 in the Copyright Office for the opera-

tion of the new registration system for sound recordings, 86 in the Congressional Research Service, and four in the Division for the Blind and Physically Handicapped. The sum of $120,000 was appropriated to enable CRS to assist the Parliamentarian of the House of Representatives to revise and update Hinds' and Cannon's *Precedents*. For furniture and equipment in the James Madison Memorial Building, $4 million was allowed and for recurring furniture and equipment needs, $435,000. An additional sum of $1,531,400 was appropriated to the Architect of the Capitol for Library buildings and grounds. Included in this amount are funds for an architectural and engineering study of the Coolidge Auditorium.

Two supplemental appropriations—the first supplying funds for the implementation of the provisions of the Equal Employment Opportunity Act of 1972 and for increased telephone and postage rates, the second for increased pay costs—brought the amount appropriated directly to the Library for fiscal 1973 to a total of $79,104,450.

Through the sale of printed cards and technical publications, applied copyright fees, and other sources, the Library deposited $9,191,000 in the miscellaneous receipts of the U.S. Treasury, 11.6 percent of the direct appropriations to the Library for fiscal 1973.

Appropriations, fiscal 1974

The Legislative Branch Appropriations Act for fiscal 1974, signed by the President on November 1, 1973, made direct appropriations to the Library totaling $82,371,150. Under Salaries and Expenses, Library of Congress, 96 new positions were allowed, including nine for the National Serials Data Program. The Congress also concurred in the Librarian's request to convert 138 indefinite positions to permanent status. The sum authorized for the Congressional Research Service included funds for the third step in the five-year program to build up its resources to meet the expanded responsibilities imposed by the Legislative Reorganization Act of 1970. Included were 94 new CRS positions. The sum of $82,500 was authorized to develop a blueprint and lay the foundations for a national bibliographic service for the blind and physically handicapped, and another $50,000 was allowed to establish two multi-state storage and distribution centers. The act also included $132,000 for the revision of Hinds' and Cannon's *Precedents* and $29,000 for the revision of the *Constitution of the United States—Analysis and Interpretation*, commonly called the *Constitution Annotated*. For structure and mechanical care of the Library buildings and grounds $1,593,800 was appropriated to the Architect of the Capitol and $196,000 was reappropriated.

Amendments to Tax Reform Act of 1969

Hearings before the Committee on Ways and Means were held in the House of Representatives with respect to legislation to reform the Internal Revenue Code of 1954, as amended. Representatives of authors' and musicians' groups, libraries, museums, and similar institutions testified or filed statements in behalf of an amendment to the Tax Reform Act of 1969, and numerous bills were introduced during the 93d Congress, first session, to provide for a tax deduction for donors of self-generated manuscripts of literary, musical, and historic value. These provisions ranged from a deduction of 50 percent to 100 percent of the fair market value. Certain bills extended the deduction to public officials and others provided that any manuscripts they produced while in the employ of federal, state, or local governments would be excluded from the charitable-contribution provisions.

Copyright legislation

March 26, 1973, was an active day for copyright legislation. Senator John L. McClellan, chairman of the Senate Subcommittee on Patents, Trademarks, and Copyrights, introduced three bills. The first was S. 1361, a bill for general revision of the copyright law. Except for effective dates, it was identical to S. 644 in the 92d Congress. Senator McClellan announced that, in response to requests, the subcommittee would hold supplementary hearings on selected issues, including library photocopying, a general exemption for educational purposes, the cable television royalty schedule, application of cable TV provisions to sporting events, and special exemptions for religious music.

On the same day, at the request of the Authors League of America, Senator McClellan introduced S. 1359, a bill to amend the present copyright law to preclude a foreign country from taking over the rights of its authors to U.S. copyright. Similar bills were introduced in the House of Representatives—H.R. 6214 by Representative Jonathan B. Bingham on March 28, 1973, and H.R. 6418 by Representative Mario Biaggi on April 2, 1973.

The third bill, S. 1360, contained a section that would provide a remedy for delays in the delivery of material to the Copyright Office, if they resulted from a general disruption or suspension of postal or other transportation or communications services.

Other legislation relating to copyright is discussed in chapter 6 of this report.

On the international copyright scene, several important actions developed. Ratification by the United States of the Universal Copyright Convention as revised at Paris on July 24, 1971, was approved by the Senate on August 14, 1972, and by the President on August 28. The United States on September 18, 1972, became the fourth country to deposit with UNESCO its instrument of accession to the revised UCC, the United Kingdom, France, and Hungary having already done so. The adherence of 12 countries is required before the 1971 revised convention can come into force. On February 27, 1973, the Soviet Union deposited its instrument of adherence to the 1952 version of the UCC, effective May 27, 1973. It thus became the 64th member of the 1952 convention, which came into force on September 16, 1955. Since the convention does not apply retroactively, Soviet adherence does not affect works published before that date. On April 11, 1973, the President transmitted to the Senate, for ratification, the convention concluded at Geneva on October 29, 1971, protecting producers of sound recordings against unauthorized duplication of their products. Countries adhering to the convention would provide international protection against the making or importation of unauthorized duplicates of sound recordings for public distribution. The President's message to the Senate recommended favorable consideration.

International copyright developments

The Federal Advisory Committee Act, signed into law by the President on October 6, 1972, concerned committees, boards, and similar bodies established to advise officers and agencies in the executive branch. Among other provisions, the act directed that the Library of Congress receive a copy of the charter of each new advisory committee, as well as copies of the reports of every advisory committee and, when appropriate, background papers prepared by consultants. At present, the reports are available to the public in the Special Format Collection of the Library's Stack and Reader Division.

Federal Advisory Committee Act

Established in 1965 by the Library of Congress and the Office of Management and Budget, the Federal Library Committee has as its purpose the concentration of the intellectual resources present in the federal library and library-related information community on:

Federal Library Committee

better utilization of library resources and facilities

more effective planning, development, and operation
of federal libraries
optimum exchange of experience, skill, and resources

A comprehensive review during the past year of the membership, functions, and structure of the committee resulted in a reorganization. Effective July 1, 1973, the permanent members of the Federal Library Committee became the Librarian of Congress, the director of the National Agricultural Library, the director of the National Library of Medicine, and representatives from each of the other executive departments, the Atomic Energy Commission, the National Aeronautics and Space Administration, the National Science Foundation, the Smithsonian Institution, the Supreme Court of the United States, the United States Information Agency, the Veterans Administration, and the Office of Presidential Libraries of the National Archives and Records Service. Six members are selected on a rotating basis by the permanent members of the committee from independent agencies, boards, committees, and commissions. Rotating members serve two-year terms. Ten regional members, also on a rotating basis, are selected by the permanent members of the committee to represent federal libraries following the geographic pattern developed by the federal regional councils. These rotating regional members also serve two-year terms and are voting members. In addition to the permanent representative from the Department of Defense, one nonvoting member is selected from the U.S. Army, one from the U.S. Navy, and one from the U.S. Air Force. These service members, who serve for two years, are selected by the DOD member from a slate provided by the Federal Library Committee. A representative of the Office of Management and Budget, designated by the director of that office, and others appointed by the chairman meet with the committee as observers. These changes increased the Federal Library Committee from 23 to 40 members.

On June 29, 1973, the Federal Library Committee contracted with the Ohio College Library Center to experiment with connecting the OCLC data base and existing support systems to a national automated telecommunications system to provide federal libraries using the service with online access to the OCLC data base through local phone connections as well as online cataloging data and printed catalog cards in individualized formats. It is anticipated that approximately 25 federal libraries will participate when the system becomes operational.

In October 1972 the FLC Public Relations Task Force issued a manual, *Guidelines for Preparing Library Handbooks*. The Task Force recognized that users of the *Guidelines* might wish to see illustrations of the points emphasized in the text and, for this purpose, assembled packets of selected library handbooks. Available on loan for a period of four weeks from the FLC office, each packet contains eight handbooks chosen to exemplify both excellence of presentation and the wide range of options open to the librarian planning a user's guide. The qualities that led to the inclusion of each handbook in the sample are briefly noted.

Three projects developed by the U.S. National Libraries Task Force on Cooperative Activities were approved by the Librarian of Congress and the directors of the National Library of Medicine and the National Agricultural Library. The first was to increase and maintain staff awareness of automation activities. To this end, each library held a seminar for staff members at the policy and technical levels to identify areas for cooperation or coordinated activity. Second, the development of a standard order form was undertaken by a committee of members of the three libraries under the chairmanship of Mrs. Jennifer Magnus. A draft form was sub-

U.S. National Libraries
Task Force on
Cooperative Activities

mitted to the Acquisitions Section of the ALA Resources and Technical Services Division at the annual conference in June. Third, a survey of subscription agencies and their services was undertaken by William Katz, School of Library Science, State University of New York, Albany. He developed a checklist of service requirements and a mechanism for ensuring dealer compliance, submitting a report of his findings and recommendations, which was under review at the close of the fiscal year.

The National Serials Data Program, which became fully operational in January 1973, functions as the U.S. national center in an international effort to achieve standardized bibliographic control of serial publications. Under the program, a serials data base is being established as a computer file, with initial input received as current cataloging from the Library of Congress, the National Agricultural Library, and the National Library of Medicine at a rate of some 14,000 titles per year. Each serial is assigned an International Standard Serial Number (ISSN), key title, and other data elements needed to provide unique identification.

National Serials Data Program

Printed and machine-readable products generated from the file are circulated to the three national libraries and will eventually be available to the American library community. In addition, copies of the title page and cover for each serial title are recorded on a microfilm aperture card, which serves both as a means of verifying information in the data base and, since copies of the card are made available to other libraries, as an important information source in its own right.

The NSDP is also establishing a corporate entry authority file, following the Anglo-American Cataloging Code. The file, which includes the form of entry used by NSDP for any issuing body associated with a serial publication as well as the forms of entry used by the three national libraries, is designed to:

document the form of name used by NSDP
ensure accuracy and uniformity in the use of any name added to the NSDP data base
give variant forms of authors' names, tracing the necessary cross-references and indicating the sources used for this information
record the necessary history of reorganizations and changes of name for an author, tracing the appropriate cross-references and citing the source for this information
list the form of name used by any of the three national libraries, when different from that chosen by NSDP
register the ISSN for those titles with which an author is associated

Another NSDP responsibility involves the establishment of a file containing general statements of the serial holdings of the three national libraries, based on reports submitted by the libraries.

All NSDP products must conform to established national and international standards, a requirement that results in a considerable amount of effort in building the files since the reporting libraries have followed a variety of recording practices. Standardization of serials data elements by NSDP and their entry into a machine-readable file will thus have far-reaching benefits not only for the three national libraries but for the U.S. and international library and information services communities as well.

Probably one of the most festive events to take place at the Library for many a year was the celebration of Lessing J. Rosenwald's 82d birthday and commemoration of the 30th anniversary of his first gift to the Library. No reader of the

Rosenwald anniversary

Librarian's annual report, the *Quarterly Journal of the Library of Congress*, or the Library's *Information Bulletin* can be ignorant of this noted bibliophile's enrichment of the collections of the nation's library. When Mr. Rosenwald gave 500 superb books to the Library in 1943, he made his intention to add to the collection a happy provision of his gift. Accordingly, the catalog of the Lessing J. Rosenwald Collection published in 1954 listed 1,267 rare books and manuscripts and approximately 300 reference books selected from a far larger total. The transfer of 700 rare volumes in June 1964 was one of the great milestones in the growth of the collection and was marked by, among other things, a special issue of the *Quarterly Journal* in July 1965. A catalog of the entire collection with additions to January 1973 is now in preparation and will contain over 2,650 entries, including a small selection of reference books.

For the double observance, the Library mounted a special exhibit of 82 outstanding books and manuscripts selected from the Rosenwald Collection. The difficulties of making the final choices will be apparent to anyone knowing the magnificence of the whole.

Transparent plastic cradles, fabricated in the Library's Restoration Office, made it possible for the viewer to see both the binding and the opened pages of the books displayed. Visitors on opening night had the further pleasure of touring the exhibition and hearing the captions amplified by the collector himself, by Frederick R. Goff, former chief of the Rare Book Division, and by William Matheson, the present chief. On that night, the Library's Great Hall was fitted out with candlelit, flower-bedecked dining tables, and the guests joined in tributes to the man whose love and pursuit of fine books and manuscripts have given not only his contemporaries, but also coming generations, a priceless source of beauty, inner satisfaction, learning, and continuing research. The exhibition continued until August 31, 1973, affording an opportunity for visitors to the Library throughout the tourist season to see the Treasures From the Lessing J. Rosenwald Collection.

Exhibits

Among other popular exhibits was Recent Major Photographic Acquisitions, which included works by Toni Frissell and Arthur Rothstein, a selection of photographs from the *Look* magazine collection, and enlarged reproductions of the six rare early daguerreotypes of the Capitol, White House, Patent Office, and other buildings believed to have been taken by John Plumbe in the 1840's. Another photographic exhibit, which opened in January 1973, displayed the work of Alfred Cheney Johnston, who for 20 years specialized in portraits of stage and motion picture stars. During the 1920's he was the official photographer for the Ziegfeld Follies. Among the personalities whose portraits appeared in the exhibit were Barbara Stanwyck, Tyrone Power, Mary Astor, Ruby Keeler, Corinne Griffith, and Dolores Costello.

The White House News Photographers Association's annual exhibition, its 30th, with its intimate shots of the President and his family and associates, Washington scenes, and political figures and events, was as popular with Library visitors as its predecessors. The wealth of materials shown and the breadth of subjects represented in the Library showcase exhibits and in the various divisional displays held during the year are reflected in the appendix on exhibits. Six traveling exhibitions were prepared and circulated by the Library from coast to coast. These exhibits were: Preservation Through Documentation, on the work of the Historic American Buildings Survey; Papermaking: Art and Craft; the 22d National Exhibition of Prints; Contemporary Photographs From Sweden; Born of the Hops, late 19th-

century beer posters; and The Performing Arts in 19th-Century America, items
relating to the theater from the 1820's to the 1890's. Also, during the year 45
libraries, museums, and other institutions borrowed a total of 823 items for use in
their own displays.

The Library's literary and musical programs have an enthusiastic and faithful
following. A new program in observance of the bicentennial of the nation's
independence bids fair to establish its own equally enthusiastic constituency. One
of the outstanding features is a series of symposia. The second in the series,
"Fundamental Testaments of the American Revolution," was held on May 10 and
11, 1973. In opening the session, Julian P. Boyd, editor of *The Papers of Thomas
Jefferson* and moderator of the symposium, told his audience:

Symposium
on the
Bicentennial of the
American Revolution

> It has often been observed that, while the origins of other nations are lost in the dim mists of
> antiquity, our beginnings can be traced almost day by day in the resolves, petitions, and
> legislative records of committees of safety, colonial conventions, and the Continental Congress,
> on whose faithful secretary, Charles Thomson, was bestowed a privilege never before granted to
> any mortal—that of recording the birth pangs of a new nation. The papers presented at this
> second symposium will focus our attention on only four peaks of this vast Himalayan range of
> records in which the Declaration of Independence towers like Mount Everest above all others.

The peaks chosen for this two-day session on the fundamental testaments were
Common Sense, the Declaration of Independence, the Articles of Confederation,
and the Paris Peace Treaty. The discussions of the four documents were presented
by Bernard Bailyn of Harvard University, Cecelia Kenyon of Smith College, Merrill
Jensen of the University of Wisconsin, and Richard B. Morris of Columbia University. The final paper, "The Fundamental Testaments Today," was delivered by
former U.N. Ambassador J. Russell Wiggins. The papers were published by the
Library in December 1973.

The first symposium, "The Development of a Revolutionary Mentality," was held
in May 1972. Topics of subsequent symposia, chosen by the Advisory Committee
on the Library of Congress American Revolution Bicentennial Program, are leadership in the American Revolution, the impact of the Revolution abroad, and the
uncompleted Revolution. The series, which is made possible through a grant from
The Morris and Gwendolyn Cafritz Foundation, has been awarded the "Official
Recognition" certificate of the American Revolution Bicentennial Commission as
well as the commission's banner.

One of the Library's contributions to the observance of the Bicentennial was
among four LC titles that won awards in the Federal Editors Association's annual
contest for outstanding government publications. A first place was taken by *The
Development of a Revolutionary Mentality*, the papers presented at the Library's
first symposium on the American Revolution. Another first place went to the
October 1972 issue of the *Quarterly Journal of the Library of Congress*. Since
1966, the FEA has awarded the *Quarterly Journal* five first places, one second
place, one honorable mention, and one best of show. The other two publications
distinguished in this year's event were *A la Carte*, which was given an honorable
mention, and a folder for the Division for the Blind and Physically Handicapped,
which placed second in its class. A slide presentation on the Card Division, prepared
by Helen-Anne Hilker, the Library's interpretive projects officer, won first place in
the audiovisual category.

Federal Editors
Association awards

The lead article in the October 1972 *Quarterly Journal*, "Monument to Civilization; Diary of a Building," by Miss Hilker, received honorable mention in a contest sponsored by the Society for Technical Communication.

In April 1973 the *Quarterly Journal* marked the 10th anniversary of the

Special issue of the Quarterly Journal Children's Book Section with a special issue that contained a lead article by Erik Haugaard, the well-known author of children's books and translator of the stories of Hans Christian Andersen. With illustrations reproduced from editions dating from 1780 to 1966 and an introduction by Virginia Haviland, head of the section, "Who Killed Cock Robin?" recalls the courtship, marriage, and sad end of that unforgettable bird. An article by Duncan Emrich on children's folklore in the Archive of Folk Song, one by Treva Turner on LC cataloging of children's materials, and one by Catherine B. Wires on books for blind and physically handicapped children completed the issue.

Monographs Among other titles published during the year were *Spanish-Speaking Africa* and *French-Speaking Central Africa;* facsimiles of the first page of Genesis from the Library's copy of the Gutenberg Bible and Captain John Smith's map of Virginia; a catalog, *The Wide World of Children's Books,* and another of the collection of Angelo Rizzuto's photographs of New York City; a supplement to *Children's Literature; a Guide to Reference Sources* and a guide to the collections and services of the Music Division. Another Bicentennial publication issued during the year was *Creating Independence, 1763-1789,* an annotated list of background reading for young people, compiled by Margaret N. Coughlan, with an introduction by historian Richard B. Morris.

Presidential papers Early in the fiscal year the six-volume *Index to the William Howard Taft Papers* was published, a necessary guide to the 658-reel microfilm edition of the collection, and the three-volume index to the 540 reels of microfilm of the Woodrow Wilson papers followed in winter 1974. The indexes to the Garfield papers, now in press, and the Jefferson papers, now in preparation, will complete the project of microfilming and indexing the Library's holdings of the papers of 23 Presidents.

Arms Control and Disarmament But annual reports must note losses as well as gains; this one must regretfully record that the last issue of *Arms Control & Disarmament; a Quarterly Bibliography with Abstracts and Annotations* was volume 9, number 2, spring 1973. The cessation of the periodical and the abolition of the Arms Control and Disarmament Bibliography Section of the General Reference and Bibliography Division followed notification of the Library by the Arms Control and Disarmament Agency that funds for the support of the project were no longer available.

Several of the Library's card files have been published in book form by G. K. Hall & Co. The largest was the *Far Eastern Languages Catalog/Library of Congress,* which reproduced some 332,000 printed LC cards for Chinese, Japanese, and Korean books and serials cataloged since 1958. The four-volume *Catalog of Broadsides in the Rare Book Division, Library of Congress, Washington, D.C.* and the first supplement to *Africa South of the Sahara; Index to Periodical Literature* also appeared in fiscal 1973, followed in the first few months of fiscal 1974 by *The Bibliography of Cartography* in five volumes. A complete transcript of the family name index in the Local History and Genealogy Room, entitled *Genealogies in the Library of Congress, a Bibliography,* was published in March 1972 by Magna Carta Book Company.

It was a record-breaking year for the *Monthly Checklist of State Publications,* prepared by the Exchange and Gift Division: volume 63, covering 1972, listed an alltime high of almost 24,000 entries and the 1972 index was the largest yet compiled. The staff of the division also compiled *Non-GPO Imprints Received in the Library of Congress in 1972; a Selective Checklist,* published in the late summer of 1973. It contains over 400 entries for monographs, 49 percent more than the issue for 1971, plus 140 serial entries. For almost six years, the division has been sending copies of the non-GPO imprints received by the Library to the office of the Superintendent of Documents, where most of them are selected for inclusion in the *Monthly Catalog of U.S. Government Publications.* The Library's *Non-GPO Imprints* lists only those publications that are not included in the *Monthly Catalog* or such other established bibliographies as *Scientific and Technical Aerospace Reports (STAR),* issued by NASA, *Government Reports Announcements of the National Technical Information Service,* the AEC's *Nuclear Science Abstracts,* or ERIC's *Research in Education.*

    In a continuing effort to keep various publics informed on developments in the application of the MARC system, the Library issued the *MARC User Survey, 1972,* the third edition of *Information on the MARC System, Manuscripts: A MARC Format,* and the *RECON Pilot Project; Final Report.* A companion volume to the RECON project report, *National Aspects of Creating and Using MARC/RECON Records,* was published after the close of the fiscal year.

    Many readers across the United States to whom the word *Dewey* is synonymous with the system of numbers by which the books in their local library are arranged would be surprised to learn that the Library of Congress had a hand in building that system. But the staff of the Decimal Classification Division works steadily at the revisions, expansions, and improvements that will be incorporated in the new edition of the *Dewey Decimal Classification.* Sales of the 18th edition have exceeded those of any of its predecessors. Meetings of the Editorial Policy Committee in October 1972 at Lake Placid and in April 1973 at the Library of Congress resulted in numerous basic recommendations for the development of the 19th edition. These were reviewed by the Forest Press and work on the next edition is well advanced. Among the areas likely to receive major attention are the life sciences, sociology, and music. In the LC classification area, the fiscal year saw the publication of the sixth revised edition of *Class Q, Science,* and the presentation of a new subclass BQ, Buddhism, issued as part of *LC Classification–Additions and Changes,* List 168.

    An important segment of the Library's publications, and one of immeasurable value to libraries, bibliographers, and scholars, is its book catalog program. The most ambitious of these publishing projects, from point of view of size, is the *National Union Catalog; Pre-1956 Imprints.* By the close of June 1973, more than 5 million cards had been edited and shipped to the printer and the catalog had reached an estimated halfway point. The publisher informed the Library that, because of their reference value, the 5,000 entries in volume 184 dealing with Freemasons had been issued as a separate publication. Two studies of the *National Union Catalog* were made in fiscal 1973. The first, a survey of reports to the *NUC* by geographical regions within the United States, revealed that library resources of several states were not well represented. To correct this situation, contacts were made with libraries in those states, their response resulting in greater participation and improved levels of reporting. The subject of the second study was the cost of processing an added location report that omits the LC card number. Although this number cannot be included on reports of titles new to the *National Union Catalog,* only 15 percent of the titles reported fall in this category. Reports that omit the

Marginal notes: Non-GPO imprints | Classification | Book catalogs

information must be arranged alphabetically and searched manually in a large control file to obtain the card number before being sent to the *Register of Additional Locations* for publication. The average cost of this operation is 17 cents for each report. On the other hand, reports received with card numbers go directly to the *Register,* bypassing the arranging and searching operations, at a processing cost of only three cents each. In view of the saving involved, participating libraries have been asked to provide the card number whenever possible.

Still another national union catalog, known familiarly as *NUCMC,* achieved maturity with the publication of the 10th volume of the *National Union Catalog of Manuscript Collections,* containing descriptions of over 2,000 collections cataloged in 1971 and cumulative indexes for 1970-71. Collections reported to date in this continuing series total some 29,400 in 850 repositories.

To provide greater flexibility and to offer the user the choice of materials best suited to his needs, *Newspapers in Microform* is now being issued in two volumes. The first, covering U.S. newspapers from 1948 to 1972, was released in October, shortly after the close of fiscal 1973. It contains almost 1,100 pages of text and reports over 34,000 titles in close to 7,500 localities of the United States, its territories, and its possessions. The second volume, covering foreign newspapers for the same period, was in press when this report was written.

A complete list of publications issued during the fiscal year, giving their availability, can be found in the appendixes.

Seventy years ago, Herbert Putnam opened his *Annual Report of the Librarian of Congress* with these words:

> The activities of the year that may be indicated by statistics are set forth in the several statistical tables embodied in the text or appendices. . . . The progress of the Library which is more significant can not be expressed in figures. It consists in the gradual perfection of its equipment and of its service, in a development of its collections appropriate to its purpose as a library for research, and in a wider appreciation and acceptance of its functions as a national library, with a duty to the entire country.

Although methods have changed, new programs have been added, and staff, collections, and services have grown, the present Librarian of Congress can second Dr. Putnam: figures are but indicators; performance is the true measure of the Library's development.

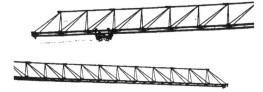

1

The Processing Department

For the third successive year, an officer of the Processing Department was honored by the American Library Association when Glen A. Zimmerman, executive officer of the department, received the Esther J. Piercy Award, an annual citation presented by the ALA Resources and Technical Services Division "in recognition of a contribution to librarianship in the field of technical services by younger members of the profession." In alphabetical order, some of the department's accomplishments thus signalized were:

□ Accumulation of over 365,000 titles in the photocomposed data base for printing catalog cards.

□ Acquisition of more than 6 million items for subsequent screening by the selection staff.

□ Adoption of the MARC format structure as an international standard.

□ Continuing analysis of technical problems involved in bibliographical control.

□ Cataloging and forwarding for printed cards of 253,000 titles.

□ Conversion of *Music; Books on Music, and Sound Recordings* to a quasi-national union catalog.

□ Development of subscriber profiles for users of the card distribution service.

□ Distribution for the first time of MARC tapes for films and other materials for projection, maps, and serials.

□ Drafting of a standard order form for use by the three national libraries and by libraries generally.

□ Elimination of a longstanding backlog of

19

printed catalog cards waiting to be adapted and filed into the shelflist.

□ Establishment of a new, improved process information file, arranged by title.

□ Exchange of personnel between the staffs of the Decimal Classification Division and the *British National Bibliography.*

□ Expansion of job-related and job-enriching instruction in cataloging.

□ Growth of the general catalogs by 1,879,000 new catalog cards.

□ Increase of 233 percent in the number of cards printed via photocomposition from machine-readable catalog records.

□ Input of some 7 million records for an automated *Register of Additional Locations.*

□ Preparation of more than 77,000 pages of camera copy for the catalogs in book form.

□ Procurement for other American libraries of 1,530,000 publications through Public Law 480 programs in Egypt, India, Israel, Nepal, Pakistan, Poland, Sri Lanka, and Yugoslavia.

□ Publication of a greatly expanded classification scheme for Buddhism.

□ Recording of 1,336,000 serial issues and the observance of the 20th anniversary of *New Serial Titles.*

□ Sale of more than 73 million printed catalog cards.

□ Shipment to the printer of the 5-millionth card for the *National Union Catalog: Pre-1956 Imprints.*

ACQUISITIONS AND OVERSEAS OPERATIONS

The National Program for Acquisitions and Cataloging (NPAC) appropriation for fiscal 1973

covered mandatory salary increases and a statutory pay raise. It also provided some additional funds to cope with inflation and devaluation but did not permit any expansion of the program. The shared cataloging centers in Austria, France, Germany, Great Britain, Italy; Japan, the Netherlands, Norway, and Spain all strove to cut costs and effect economies. The issuance of more selective guidelines for NPAC bookdealers served to eliminate the acquisition of titles of only marginal value. The regional acquisitions offices in Brazil, East Africa, and Southeast Asia increased their overall acquisition of materials. After the dissolution in 1971 of the Shared Cataloging Committee of the Association of Research Libraries, there was little structured communication between ARL and LC concerning NPAC. But the dialog with the former committee had been useful and, as a result, an ARL standing advisory committee has been established. It will meet twice yearly to keep LC apprised of research library commitments, shifts in area studies, budgetary factors, and other pertinent information, as well as advising on priorities in acquisitions and cataloging. William J. Welsh, director of the Processing Department, was elected director-at-large of the ALA Resources and Technical Services Division.

Public Law 480 Program

On November 7, 1972, the 10th anniversary of the Public Law 480 program was marked by a luncheon in the Whittall Pavilion honoring U.S. Representative John Dingell of Michigan, whose amendment to Public Law 83-480 enabled the Library to initiate the program, and Mortimer Graves, executive director emeritus of the American Council of Learned Societies, who was instrumental in formulating the idea of the program and in organizing support for it among scholars and librarians. During its first decade the program acquired for LC and some 350 other American libraries over 16 million monographs and serial issues from Egypt, Ceylon, India, Indonesia, Israel, Nepal, Pakistan, Poland, and Yugoslavia.

Though the new Polish program was formally initiated in January 1972, it did not move into high gear until the following summer, after procedural details had been worked out and tested. By the end of fiscal year 1973, the program was in full operation and the number of participating libraries had increased from 12 to 18. The arrangements made with Ars Polona-Ruch, the official Polish export agency, have enabled the program to develop smoothly and effectively. The number of claims for missing or defective materials has been gratifyingly minuscule in relation to the very large volume of publications being acquired.

The Cairo office identified, acquired, cataloged, listed, and shipped to the Library of Congress and 24 other U.S. libraries a wide variety of publications from Egypt and other countries of the Middle East. It operated under the general supervision of an acting field director who spent a week each month in Cairo in addition to his regular assignment. The international book fair held in Cairo in January 1973 proved a valuable source of books from the surrounding region. Because of a continued shift from Cairo to Beirut as the chief publishing center of the area, overall acquisitions declined by about 12 percent.

Working under the successive direction of three energetic and imaginative field directors, a remarkable group of Indians and Americans in New Delhi has, since 1962, acquired for American research libraries over 8 million items from India, Sri Lanka, and Nepal. Nearly 6,000 serial titles are made available for selection and the *Accessions Lists*, which constitute the only comprehensive current lists of research publications available from those nations, are distributed to over 600 libraries in 40 countries. The microfilming laboratory installed in 1967 is now filming 93 newspapers from India, 12 from Pakistan, four from Nepal, six from Ceylon, and 30 from Indonesia; as well as gazettes from all these areas. The result of this intensive activity is the development in the United States of resources for South Asian studies unsurpassed anywhere in the world. For greater flexibility, participating libraries may now receive either a comprehensive set of publications or a basic set which has been pruned of

the less essential categories. Members of the Documents and Acquisitions Sections visited government offices, universities, and other institutions in all the northern states of India and in the southern states of Kerala and Tamil Nadu. A shortage of paper for printing and communal disturbances reduced the number of books published in Sri Lanka.

In February 1973 the Karachi office moved from the ground floor of the American consulate to sunny, pleasant, and more commodious quarters on the second floor. Many new journals appeared in Pakistan and the publishing of monographs, particularly in the regional languages, picked up during the second half of the year. Total receipts topped those of fiscal 1972. In addition to the 12 monthly issues of the *Accessions List: Pakistan*, the second quinquennial index (1967-71), and the 1972 cumulative list of serials, both 25 percent larger than their predecessors, were prepared and distributed.

Coverage of Bangladesh continued under a multiple-copy program supported jointly by 15 participating libraries and the Public Law 480 program. Administered from New Delhi, it acquired publications through the Library's blanket-order dealer in Calcutta and processed them in New Delhi before shipment. As the year closed, it was determined that the quantity and quality of publications being acquired were not commensurate with the investment of time and money required, and participants were informed that this program would end early in fiscal 1974.

With the termination of the Public Law 480 program for Israel, the Tel Aviv office was permanently closed at the end of May 1973. It was established in 1963 by Harry R. Stritman, who served as field director for the duration of the program. Under his imaginative and able leadership, the office acquired for the Library of Congress and over 20 other major libraries more than 1,660,000 items, consisting of monographs, periodicals, and newspapers, and provided preliminary cataloging copy for virtually all titles acquired. It also compiled, produced, and distributed the monthly *Accessions List: Israel*, which quickly became recognized as an indispensable guide to current Israeli publications of research value. The program was perforce terminated when Israel was removed, in 1972, from the list of countries in which United States-owned foreign currencies were available for program purposes.

A similar situation prevailed in Yugoslavia in September 1972 when all Public Law 480 dinars were frozen. Participants were notified that the Belgrade office could no longer acquire monographs for them and that subscriptions would not be renewed for calendar 1973. It was hoped that partial provision of publications might eventually be resumed, but the plan did not prove feasible. The possibility of administering a multiple-copy acquisitions program supported by participating libraries was considered but rejected on the grounds that commercial sources of supply are available. Funds were requested to continue the office in fiscal 1974 as a regional acquisitions office under the National Program for Acquisitions and Cataloging, but the request was denied.

The Belgrade office was therefore scheduled to close at the end of August 1973.

It should come as no surprise that the Public Law 480 program appears to have passed its zenith and is now on the wane. This direction was determined in 1968 with the passage of an amendment to the original legislation requiring that payment for future sales of surplus agricultural commodities must be in U.S. dollars rather than in the foreign currencies previously accepted.

Frank M. McGowan, chief of the Overseas Operations Division, spent 10 days in Rio de Janeiro in July 1972 reviewing the work of the office there with the field director and local staff. In February and March 1973 he visited LC offices in Nairobi, New Delhi, Dacca, and Jakarta, stopping briefly in Calcutta, Kuala Lampur, and Singapore to meet with book dealers and librarians.

Once again the Library is pleased to express its

Public Law 480 Acquisitions, January 1, 1962–June 30, 1973

Country	Commercial and institutional publications			Government publications		Total, fiscal 1973	Total, January 1962 to date
	Newspapers	Serials	Monographs	Serials	Monographs		
Arab Republic of Egypt	67,482	29,021	22,580	11,429	1,466	131,978	2,444,367
India (includes Sikkim & Bhutan) [1]	121,087	493,320	121,963	161,007	9,043	906,420	8,449,511
Indonesia							[2] 992,336
Israel [1]	3,059	5,030	19,207	3,586	2,220	33,102	[3] 1,664,777
Nepal [1]	6,449	21,034	2,197	1,712	273	31,665	[4] 256,328
Pakistan [1]	78,323	112,364	16,709	18,878	5,266	231,540	2,132,213
Poland	22,000	52,200	24,400			98,600	[5] 131,100
Sri Lanka [1] (formerly Ceylon)	7,428	7,552	4,211	4,459	629	24,279	[6] 153,382
Yugoslavia	21,375	41,468	9,749			72,592	[7] 1,082,707
Total	327,203	761,989	221,016	201,071	18,897	1,530,176	17,306,721

[1] Including English-language program acquisitions
[2] From July 1963 through June 1969
[3] From July 1963
[4] From July 1965
[5] From January 1972
[6] From July 1966
[7] From March 1967

gratitude to the Department of State for cooperation and assistance in Washington and abroad. In addition to providing administrative support to the Library's overseas centers, the department also assists in publication procurement from many areas of the world and serves as the official channel for discussing with other governments bilateral agreements for the exchange of official publications.

Purchases

A suggestion by Jennifer V. Magnus, assistant chief of the Order Division, that the Library of Congress, National Agricultural Library, and National Library of Medicine develop a standard order form for their common use led to her appointment in November 1972 as chairman of a Federal Library Committee working group. At the January 28-February 3, 1973, meeting in Washington of the American Library Association, the working group was encouraged by representatives of publishers and distributors. A preliminary draft was prepared and was under discussion at the end of fiscal 1973. Subcommittee 36 of the American National Standards Institute's Committee Z-39 was formed in March, with Mrs. Magnus as chairman, to pursue the development of a standard order form on a national level; Mrs. Magnus gave a paper on the topic at the Pittsburgh meeting of the Special Libraries Association in May 1973. A standard form for use in ordering library materials would reduce clerical effort and errors, speed book ordering procedures, provide publishers and dealers with easy access to data necessary for prompt handling of orders, and ensure compatability of records between libraries.

Work is in progress on the third of the four scheduled tasks of the Order Division automated system. It will bring under control all records pertaining to purchase subscriptions and is scheduled for completion in January 1974. Accomplishments to date include the completion of all input procedures, codes, forms, file establishment specifications, file management specifications, the design of all output reports, and

program specifications. Programs for task 3 are in the process of being coded and tested. Previously completed tasks have provided for collecting and printing data for regular and new subscription orders, creating a permanent machine-readable file of these orders, and using the collected data for management information. Robert C. Sullivan, chief of the Order Division, was elected vicechairman and chairman-elect of the newly formed Resources Section of the ALA Resources and Technical Services Division.

Among the noteworthy purchases of the year were a collection of letters from Sigmund Freud to Karl Abraham, letters of Presidents Grover Cleveland, Calvin Coolidge, James A. Garfield, Ulysses S. Grant, Benjamin Harrison, Andrew Jackson, William McKinley, James Monroe, Theodore Roosevelt, George Washington, and Woodrow Wilson, and six early architectural daguerreotypes.

Exchanges

The Library's exchange program now covers every nation in the world, centering on official agencies, international organizations, semiofficial bodies, and educational and research institutions of all types that have publishing programs and are willing to exchange their publications for the U.S. government documents and the duplicates the Library has to offer. One of the most important activities is a continuous review to determine whether promised materials are regularly received, commitments on both sides are lived up to, and an adequate balance is maintained. For the past several years the Exchange and Gift Division has been engaged in a systematic survey of the Library's exchange relations. Three of the four exchange sections have completed their area reviews and are now programing a continuing survey within a two-year cycle. A prime objective is to assure that there is an equitable exchange of official publications with the other nations which have entered into bilateral or multilateral agreements with the United States and that the full sets (14,000 documents a year) and partial sets (2,000 documents a year) are matched by returns of comparable comprehensiveness and quality, though an exact balance in quantity is not necessarily required. All these agreements were scrutinized and, in 13 instances where receipts fell short of reasonable expectations, a group of 14 major government publications was substituted for the larger sets. At the close of the fiscal year, 52 full and 43 partial sets were being sent.

A notable product of the visit by Chi Wang of the Orientalia Division to China in the summer of 1972 has been the revival of contacts with the National Library of Peking. All exchange relations with the People's Republic of China had been suspended since the early 1950's. Shortly after Dr. Wang's return an initial shipment of books arrived from the National Library and, as a gesture of reciprocity, the Library of Congress sent books thought to be of special interest to the National Library. A second interchange of materials was concluded early in 1973. Receipts from the Democratic People's Republic of Korea, the Mongolian People's Republic, and the Democratic Republic of Vietnam all increased during the year and those from Cuban agencies and institutions reached an alltime high. Very welcome also were publications from Qatar, Yemen, Oman, and the United Arab Emirates.

In cooperation with the American Association of Law Libraries (AALL), the Exchange and Gift Division successfully completed the program, begun last year, to distribute 21,000 duplicate state reports and session laws to 639 law libraries throughout the United States. It also collaborated with the Geography and Map Division in setting up exchanges to utilize the Library's duplicate panoramic maps and with the Prints and Photographs Division in arranging exchanges involving duplicate prints, photographs, and posters.

The Federal Advisory Committee Act went into effect on January 4, 1973. Under its provisions each advisory body must file with the Library of Congress a copy of its charter and eight copies of its reports. By the end of the fiscal year 988 charters had been received and 25 reports.

When the 1971 issue of Non-GPO Imprints Received in the Library of Congress was distributed,

a notice was inserted requesting comments on the usefulness of the publication. Their tenor was that publication should continue until the Monthly Catalog of United States Government Publications attains complete coverage. The 1972 issue will be published in the fall of 1973.

To collect state documents and make them available on as comprehensive a scale as possible is one of the essential services of the Library of Congress. Though the Monthly Checklist of State Publications is still not a complete record, it is broadening its coverage. Ten years ago it listed some 17,000 titles; last year more than 25,000 titles were listed. States designating the Library of Congress as a depository for their documents number 45.

Documents Expediting Project

With five new members—the State Historical Society of Wisconsin, University of Arkansas, University of Cincinnati, Minneapolis Public Library, and Brooklyn College—the number of subscribers increased to 141 university, public, and special libraries in 44 states. They received from the project, administered as a unit in the Exchange and Gift Division, some 382,000 difficult-to-obtain nondepository U.S. government documents, an increase of 21 percent over fiscal 1972. The number of special requests handled approached 7,000. Of these, 73 percent were filled by supplying the wanted material and 8 percent by providing information on the source of supply.

Gifts

Because of the continuing adverse effect of the Tax Reform Act of 1969, which denies any significant tax advantage to donors who present their own creative work, many persons continued to place materials on deposit with the hope that the law will eventually be changed. The heirs of notable figures as well as collectors enhanced the Library's holdings with their gifts. Additions were made to the papers of Clinton Anderson,

Marcia Davenport, Sigmund Freud, George Gamow, Frederick J. Libby, James A. Michener, Ludwig Mies van der Rohe, Ogden and Whitelaw Reid, and Robert A. Taft, and to the musical manuscripts of George Antheil, Ernest Bloch, and George Gershwin, among others. New acquisitions included papers of Goodman Ace, Verner W. Clapp, Hamilton Fish, Alma Gluck, Herman Hollerith, Katie Louchheim, Agnes E. Meyer, Helen Traubel, and Edoardo Weiss, some notable collections of films and sound recordings, and the original of Calvin Coolidge's "I do not choose to run" message. Some of these, as well as other gifts, are described more fully in issues of the *Quarterly Journal of the Library of Congress* and are also mentioned in chapter 3.

AUTOMATION ACTIVITIES

Automation projects in progress in various units of the Processing Department have been coordinated by a judicious mix of library- and computer-oriented staff in the MARC Development Office. These projects involved the creation and maintenance of machine records in the MARC Editorial Division, work on the master guidelines and research in other areas of technical processing in the Technical Processes Research Office, the MARC Distribution Service and the use of photocomposition for printing cards and book catalogs in the Card Division, an automated acquisition system in the Order Division, films catalog and the *Register of Additional Locations* for the Catalog Publication Division, an automated subject headings system in the Subject Cataloging Division, MARC serials input for the Serial Record Division, and the automated Process Information File for the Descriptive Cataloging, Shared Cataloging, and Catalog Management Divisions. In the Reference Department, the Geography and Map Division, Prints and Photographs Division, Science and Technology Division, and Division for the Blind and Physically Handicapped received varying degrees of assistance on the input and printing of MARC records for their special requirements. Monthly meetings with the Information Systems Office coordinated

hardware and software requirements and procurement.

Henriette D. Avram, chief of the MARC Development Office, and several other members of its staff worked closely with groups concerned with automation in the American Library Association, the International Federation of Library Associations, and the International Standards Organization. The work in the area of standards has culminated in the adoption of the MARC format structure as an international standard. The office continued to disseminate information about its activities through the Library's publication program and through the professional journals. A new communications format for manuscripts, several addenda to existing communications formats, a preprint of a new edition of the serials format, and the final report of the RECON pilot project were issued.

The original guidelines for an automated core bibliographic system were refined to include functions utilizing a machine-readable Process Information File, name and subject reference files, and the expanded MARC files. Completed were tasks to calculate the size and growth factor of all files, estimate the requirements for online terminals and printers, and gauge the volume of activity in each file or combination of files.

A phased implementation plan for the automated Process Information File has been developed. The first phase will include the capability of searching online by LC card number and author/title or title search keys, as well as inputing and updating bibliographic and status information for English-language monographs processed by the Preliminary Cataloging Section of the Descriptive Cataloging Division. Subsequent phases will incorporate into the file the records from the Shared Cataloging Division and records for other languages and other forms of material. Specifications for file organization, search keys, and automatic assignment of LC card numbers have been completed. It is anticipated that, in the future, machine-readable files from the Order Division and foreign national bibliographies will be input to the system, and the machine-readable PIF records in appropriate languages and forms of material will, in turn, be

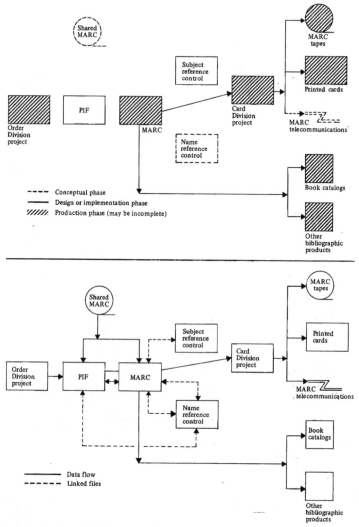

The first figure depicts the core bibliographic system described in the master guidelines as it now exists. The second figure represents the system with its components linked together, as planned for the late seventies.

updated to become MARC records.

Lucia J. Rather, formerly the MARC Development Office's senior library information systems specialist, was appointed to the newly created position of assistant chief.

CATALOGING

Fiscal 1973 virtually equaled fiscal 1971, the previous banner year, for number of titles cataloged for printed cards. In 1971 some 255,000 titles, exclusive of maps, were completed. The level of cataloging production remains at approximately a quarter of a million titles a year. Between fiscal 1965 and fiscal 1973 the number of books cataloged annually increased from 110,000 to over 253,000. This increase is due to the implementation of the National Program for Acquisitions and Cataloging in the spring of 1966.

Cataloging in Publication

In July 1971 the Library of Congress and the American publishing industry embarked on one of the most significant cooperative efforts in the history of bibliographical control—the Cataloging in Publication Program (CIP). Under it, standardized cataloging data is provided on the copyright page of current titles, and librarians speed the books to their readers, avoiding original cataloging costs. During its second year the number of cooperating publishers increased from 200 to 405 and titles processed from 6,500 to 12,000.

Since over 18,000 current titles are now available with CIP data, the impact of the program is increasingly felt in libraries throughout the country, and many letters attest to the reduction in cataloging costs and processing time. Librarians in Canada, Germany, Great Britain, India, Israel, and Sweden have indicated that they are considering similar programs.

As of June 1973 approximately 55 percent of the U.S. book trade production included CIP data, and the recent addition of several of the major publishing houses suggested that coverage would soon approach 80 percent. Over 70 per-

cent of the leading medical book publishers have joined the program and of the 12,000 titles cataloged during the year, more than 1,000 were jointly processed by the National Library of Medicine and the Library of Congress under a cooperative agreement inaugurated in May 1972. The biomedical titles are listed in NLM's *Current Catalog Proofsheets* and distributed twice a week to some 4,000 libraries and institutions which subscribe to this service for the selection and prepublication ordering of medical books. The titles appear in these listings approximately four months in advance of publication date. The goal of the program is inclusion of CIP data in all current books. Preliminary planning is under way to extend CIP to include selected federal government documents that are widely acquired and cataloged by libraries, beginning gradually, agency by agency and title by title, without diminishing the continuing emphasis on phasing-in the remaining trade book publishers.

Inclusion of CIP entries on MARC tapes proved immediately useful not only for cataloging but also for acquisitions and for current awareness services. *Publishers Weekly* has expanded its use of CIP information in its "Weekly Record" section. In support of the program, the ALA ad hoc committee on Cataloging of Children's Materials in May 1973 sent letters of appreciation to participating publishers, thanking them for this effort to help libraries effectively serve young readers.

To assist in identifying the participants and the product, the CIP logotype was distributed to publishers in November 1972 and librarians are urging its use in sales catalogs and advertisements, since it alerts librarians to titles which contain CIP data and will therefore be less expensive to process.

Machine-Readable Cataloging Copy

In July 1972 the MARC Editorial Office was extensively reorganized and renamed the MARC Editorial Division. The increasing sophistication of the MARC processing procedures and the expanding scope of the operation have created

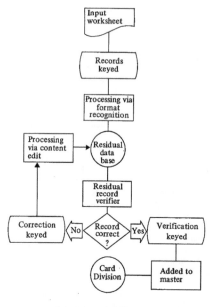

Processing MARC records

a catalog in book form. The preliminary steps in their processing—conversion of the records to machine-readable form, creation of a prototype book catalog, and selection of records for the first half of calendar 1973—have been completed.

Descriptive Cataloging

A significant change in the organization of the Descriptive Cataloging Division was effected in February 1973 with the separation of the former English Language Section into three coordinate sections. This reorganization decreased the span of supervisory control and promises to improve staff capabilities by offering the staff of each section an opportunity to work with materials presenting a greater variety of cataloging problems. Staffing has been reasonably stable, with 86 percent of the staff having at least one full year's experience in the division. The decrease in cataloging arrearages and particularly in reviewing arrearages in most of the sections may well be a happy consequence.

exacting training demands for both the existing staff and for all new staff members. Accordingly, a great deal of attention is being given to perfecting MARC training programs. Advantage is taken of all relevant training available at the Library or sponsored by other organizations. The training presented by the division itself is carefully scrutinized. Evaluations are solicited from participating staff members and from those who later review their work, in an effort to refine and enrich subsequent classes. As one result, a backlog of almost 11,000 records which had been typed but not verified had been reduced by the close of the fiscal year to 3,000 records. The input of French-language monographic records began in June 1973, and the first weekly tape containing French records was distributed shortly thereafter. The audiovisual records processed by the MARC Editorial Division are being used to create

The International Standard Bibliographic Description (ISBD) for monographs figured prominently in the technical rule development work of the division. Bulletin 105 of *Cataloging Service* is devoted almost exclusively to a résumé of the standard, prepared by staff assistant Robert Hiatt and illustrated with "before" and "after" examples showing the effect upon Library of Congress cataloging. Bulletin 106 describes the plans for implementation of the standard at the Library. A necessary prelude to the implementation has been the revision of chapter 6 of the *Anglo-American Cataloging Rules,* a project that has required painstaking attention. With a few minor exceptions, the revised rules for description for the North American text have been approved by the descriptive cataloging committee of the American and Canadian library associations. The rules accepted at the June 1973 meeting are the result of careful drafting and redrafting by principal descriptive cataloger Paul Winkler and thorough review by cataloging and library automation experts from the Processing Department and from the cataloging committees. Final approval, however, and the preparation of the manuscript for publication by the American Library Association were, at the close of the fiscal year, awaiting the recommendations expected from the reconvening of the Working Group on the International Standard Bibliographic Description at Grenoble in August 1973. Meanwhile, plans were already under way for the training of the staff in the application of the revised rules.

In April 1973 the division's Descriptive Cataloging Standards Committee submitted its final report. It had been created the year before to recommend standards for evaluating the performance of descriptive catalogers in career positions. The serious thought and conscientious work of the committee are readily apparent in the detailed standards and procedures recommended to assist supervisors in making objective evaluations for promotions and within-grade increases.

The first printed cards in Sindhi were produced. The photocomposition of Chinese and Korean entries in the Library's Tokyo office proved technically feasible but the facility is at present unable to absorb the additional workload.

Elizabeth L. Tate, returning to the Library from the National Bureau of Standards where she had been chief of the Library Division, succeeded Joseph H. Howard as chief of the Descriptive Cataloging Division.

Shared Cataloging

During its seventh year the Shared Cataloging Division cataloged some 114,000 titles, a small increase over fiscal 1972. The number of titles awaiting cataloging dropped from 21,000 to 10,000. The reduction of backlogs was most apparent in the German, Italian, Scandinavian, and Slavic Sections. Out-of-scope titles were weeded from the acquisitions control files, making them more compact and easier to use. The Series File, a control file for all titles appearing in a series except those in the Japanese language, was revised, and improved procedures were established for its maintenance. The program for get-

ting final camera copy for Japanese cards printed in Tokyo continued to flourish and over 9,000 cards were printed. The cooperative arrangement with the National Agricultural Library (NAL) was resumed. Under it books purchased in western Europe by NAL are processed by the shared cataloging centers and sent to Washington for cataloging by the Library of Congress and subsequent forwarding to the National Agricultural Library.

Subject Cataloging

Nearing completion, in cooperation with the MARC Development Office, is the conversion of subject headings data into a MARC format that will allow all future editions and supplements to the subject headings list to be produced by an automated system. The project is in the concluding phase of creating a single machine-readable file of data from the seventh edition merged with data from the supplements through December 1972. Since January 1973 the Editorial Section of the Subject Cataloging Division, in addition to proofreading and correcting the records, has also been keying data directly into the automated subject headings processing system. Changes are entered in weekly cycles and accumulated on a data base to produce the quarterly supplements to the subject headings list.

One out of every 20 books cataloged by the Library results in the establishment of new subject headings or classification numbers. During fiscal 1973 the division processed 11,500 newly established headings and 10,000 new class numbers. The sixth edition of *Class Q: Science,* distributed in March 1973, incorporated considerable material not heretofore published. The development of nuclear physics during recent years required a noticeable expansion and rearrangement of topics in subclass QC (Physics). Detail has been incorporated into the arrangement of works in genetics and virology, where only broad classification was possible before. Subclasses QK (Botany) and QL (Zoology) have been greatly enlarged by printing virtually exhaustive lists of the various taxa representing the level at which classification is effected. The development by cataloger Kenneth Tanaka of a classification for Buddhism, from a section in BL (Religion) into a separate subclass, BQ (Buddhism), is a reflection of the increasing amount of material received by the Library from Asia in the past decade. The new BQ subclass appeared in an appendix of the October-December 1972 issue, List 168, of *LC Classification—Additions and Changes*. Arrangements were completed with the National Library of Canada for the assignment for an indefinite time of a law cataloger from its staff to work on developing subclass KE (Law of Canada). With the aid of seven work-study students from Kalamazoo College and Northeastern University, the Shelflisting Section adapted and filed into the shelflist a backlog of 663,000 printed cards, thus eliminating, in all classes except P (Language and Literature), a longstanding arrearage.

The continuing high level of individual production enabled the division not only to handle the current influx but also to make substantial inroads on a burdensome backlog of material awaiting subject analysis. Incunabula and microforms, types of materials which the Library of Congress has never shelved in its classified collections, are now being provided with bracketed class numbers for the benefit of those libraries which wish to arrange these materials by topic.

Charles C. Bead retired as chief of the Subject Cataloging Division after more than 29 years of federal service. He devoted his Library career to the field of cataloging and classification, serving with distinction in both the Descriptive and Subject Cataloging Divisions. Edward J. Blume, assistant chief of the division since 1970, was named to succeed Dr. Bead and his position, in turn, was assumed by David G. Remington, formerly director of library services for Bro-Dart's western division.

Cataloging Instruction

In response to requests from seven different divisions, the course which introduces staff members to the Anglo-American cataloging rules was

offered four times during the year. Other basic courses offered were a general one on the effective use of the card catalog, another on filing, a third on searching, and an introductory one for processing assistants. Two courses were modified to include specific job-related material for the benefit of the Additions and Corrections Unit of the Catalog Management Division and the Shelflisting Section of the Subject Cataloging Division. One new course, designed for beginning subject catalogers, was offered twice. In all, 136 staff members received instruction.

Decimal Classification

An exchange of personnel between the Decimal Classification Division and the *British National Bibliography* was a landmark in Anglo-American library relations; it was between people at the operating rather than at the management level but, even more significant, it was between people engaged in activities having national and even worldwide effect. Melba D. Adams, LC decimal classification specialist, worked at the *BNB* from July 27 to August 25, during which time she provided consultation on the use of the classification and observed and participated in the *BNB*'s methods of subject analysis. R. Ross Trotter, head of the Dewey Classification Section at the *BNB*, worked at the Library from October 10 to November 24, advising on British requirements in the classification and participating in both application and development of the system. This exchange between the Library of Congress and a unit of the British Library promoted understanding on each side and more consistency in the application of the system, thus serving the needs of the thousands of libraries throughout the world that use the decimal classification. The trips were made possible by grants from the *British National Bibliography* and the Forest Press, publishers of the *Dewey Decimal Classification*. During a visit by Janet Braithwaite of the National Library of Australia, which publishes the *Australian National-Bibliography*, an agreement was reached for an interchange of detailed advice on the classification of specific titles, similar to that in effect for several years with the *BNB*. The Editorial Policy Committee held two meetings, at Lake Placid, N.Y., and in Washington, at which it discussed the shape of the future and made several recommendations to the Forest Press. John A. Humphry, president, and Richard B. Sealock, executive director of the Forest Press, visited Great Britain in company with Benjamin A. Custer, chief of the Decimal Classification Division, to participate in one committee and three public meetings. Mr. Custer also spoke at an institute on the 18th edition held in Los Angeles at the University of Southern California and took part in a colloquium on the same subject sponsored by the State University of New York at Albany.

The 18th edition was favorably reviewed in American, Australian, British, Canadian, and South African library journals. Despite smaller book budgets in many libraries, it continued to outsell the 17th edition by a wide margin. Work on the next edition is well advanced. Among the areas likely to receive major attention are the life sciences, sociology, and music. In another step toward the new edition, the staff compiled a "reverse index" to the 18th edition, arranged by class number and by terms referred to. They also compiled a detailed chronological and classified manual of editorial criteria, rules, and policies.

PROCESSING SERVICES

The production and distribution of Library of Congress printed catalog cards, the maintenance of the Library's general card catalogs and special files, the publication of its catalogs in book form, the cataloging and recording of serials received by the Library, and the editing for publication of *New Serial Titles* are the principal functions of this area of the department.

Card Distribution

To the processing of machine-readable order slips and the photocomposition of catalog cards were added an expanded MARC distribution service and an automated control system for the book catalogs. The photocomposed data base now has over 365,000 titles which may be used to print catalog cards. The total number of cards produced via photocomposition from MARC records increased from 9 million in fiscal 1972 to 30 million in fiscal 1973. In September 1972 the Card Division began the sale and distribution of MARC tapes for motion pictures, films, and filmstrips cataloged by the Library. In April 1973 the MARC Distribution Service expanded its coverage to include single- and multi-sheet thematic maps, map sets, and maps treated as serials. The Library catalogs about 5,000 maps each year in these categories and for the first time map catalog records are available to subscribers both in a machine-readable form and on printed cards. The first MARC tapes containing cataloging information for serials were distributed in June 1973. They contain records for newly cataloged serials in all roman-alphabet languages. Subscriber records are being converted to machine-readable form. Subscriber profiles have been developed and are being used to produce renewal notices, mailing labels, audit lists for items shipped, and invoices. They may also be used to review the status of an account. This change will enable the Card Division to handle existing services more efficiently and allow for easier implementation of new ones.

The shortage of skilled typists and the difficulty in recruiting them led the Card Division to set up its own refresher courses for staff members with some typing experience. The training thus provided enabled the division to fill several vacancies. All the items sold by the Card Division were subjected to standard cost analysis to establish a more balanced set of prices for the various services.

Under the "All-the-Books" Plan, publishers provided the Library with advance copies of over 24,500 current titles for cataloging and also printed the Library's card numbers in most of them. To maintain direct contact with subscribers, Card Division staff members took part in the 1972 conference of the Southwestern/ Southeastern Library Association Regional Conference as well as the 1973 midwinter and annual

conferences of the American Library Association.

Loran P. Karsner retired as chief of the Card
Division after more than 40 years of government
service, almost all of which were spent in the
Card Division. He made many contributions toward improving the methods and technical operations of the card distribution services to the
Library of Congress and the library and scholarly
communities. Paul E. Edlund, executive officer
in the Processing Department, was named to succeed him. Mr. Edlund has served for 17 years in
the Processing, Reference, and Administrative
Departments.

Card Catalogs

Under consideration for several years, a Process
Information File arranged by title was established in December 1972. A number of reasons
were involved. The title is the most direct approach to a book and its use eliminates guess-
work as to choice and form of author entry. If a
client has garbled the title, it is perhaps less serious in a large file ·than if he has garbled the author entry. Authors may alter their names for
various reasons but the title of a book remains
stable. The old main-entry file was frozen and
moved from open trays on tables to catalog cases
to provide space for the new file. Reaction to it
has been favorable, and the staff servicing it
answered more than 83,500 inquiries during the
fiscal year.

The addition of 1.75 million cards each year to
the Library's two principal catalogs taxes both
floor space and equipment. Space is most critical
for the Official Catalog. A study of its needs
through December 1976 estimated that the
yearly addition of 14 units of 75 trays each will
be required for its maintenance. The Main Catalog was provided with 10,000 new guide cards
and its lighting was improved. ·

In addition to its now customary participation
in the work-study program of the D.C. high
schools, the Catalog Management Division
accepted four young people enrolled in the Public Service Career Trainee Program. All were

eager to learn, performed well, and are being
placed in permanent positions. A paper by Barbara M. Westby, chief of the division, was featured at the seminar on "The Services of
Processing Agencies" sponsored by the New
York Metropolitan Reference and Research Library Agency (METRO) in May 1973.

Catalogs in Book Form

All numerical listings in the *National Union
Catalog–Register of Additional Locations* are
now being processed through an automated
system. The initial input phase has been completed, with some 7 million locations dating from
1968 and later. Programs have been written by
the MARC Development Office to edit and
merge these records into a master file. The 1967
and earlier locations had already been processed
by manual methods. These locations, numbering
approximately 4.6 million, and the 7 million
automated locations should be published in 1974
in the 1968-72 cumulation of the *Register*. The
growth of the *National Union Catalog* itself is
depicted in the accompanying graph.

In the last months of 1972 discussions between
the Library of Congress and the Music Library
Association culminated in a decision to include
in *Music and Phonorecords* reports from seven
college and university libraries in the United
States and Canada: Bowling Green State University, University of Chicago, University of North
Carolina, Oberlin College, Ohio State University,
Stanford University, and University of Toronto.
These institutions were chosen because their collections complement those of the Library of
Congress, their cataloging procedures are in har-
mony, and they have the interest and resources
to make continuing contributions. The enlarged
publication thus became a quasi-national union
catalog and was renamed *Music, Books on Music,
and Sound Recordings.*

During 1972 the Descriptive Cataloging Division began cataloging transparencies and slide
sets, and catalog cards for these materials appeared during the latter part of the year in *Motion Pictures and Filmstrips.* Since 1973 was the

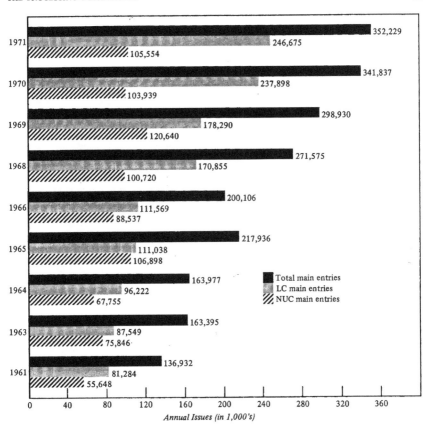

Growth of the annual issues of the National Union Catalog

first year of the next quinquennial cumulation, it seemed timely to choose a title for the catalog that would describe its contents more accurately. *Films and Other Materials for Projection,* though somewhat complicated, is accurate and comprehensive enough to permit the addition of other visual materials without a further change of name. The six-month cumulation for January-June 1973 will be the first book catalog to be produced by LC directly from MARC records.

The long-awaited seventh edition of *Newspapers on Microfilm,* now titled *Newspapers in Microform* to reflect the greater variety of techniques represented, is being published in two parts to provide greater flexibility and to offer the user a choice of materials better suited to his needs. The first volume, *Newspapers in Microform: United States, 1948-1972,* with 34,000 titles in 7,500 localities as reported by 845 libraries and 48 commercial firms, was released in October 1973. The second volume, *Newspapers in Microform: Foreign Countries, 1948-1972,* containing almost 9,000 titles reported by 522 libraries and 40 commercial firms, was sent to the printer soon after the close of the fiscal year.

Compiled in the Descriptive Cataloging Division from reports provided by other U.S. repositories, the 1971 volume of the *National Union Catalog of Manuscript Collections* is the 10th in a continuing series designed to bring under bibliographic control manuscript collections housed permanently in American institutions that are regularly open to scholars. Off the press in April 1973, it reports some 2,000 collections located in 151 repositories and brings the total number of collections described to date to over 25,000 representing holdings in 850 institutions.

As of June 30, 1973, the National Union Catalog Publication Project had edited and shipped to the publisher in London over 5.2 million cards. This extended the edited portion of the file through "Konusov, A. P." and brought the *National Union Catalog: Pre-1956 Imprints* close to the halfway point. Subscribers had received 265 bound volumes, with coverage through "International Harvester Company of America," and an additional 27 volumes were in the process of being printed. The most notable editing accomplishment was the completion of the many complex files of entries beginning with the letter "I." These included the "International" and "Institute" headings; many jurisdictions, e.g., Illinois, India, Indiana, Iowa, Ireland, Italy; and the numerous Arabic authors whose names begin with the word "Ibn." Because of its reference value the portion of volume 184 containing the 5,000 entries under "Freemasons" has been issued as a separate publication. Work on the Bible entries progressed steadily but slowly, due to the extraordinary complexity of the file and the thoroughness with which it is being edited. Publication of the four Bible volumes will be delayed until the rest of the catalog has been completed. In this way the volumes will be as complete as possible, with a minimum of supplementation required.

Serial Record

Characterized by Andrew Osborn in his *Serial Publications* as the world's largest, the Library's Serial Record Division records the receipt of serial issues in the roman, Greek, and Cyrillic alphabets and forwards them to appropriate units for immediate use or further processing. In fiscal 1973 the division received 1,325,000 issues, handled 1,336,000 (by dipping into the backlog), and closed the year with an onhand figure representing less than three day's workload. Though smaller than last year's total, 1,336,000 is still a formidable number. If the issues were placed neatly on top of one another in one of the Library's courtyards, they would make up a pile more than five miles high. Probably more information is put into the Serial Record than is ever retrieved but the statistics on use are nevertheless impressive: the staff answered more than 64,000 telephone and written inquiries during the year. Other statistics—over 11,000 new entries made for the visible files, almost 8,000 printed cards for current titles—are also gratifying, since they represent currency in these operations. Since 1971 the printed card copy prepared by the division's catalogers has generated reports to *New Serial Titles.* In February 1973 its bibliographic services were expanded to provide data for all newly cataloged entries to the new MARC-S project and to the National Serials Data Program. The MARC-S project is converting the data for all serials in the roman alphabet; entries in other alphabets may be added later. As of June 1973 some 1,200 entries had been input into the machine-readable records which are available on tape through the MARC Distribution Service.

In 1973 *New Serial Titles,* the national union list, marked its 20th anniversary. The staff continued to assist the R. R. Bowker Company in preparing the 1950-70 cumulation, which will contain some 230,000 entries, making it the largest serial bibliography ever published in a single alphabet. The present champion is the *Union List of Serials* with over 156,000 entries.

The division shared with other units a greater interest in training, improving communication with the staff at all levels, and carefully analyzing appointments, performance ratings, and promotions, placing special emphasis on these activities. On-the-job training took on a new dimension when 50 library technicians in the Processing and Reference Section went on a split-day schedule, dividing their time between two of the following units: Accessioning, Editorial and Reference, and Searching and Visible File Cataloging. Despite the initial shocks of blast-off, the crew members adjusted quickly and managed to keep all systems go.

Samuel Lazerow left the Library to become a vice president of the Institute for Scientific Information. He was succeeded as chief of the Serial Record Division by Joseph H. Howard.

TECHNICAL PROCESSES RESEARCH

As part of its program for investigating devices for bibliographical control, the Technical Processes Research (TPR) Office undertook the following studies:

An analysis of the characteristics of the LC subject headings on 5,800 MARC records to determine their form, patterns of occurrence, printing status, and frequency of use over a period of years.

A study of the extent to which the Library of Congress and the *British National Bibliography* agree in their assignment of LC class numbers, LC subject headings, and Dewey decimal class numbers. The findings show a sufficiently high degree of compatability to justify exploring ways to broaden the areas of agreement with potential benefits to both agencies.

A consideration of the feasibility of a rotated display of LC subject headings as an aid to catalog use and an estimate of its size under alternative conditions.

A projection of the cataloging workload that would result over a four-year period if the policy of superimposition were abandoned for current imprints.

A critical evaluation of the International Standard Book Number system as a means of controlling LC catalog records. The practicality of this suggestion was tested by examining the relationships that can exist between book trade items and catalog records, the consequences of the mixed numbering system that would result, and the life expectancy of ISBN in its present form.

As a contribution to the design of an automated Process Information File, TPR undertook to define the characteristics of the most efficient indexes for such a file. The basic problem is how to achieve the greatest degree of discrimination in online searching with the minimum effort in inputing a search query. The effectiveness of various formulations of indexes was tested by simulated searches against the 553,000 LC entries in the 1963-67 cumulation of the *National Union Catalog,* and in the case of full titles, against the LC Official Catalog. The findings indicate that searches based on the first three letters of the main entry and the first three (other than an initial article) of the title—3-3 keys—are more efficient than searches involving either personal surname plus first initial or corporate name. A subsequent computer analysis of the distribution of 3-3 keys for the entire MARC data base confirmed their high discriminating ability.

In planning for the automated core bibliographic system, TPR continues to be actively engaged with the MARC Development Office. This activity involves both conceptualizing the system and estimating hardware requirements.

John C. Rather, specialist in technical processes research, was named as LC liaison to the Committee on Computer Filing of the ALA Resources and Technical Services Division. His paper outlining an approach to the standardization of filing arrangement was accepted by the committee as a working guide.

Richard S. Angell, chief of the Technical Processes Research Office since its establishment in 1966, retired on June 29, 1973, after 27 years of service in the Library. As chief of four divisions (the others being Copyright Cataloging, Descriptive Cataloging, and Subject Cataloging) during his Library career, he acquired a range of experience that has rarely been equaled. His many contributions to the improvement of catalog control on a national and international level were based on a profound understanding of its theoretical and practical aspects.

2

The Congressional Research Service

Completing its 59th year of service to the Congress in fiscal year 1973, the Congressional Research Service has grown from a small staff responsible for compiling legal indexes and digests in the early part of the century to an organization of over 500 persons responsible for more than 181,000 congressional requests annually. Its correspondingly expanded mission has been characterized most recently by an emphasis on indepth research and analysis, as well as reference support, increased assistance to Members in their legislative responsibilities, and anticipation of public policy issues as they relate to congressional research needs.

The growth of the Service and the changing nature of its operations are essentially rooted in the dramatic changes of 20th-century America. Several terms have been applied to conditions in the latter third of this century that connote the need for sweeping change: knowledge explosion, energy and pollution crises, population bomb, technological revolution. Although popular slogans may not accurately reflect the realities, most individuals and organizations have not been

immune to the demanding, crisis-oriented semantics of our time and at least some of the pressure for reexamination they create. Whether by intent or by default, modern society is becoming more complex, more interdependent, more aware of the existence of alternatives and of the need to make informed choices. Business and educational and governmental institutions are both creating and responding to changing perspectives and realities of the times. An organization whose function is to acquire, distill, and transmit information on diverse subjects, ranging in scope from the parochial to the international, must be particularly sensitive to these trends.

The growth of the Congressional Research Service is most directly attributable to the expanded information requirements of the Congress. In the Legislative Reorganization Act of 1970 (Public Law 91-510), the Congress authorized an increased emphasis on indepth research and analysis as well as continued provision of traditional CRS services; more extensive support for congressional committees, including analytical assistance relative to legislative proposals and the

37

maintenance of continuous liaison with all committees; and the preparation of subject and
terminating program lists. Fiscal year 1973 com-
pletes the second year of a five-year program to
implement these expanded responsibilities.

Changing patterns and emphases characterized
the past year in the continuing effort to improve
CRS methods for responding to congressional
needs. The Service is placing an increasing reliance on automated techniques to handle routine,
once-manual operations; it is moving toward
interdisciplinary approaches and interdivisional
organizational arrangements to handle increasingly complex legislative issues; and it is placing
greater emphasis on establishing more effective
communication channels within CRS and with
outside organizations. The Service has been flexible not only in increasing the amount and range
of its activity but also in creating an inherently
resilient organization, one which can utilize new
information sources and respond rapidly and
effectively to new demands. This report on the
fiscal year explores the major analytical and
research work of the Service's eight subject divisions, documentation and status of legislation
activities, information and reference services, and
general administration.

ANALYTICAL AND RESEARCH SERVICES

More than 21,000 requests from congressional
committees were received by the Service during
the last fiscal year. In response to the directive of
the Reorganization Act that CRS, upon request,
advise and assist committees in the analysis,
appraisal, and evaluation of legislative proposals,
the Service identified 220 of these requests as
major research projects to be tracked by the
assistant director for policy analysis. Each project had a direct connection with legislative proposals or with existing legislation, required
substantial analysis, and represented a significant
investment of high-level manpower. An analysis
of the congressional use of the 220 projects
revealed that approximately 40 percent provided
background information, analysis of issues, or
both; 30 percent involved analytical reports or
assistance specifically in connection with hear-

ings; 20 percent related to the development or
analysis of pending or enacted legislation; and 10
percent contributed to congressional documents.

The projects are significant for their collective
coverage of an extensive range of issues pending
before the Congress and for the interdivisional
approach necessary to ensure comprehensive
treatment of a number of them. This is illustrated by the following examples of projects
undertaken in the past year.

The Central City Problem and Urban Renewal Policy

This study, resulting in a committee print of the
same title, was undertaken at the request of a
subcommittee of the Senate Banking, Housing,
and Urban Affairs Committee and incorporated
substantive contributions from four CRS divisions. The emphasis of the study was upon the
history, operations, and policies of the urban
renewal program and the related model cities
program. Its objective was to provide a comprehensive report that would identify the issues and
assist in the evaluation of existing and proposed
policies and in the formulation of new ones. The
Service's senior specialist in housing coordinated
the study and worked primarily with researchers
in the Economics Division on sections pertaining
to the urban renewal program and the social and
economic characteristics of central cities. Analysts in the Education and Public Welfare Division contributed material on manpower training
and law enforcement. The Environmental Policy
Division submitted a 35-page component on the
impact of environmental pollution upon the
inner city in general and upon residents living in
conditions of poverty in particular. The Government and General Research Division prepared a
comprehensive survey of the literature on the
history and current conditions of the central city
and contributed to the section on social and economic characteristics.

Environmental Policy Legislation in the 92d Congress

Undertaken for the Senate Interior and Insular
Affairs Committee, this project resulted in a
committee print entitled *Congress and the Na-*

THE CONGRESSIONAL RESEARCH SERVICE

tion's Environment, complementing an earlier volume that analyzed the environmental policy activities of the 91st Congress. The chapters of the print are grouped under three main sections—natural resources, pollution, and management aspects—and present a concise analysis of congressional effort in such major policy areas as air pollution, public lands, and energy. Each chapter contains an analysis of legislation enacted, brief descriptions of other legislative proposals, highlights of hearings, recommendations from major policy reports of interest to the Congress, and bibliographies of congressional documents prepared by the Library Services Division and based on the CRS automated bibliographic data base. The Environmental Policy Division coordinated the report and researchers within the division contributed most of the chapters. The chapters on radiation hazards and noise abatement were contributed by staff members of the Science Policy Research Division.

Foreign Policy Implications of the Energy Crisis

An illustration of the type of support CRS renders to congressional committees and subcommittees in connection with hearings and, in this case, for hearings with a symposium format can be found in this project undertaken for the Foreign Economic Policy Subcommittee of the House Foreign Affairs Committee. Staff members from four CRS divisions provided basic background and source material to subcommittee staff before the hearings. They conferred extensively with the staff on the proposed subject matter for the hearings, the symposium format, the witness lists, and the design of the CRS summary and analysis of each session. Following each session, the Service summarized the prepared statements and discussions of the panelists and provided an analysis of conflicting points of view, an examination of the central points made, and a listing of important questions and possible areas of congressional concern. The hearings, conducted in September and October 1972, covered three major areas: current trends and an overview of the energy situation, a survey and analysis of alternative energy technologies, and

the foreign policy ramifications of the energy crisis. The CRS summaries and analyses of the sessions made up some 100 pages of the published committee hearings. The Service's divisional contributions were directed and coordinated by a senior specialist in international affairs. Specialists from the Science Policy Research Division prepared the section on "Current Trends and Overview" and part of the one on "Alternative Energy Technologies"; a specialist in the Environmental Policy Division also contributed to the latter; analysts from the Foreign Affairs Division prepared the section, "Foreign Policy Ramifications," and a glossary of technical terms; and the Library Services Division compiled the selected bibliography.

School Finance

At the request of the Subcommittee on Education of the Senate Labor and Public Welfare Committee, a project was initiated to provide background materials for future hearings on various aspects of school governance and finance. The Service developed 11 papers, which are tentatively planned for publication as a committee print or Senate document. Responsibility for preparation of the papers was apportioned among four CRS divisions. The Education and Public Welfare Division coordinated the project and concentrated on such subjects as a definition of equality of educational opportunity, the relationship of expenditures to educational quality, and the current state school finance programs and proposals for their reform. The Economics Division contributed papers on the tax structure supporting education and possibilities for reform, and on potential yields of taxes levied at various governmental levels. The American Law Division studied the legal challenges leveled at current school financing arrangements and their implications for the federal government. The Government and General Research Division concentrated on the structure of the governance of education and possibilities for change, in addition to analyzing alternative federal grant programs, for example, categorical vs. general grants, and possible delivery systems. An additional aspect of the study, the establishment of a school finance data bank for use in analyzing federal aid-to-education proposals, was contracted out by CRS..

In addition to extensive assistance to committees, the Service continues to provide analytical support to Members of Congress and frequently prepares reports in anticipation of congressional demand. Overall, more than 500 major Member, committee, and anticipatory projects, each requiring more than 10 days of analysis, were completed during this fiscal year. The diversity of reports prepared by the Service is illustrated by the following examples: federal housing delivery systems; federal programs for the control of drug abuse; budget reform proposals and issues; analysis of multilateral commodity arrangements and world food reserve agreements; the 1973 gasoline shortage; executive privilege; newsmen's privilege; Indian lands; the dispute between the Navajos and Hopis; major federal legislation affecting women's rights enacted between 1963 and 1973.

Numerous multilithed reports are prepared by CRS each year on subjects for which there is a recurrent or anticipated demand for materials. In the past fiscal year, there were multilithed analytical surveys of state and federal laws governing elections, the practice of abortion, and the regulation of obscenity. Background and policy studies were produced on wastepaper recycling, the F-14 fighter procurement program, the work of the Appalachian Regional Commission, the ABM defense of Washington, U.S. commitments to NATO, trends in uses and sources of federal budget funds over 10 years, and European housing policies and programs. More descriptive, less analytical reports were produced on major natural disasters in the United States from 1959 to 1972, acupuncture in America, U.S. flag law, and issues related to Alaska oil.

Contracting Authority

To assist CRS in meeting its research obligations to Congress, the Legislative Reorganization Act

authorizes the employment of outside consultants or organizations when the permanent employment of experts in specialized areas of knowledge is not justified or warranted by continuing congressional need. Substantive criteria and procedures for utilization of the contract authority have been specified by the Service and were applied for the first time in this fiscal year. An appropriation of $194,000 for the purpose permitted the Service to enter into 17 contracts, of which 15 were generated by committee requests:

Preparation of Lists of Subjects and Policy Areas

The Legislative Reorganization Act, as amended, directs the Service to prepare for each congressional committee at the opening of a new Congress "a list of subject and policy areas which the committee might profitably analyze in depth...." The purpose of the lists, as stated in the House Rules Committee report accompanying the 1970 bill, is to assist congressional committees with advance planning for research required during the course of the Congress, and at the same time alert the Service to the needs of committees so that it will be able to provide timely and effective assistance. The liaison and reciprocation aspects of the list-preparation process was made explicit in the House report: "We expect the CRS to work closely with the committee and its staff in the preparation of that list."

During the past fiscal year, CRS had its initial experience with the preparation and transmittal of subject and policy area lists for the 93d Congress. The Service established 37 ad hoc teams consisting of 144 persons, 30 percent of its total research staff, who devoted over 600 man-days to the task. Individual teams consisted of staff knowledgeable in most aspects of a committee's jurisdiction and in many cases were composed of personnel from several divisions. Normally, a team worked under the direction of a single coordinator, usually a senior analyst, who was the chief CRS spokesman in discussions with committee staff. Based on thorough and systematic evaluations of all relevant sources of information, the teams prepared comprehensive preliminary lists of subjects and policy areas of interest to a given committee. These lists were discussed with committee staff, modified on the basis of the discussions, and submitted in final form in the early spring of 1973.

Committees were given the option of receiving selected lists, consisting only of subjects with which the Service could provide assistance, or comprehensive lists, which included but were not limited to those subjects. The final product, unless specifically requested otherwise by a committee, included a summary list of agreed-upon subjects and policy areas, a one-page description of each subject to explain the reasons for its inclusion and provide additional sources of information, and, to the extent feasible and desired by the committee, additional materials to supplement and illustrate the one-page treatment. A total of 45 lists were prepared and sent to 46 committees; the average list contained 18 subjects and the lists and additional background reports averaged 20 pages in length.

The preparation of lists of subjects and policy areas has had at least two beneficial returns for the Service as it seeks to achieve the objectives of the Reorganization Act. The act directs the Service to maintain continuous liaison with all congressional committees, making known and available its services and resources. Expedited largely by the preparation of lists and consequent consultation between CRS and committee staffs, liaison was achieved with virtually all congressional committees in the past year. A more formalized liaison network is expected to be implemented in the next year as the result of a thorough review and evaluation of the list-preparation process. The lists also encouraged further committee use of CRS analytical resources; it is estimated that they generated some 80 committee research projects. Thus, the initial experience with preparation of subject lists and associated background reports had a significant impact on furthering the Service's accessibility and utility to congressional committees.

Cooperative Projects with Other Agencies

A number of cooperative arrangements with the

General Accounting Office have been developed by CRS in accordance with the House Rules Committee report accompanying the 1970 Reorganization Act, which provides that CRS and GAO "shall exchange information freely, collaborate whenever feasible...." In the past fiscal year, two mutual exchange briefings were held between representatives of the CRS Foreign Affairs Division staff and the GAO International Division on the organization and subject coverage of each. Staff meetings have also been held to provide for regular information exchange and to plan future cooperative arrangements. As a result of closer liaison, a number of substantial projects were undertaken with GAO in the past year. The GAO Office of Federal Elections requested that the CRS American Law Division undertake the collection, indexing, and abstracting of federal and state legislation and federal court litigations pertaining to or affecting election laws within each state. Accordingly, under contract agreement between GAO and the Library of Congress, the American Law Division began in January to index and abstract all state legislative information received from GAO and submitted its first report, covering January-June 1973, at the end of fiscal 1973. The GAO printed copies of the report and distributed them to all state governors, secretaries of state, leaders in state legislatures, Members of Congress with oversight responsibility in the election area, and interested organizations. Under terms of the contract, CRS is responsible for submitting monthly reports to GAO, supplemented by quarterly and annual compilations. The more significant state and federal legislation and federal litigations are supplemented by analysis.

The Service's Environmental Policy Division has cooperated with GAO on projects relating to implementation of environmental legislation. In a project for the Senate Public Works Committee, CRS is identifying and analyzing, on a continuing basis, all significant policy positions taken by the Environmental Protection Agency on implementation of the Federal Water Pollution Control Act amendments. The committee's oversight of the act's implementation by EPA is now being supplemented by GAO's access to internal executive documents and the analysis and evaluation provided by a CRS environmental policy analyst. Regular meetings with representatives from the committee, GAO, and CRS, in connection with projects related to the oversight function, have assisted in establishing closer relationships between the three staffs.

The Technology Assessment Act of 1972 (Public Law 92-484, enacted in October 1972), created an Office of Technology Assessment within the legislative branch "to provide early indications of the probable beneficial and adverse impacts of applications of technology and to develop other coordinate information which may assist the Congress." The policy and leadership component of OTA is the Technology Assessment Board. The director of CRS and the comptroller general are statutory members of the board's advisory council. The legislation authorizes the Librarian of Congress to make available to OTA any services and assistance from CRS as may be appropriate and feasible. The relationships between OTA and offices of the legislative branch are still at a formative stage, but the Service anticipates the development of constructive cooperative arrangements with OTA in the future.

Constitution Annotated

The seventh edition of *The Constitution of the United States of America–Analysis and Interpretation,* to be published as S. Doc. No. 92-82 of the 92d Congress, was completed in May and sent to the Government Printing Office. Prepared by the American Law Division, the new edition is some 2,000 pages long and represents a substantial revision and updating of the 1964 edition. The volume presents a clause-by-clause annotation and analysis of the Constitution's meaning as revealed in the decisions of the Supreme Court since 1789 and in the practice and policy of Congress and the President. The previous editions have fulfilled a substantial need in Congress, at the bench and bar, and in the scholarly community for many years, and Congress has responded

to this fact by authorizing in Public Law 91-589 regular decennial editions and biennial supplements to keep the text current, placing responsibility for the preparation of this major work on CRS.

DOCUMENTATION AND STATUS OF LEGISLATION

A paramount congressional interest is in the progress of legislation and an overriding concern of the Congressional Research Service has been to improve the currency of this information. Efforts in this regard have included inauguration of new operations arising from the Legislative Reorganization Act of 1970 and improvements in ongoing programs.

Terminating Program Lists

In addition to the subject and policy area lists, the 1970 act directs the Service to make available to all congressional committees at the opening of each new Congress "a list of programs and activities being carried out under existing law scheduled to terminate during the current Congress, which are within the jurisdiction of the committee. . . ." Beginning in late 1971, the American Law Division examined over 4,000 statutes enacted during the preceding 10 years and by December 1972, had identified some 730 programs and activities scheduled to terminate during a specified year. Over half of these programs relate to authorization of appropriations. Some 23 percent provide general authority for programs operated by executive branch agencies. Other categories include termination of commissions, loan authority, tax authority, reservations of land, pensions, and reporting requirements.

Following identification of terminating programs, the Service prepared lists of the 458 programs and activities scheduled to expire during the 93d Congress and transmitted the lists to 32 House, Senate, and joint committees of Congress. Each committee packet included basic identifying information on the programs relating to its jurisdictions and a legislative history or more extensive background report. The House and

Senate Appropriations Committees requested and received the complete listing of programs scheduled to expire during this Congress. Preparation of-the lists involved a substantial contribution from the American Law Division and, in many cases, preparation of background reports by the subject divisions. The entire process, directed and reviewed in the Office of the Director, was a pioneer and time-consuming undertaking. It is now being evaluated for effectiveness and for possible refinement.

Purpose and Effect Memoranda

A Legislative History Unit was established in the American Law Division to fulfill another directive of the Reorganization Act, the preparation of memoranda, upon request of a Member or a committee, specifying the purpose and effect of legislative measures that are scheduled for congressional hearings. In addition to primary source materials, papers and reports prepared by CRS divisions relating to legislative histories are being collected and indexed by the unit on a continuing basis. The collection will aid CRS researchers in locating prepared materials to answer inquiries and will be a valuable working tool in preparing future memoranda. Although over 200 requests·for legislative histories were received by the unit this fiscal year, only a few related to pending measures; most of the inquiries pertained to the history of earlier enactments. To assist in the preparation of legislative histories, the Service currently possesses the computer capability to retrieve legislative status data on pending bills. Further efforts are under way to link the preparation of legislative histories to relevant bibliographic lists· of congressional reports and documents, legal and other professional journal articles, notations in the press, executive department reports, interest group statements, and appropriate CRS multiliths.

Bill Digest

The *Digest of Public General Bills and Resolutions* was first prepared in 1936 for the second session of the 74th Congress and has provided summaries of the public bills and resolutions for each succeeding session of Congress. Since 1970, the Service has used computer programs to access the *Bill Digest* information base by means of two cathode ray tube terminals and associated printers located in the American Law Division. Six units were installed in other CRS divisions this year and there are plans to install another, which will bring the total in the Service to nine. This online capability permits rapid retrieval of *Bill Digest* information files and provides a valuable tool to support research. The CRT system can be used to query the file in five ways: by bill number, subject, bill sponsor, bill cosponsor and, as of this fiscal year, by congressional committee. Other data bases will similarly be retrievable via CRT in the near future.

At the request of Senator Howard Cannon, chairman of the Senate Committee on Rules and Administration and vice chairman of the Joint Committee on the Library, the Service made arrangements this spring for the installation of CRT terminals in the offices of seven Senators. This is a pilot venture for evaluation and planning of future congressional video access to *Bill Digest* and other information contained in CRS data banks.

Major Legislation of the 93d Congress

Complementing the *Bill Digest* is another publication which has been retitled and substantively altered in the past year. *Major Legislation of the 93d Congress* (MLC) was formerly the *Legislative Status Report,* which provided legislative status and content information on selected major bills before the Congress. Following interviews with congressional users, it became evident that this report was primarily used to answer various forms of· the question: "What is Congress doing about . . .?" and to provide content for newsletters, speeches, and responses to constitutent mail.

To serve these and other purposes more effectively, the report has been augmented to provide, in addition to bill content and status data, relevant information on major legislative issues with identification of presidential messages, court cases, CRS multilithed reports, and other appropriate and available reports relating to those issues. The American Law Division obtains contributions from other subject divisions to ensure a comprehensive treatment of the subjects and issues covered in its summaries. The report continues to be issued at the end of each month and is supplemented by the weekly *Legislative Status Checklist.* The revised report was issued in April, May, and June of fiscal 1973, each issue treating some 300 major bills organized by subject area.

INFORMATION AND REFERENCE SERVICES

The Service has expanded cooperative arrangements with outside organizations and agencies to provide the Congress with the most recent information available on current national issues and programs. In cooperation with the Advanced Study Program of the Brookings Institution, a series of seminars for Members of Congress and a separate series for the senior professional staffs of congressional offices and committees were initiated in fiscal 1973. Approximately once a month, nationally prominent specialists in various subject areas were invited to meet in the evenings with interested Members, or alternatively with congressional staff. The seven seminars held for Members attracted an overall attendance of 150 Senators and Representatives and included discussions on U.S. relations with China, perspectives and considerations in welfare reform, crime prevention and law enforcement, energy and the environment, issues and alternatives relating to national housing programs, quality and inequality of education, and economic policies and controls. The three seminars for congressional staff, covering legislative implications of the election results, energy policy options, and options for federal policy on health delivery systems, were held in multiple sessions and drew an overall attendance of 275 persons. Both series were well received and will be continued in the coming fiscal year.

At the request of the Senate Subcommittee on Housing and Urban Affairs, the Service, in con-

junction with the National Planning Association and Resources for the Future, Inc., undertook the development and sponsorship of a series of eight informal seminars on issues related to national growth policy. The evening seminars were held at the Library of Congress from February through May 1973 and featured speakers from diverse social science fields. Members and staffs from some 30 congressional offices participated in the discussions of national settlement patterns, metropolitan growth, rural development, and other related subjects. A CRS multilithed report summarizing the remarks of the principal speakers and the discussions among participants was prepared, and there are plans to resume the series next year.

In response to requests from a number of Representatives and Senators, panels of experts in the tax field were invited to speak to congressional staff on basic tax issues. The CRS senior specialist in taxation and fiscal policy was appointed chairman of a planning committee that included staff representation from congressional offices. Over 100 persons attended each of four seminars and discussed budgets and tax systems of federal, state, and local governments, theories of taxation and distribution of the tax burden, federal tax legislation in 1973, and structure and logic of the Internal Revenue Code.

Reference Requests

Serving as the reference and general information arm of the Service, the Congressional Reference Division (CRS C) responded to over 118,000 inquiries, or approximately two-thirds of the requests handled by CRS last year. Receiving roughly a request a minute, the division answered 56 percent of all Member inquiries directed to CRS, 53 percent of all committee requests, and 85 percent of the constituent inquiries. Since fiscal year 1971, there has been a 17 percent increase in Member and committee requests handled by the division and a 16 percent decline in constituent requests.

Congressional interest in the Watergate hearings has created considerable challenge for the

CRS C staff. Since January 1973, two staff members have worked full time on the "Watergate Notebook," which contains clippings of all relevant articles in selected newspapers and had grown to some 3,400 pages by the end of the fiscal year. Particularly since the hearings began in May, the "Watergate team" has been besieged by requests for biographical, chronological, and other background information. All sections of the division, including the reference centers and Congressional Reading Room, have shared in the Watergate-generated workload.

The division has now developed giveaway kits on 105 subjects. Five added this year provided information on amnesty, child abuse, ecology, the energy crisis, and strip mining. Over 18,000 kits were sent out in the past year, most often in response to constituent requests; most popular were those on abortion, Congress, drugs, pollution, and women's rights. There were over 3,500 requests for CRS multilithed reports, and the requests for copies of government publications, particularly bills and public laws, showed an increase of 21 percent over the previous year.

Information Centers

The Congressional Reading Room and the CRS reference centers provide Members of Congress and their staffs with readily accessible collections of reference books, current periodicals, and CRS multilithed reports, as well as with the services of trained librarians.

The Congressional Reading Room, located in the Main Building of the Library, continued to experience a growth in both in-person and telephone business, particularly in the number of urgent "hotline" requests. Over 15,300 requests were handled during the fiscal year, of which some 11,300 were for hotline service.

In an attempt to provide faster and more accessible service to Congress, CRS opened its first reference center in the Rayburn House Office Building early in 1971. The operation was expanded with the conversion of the Loan Division Book Room in the Russell Senate Office Building to a CRS reference center in January 1973. From

the beginning business in the new center was brisk, and the two librarians from the Congressional Reference Division who manned the operation with the help of two messengers and one Loan Division attendant were at times hard pressed to handle the volume of work.

The Rayburn center saw a steady increase in the number of reference requests and staff visitors during the year, handling nearly 9,000 requests for service during fiscal 1973. In its first six months, the Senate reference center in the Russell Building processed over 3,000 requests. In February, facsimile transmitters were installed in both centers to transmit such materials as copies of articles or statistical data between the centers, CRS C, the Congressional Reading Room, and congressional offices. The transmitters also expedite newspaper queries by enabling the rapid receipt of articles from newspaper offices or other news sources throughout the country. The Rayburn center has a microfilm reader-printer which permits direct access to microfilmed newspapers located in the Congressional Reference Division. The opening of a third center is contemplated for the Longworth House Office Building early in fiscal 1974.

Special Services

Requests for graphics and translations are handled by two small but important units of the Service with supplemental assistance from other offices of the Library. The CRS visual information specialist prepared over 100 individual graphics items and 85 other assignments were met through contractual services. Illustrative of the types of graphics services provided by the Service are the following requests received in fiscal 1973: several congressional district maps for use by Members; a series of five charts pertaining to world oil and gas production and consumption; a map of the United States showing the coverage of television stations owned and operated by the major networks, by area and number of households; graphs depicting authorizations and appropriations for water pollution construction grants; and 11 original drawings illustrating some of the major accomplishments of the 92d Congress.

The material requested for translation is diverse, ranging from simple correspondence to complex scientific and technical publications, legal documents, and diplomatic and political reports. In the past year the six CRS translators responded to over 2,600 congressional requests, a slight increase over the previous year.

In addition to these special services, CRS annually assembles and provides excerpts and bibliographic data on the national high school and college debate topics. Materials are currently available on next year's high school topic, "What should be the role of the Federal government in extending public assistance to all Americans living in poverty?"; and on the college debate topic for fiscal 1973, "Resolved: That the Federal government should enact a program of comprehensive medical care for all United States citizens."

Library Services Support

As the Service augments its professional research staff and the scope of its analytical and policy-related services to Congress, a particularly valuable and expanding support capability for all CRS operations is found in the Library Services Division. Composed chiefly of professional reference librarians who have responsibility for the acquisition, processing, and distribution of research materials and periodicals within the Service, this staff has expanded its services to accommodate more fully the information needs of subject division personnel and indirectly (and frequently directly) the needs of congressional staffs. An important innovation of the past year consisted of detailing, on a pilot basis, a library technician from the division to each of four subject divisions to assist them in developing their book and periodical reference collections and maintaining information files and to serve as liaison between the subject divisions and Library Services. The technicians, trained in the Library Services Division, are under the supervision of its assistant chief. This experimental program has

been highly successful in improving communications by informing the participating subject divisions of available library resources and alerting the Library Services Division to subject division needs. The program will be extended to all subject divisions in fiscal 1974.

The fourth edition of the Legislative Indexing Vocabulary (LIV), containing over 5,000 entries, was issued in this fiscal year. The format employed in this vocabulary is similar to that used in the list of LC subject headings, and collaboration with the staff of the Library's Subject Cataloging Division has resulted in a high degree of compatibility between the two systems.

The Service's Selective Dissemination of Information (SDI) system provides bibliographic citations to current articles and publications on public policy topics. The system is continually updated by bibliographers who screen some 4,000 periodicals, government documents, and private research organization publications, as well as CRS written products, for significant material of interest to Congress. There are currently 106 congressional subscribers to the SDI, and over 1,400 congressional requests for cited materials were received by the Service this year. The popularity of the SDI was substantiated by a recent CRS survey to ascertain the usefulness of the system to congressional staff.

Some 440 on-demand bibliographies were produced from the SDI data base this year, compared to 102 in fiscal 1972. Of these, 234 were in direct response to congressional requests and the rest were used to support research within the Service. New search techniques such as batching— the ability to search the data base for more than one bibliography at a time—and a more precise search capability have accelerated and improved access to the bibliographic data base. For the first time, the Library Services Division prepared author and subject catalogs that consolidated all bibliographic citations to publications of the General Accounting Office. Also for the first time, specialized catalogs were prepared containing bibliographic citations on issues of special interest to the subject divisions. Topics of these 18 catalogs included agriculture, Congress, the environment, and veterans.

ADMINISTRATION

To provide for continued implementation of the Service's expanded responsibilities under the Legislative Reorganization Act, Congress funded 86 new positions in fiscal year 1973. Of these, 48 were allotted to direct implementation of new and expanding responsibilities: 31 to the provision of indepth analysis for the Members and committees of Congress, including six new senior specialist positions in the fields of federal budget, engineering and public works, public administration, urban affairs, American public law, and transportation and communications; 12 to the preparation of lists of subjects and policy areas for committees; one to the compilation of lists of terminating programs; and four to the preparation of purpose and effect memoranda. The remaining 38 new positions were allocated to library services and administrative support of these new activities and to improvement and expansion of traditional CRS services.

Training and Communication

Several innovations in training and internal communications have been brought about by the accelerated growth of CRS staff. The orientation program for new staff members has been considerably expanded in the past year, and for the first time an inservice course on congressional operations and legislative procedures was offered to all staff. The course was presented in a series of six one-hour lectures featuring speakers from both within and outside the Service; future courses of this nature are being planned, including one on the federal budget process. The Service also initiated a monthly speakers' forum in September 1972, inviting noted specialists·from relevant professional fields to discuss current issues with interested CRS staff.

Overall, 456 staff members participated in the inservice training programs, including orientation, and 134 in courses outside the Library. The latter, offered by local universities, the U.S. Department of Agriculture Graduate School, and the U.S. Civil Service Commission, provided professional, technical, or administrative training for staff from all CRS divisions. Additional staff development occurs through attendance at professional conferences; 94 staff members attended 109 professional conferences in the past year, in numerous cases participating as speakers or panelists. To assist the career development of nonprofessional staff, the Service, in cooperation with the Library, has developed "Program Crossover," designed to enable transfers into professional career ladders through on-the-job and selected academic training over a two-year period. The program is scheduled to begin in September 1973.

Following a CRS conference in June 1972 on many issues relating to productivity and work environment, several measures were implemented during fiscal 1973 to improve internal communications. In addition to the weekly director's meeting with division chiefs, every fourth week the director and deputy director meet with the assistant chiefs of each division to discuss current activities and policies. Each division has held more frequent staff meetings, and the research production assistants from each division have regular meetings to exchange ideas and develop methods for improving division procedures. Additionally, monthly meetings were initiated to facilitate interdivisional approaches to major projects and to discuss research methodologies.

A second CRS conference was held in May 1973 to evaluate the Service's procedures and performance to date in implementation of certain of the Reorganization Act provisions. The conference discussions have stimulated planning and evaluation efforts, which are expected to be reflected in the accomplishments of fiscal 1974.

Automation

For the past five years, CRS has been engaged in analyzing its work procedures to identify those areas that appear to have the greatest potential for improvement through the application of automated data processing techniques. In this fiscal year, a significant number of these applications came to fruition, and these, added to the Service's initial experience with contracting for outside computer services for use inhouse, made 1973 a dramatic year for automation in CRS.

The new automated applications assist in five areas: tracking of pending legislation (the *Bill Digest* information base); bibliographic control of published materials relating to national issues (the bibliographic data base); the production of specific research products; administrative and management controls; and provision of information from outside data banks and computer programs. These last three are discussed in turn.

During the fiscal year, an increasing number of CRS reports were placed in the computer to be constantly updated but printed out only when required. Examples of these applications are printouts of terminating program lists by date of termination, by Senate and House committee with oversight responsibility, by subject of the program, and by the CRS division responsible; storage of daily chronological events by the Foreign Affairs Division so that when crises occur, instantaneous background briefing chronologies can be produced, tailored to fit either a specific country, general geographic area, or particular time span; and the employment of report storage and update programs to produce directories of, for example, executive branch publication offices, advisory commissions, and committees.

Since 1915, the Service has kept records on the number of inquiries received and kinds of responses given. These statistical records were placed in the computer in the early sixties, and have since been made increasingly sophisticated and useful to the management of CRS. Completely rewritten statistical programs were adopted at the beginning of fiscal 1973. The result is the most flexible and comprehensive statistical and administrative reporting system the Service has ever had. The work of CRS can now be examined and correlated not only in terms of how much work was done in what amount of time but also by such aspects as the form in which an inquiry was answered, the type of work required, and the subjects involved. Similarly, the data base provides monthly reports on the length of time inquiries are in the Service and on allocation by budget program of manhours and number of requests.

Fiscal 1973 also marked the initial CRS use of outside data banks and programs to supplement existing information sources. The Service acquired automated access to over 400,000 citations in the National Library of Medicine MEDLINE data bank from which the Education and Public Welfare and Science Policy Research Divisions drew biomedical information; the use of the Service Bureau Corporation's computer services, which include data analysis programs as well as access to the economic data maintained by the National Bureau of Economic Research and to program expenditure data of the Department of Health, Education, and Welfare; and the *New York Times* Information Bank, with indexes and abstracts of all *New York Times* news articles published since 1970.

Quality Control and Evaluation

Confucius reputedly was determined to eradicate a biased mind, arbitrary judgments, obstinacy, and egotism. The CRS quality control effort is comparably ambitious as it reinforces, through policy review of CRS products, the Service-wide effort to eradicate partisanship, advocacy, and subjectivity. It further evaluates the appropriateness and responsiveness of completed work. This small staff in the Office of the Director was expanded in size by the addition of another reviewer and the scope of its activities extended to policy and substantive review of major CRS written products, including multilithed reports, committee prints, subject and terminating program reports, substantive memoranda, and speeches. The staff also seeks to ensure that outgoing work meets CRS standards of intelligibility and format, as outlined in the two departmental manuals on preparation of CRS reports and bibliographic form, and arranges for peer review of interdisciplinary reports.

The Service initiated feedback surveys this year to determine the usefulness and reception of its response to congressional inquiries. One-week sample surveys were conducted in August and March by attaching a return-mail evaluation card to each completed response. Although there were significant differences between the sample size and composition of CRS and congressional staff in the two surveys, in both, 61 percent of the CRS responses were rated "superior," 37 percent "satisfactory," and 2 percent "unsatisfactory." The ratings on committee work were notably higher in March, with 9 percent more of the cards rated "superior." Over 96 percent in both surveys responded positively to questions on the relevance and timeliness of responses. About 45 percent of the cards in both surveys bore comments in the space provided; some 75 percent of these were favorable, 18 percent expressed or implied some form of criticism, and 7 percent provided suggestions or were neutral in tone. The results of the surveys were tabulated, analyzed, and distributed, with a sampling of congressional comments, to all CRS staff. In addition to providing the Service with a valuable cross section of reaction to its work by those who frequently request assistance, several constructive suggestions were received and researchers were provided with an immediate and meaningful appraisal of their work. Applied sparingly, these and other evaluation techniques can assist CRS in maintaining and improving the quality of its service to Congress.

Even in this necessarily brief review of the past year's activities and accomplishments, it is evi-dent that the Congressional Research Service has moved a great distance, not only since 1914 but more especially in the last year. The demanding and often hectic environment that has always characterized this response-oriented organization has been accelerated by the rapid growth and changing nature of its operations. The pressures on those in the firing line of rush deadlines, in the midst of numerous projects, with memoranda and reports to write, phone calls to answer, and congressional sessions to attend, are greater.

Perspective and encouragement are gained by recognition that the Service is the largest organization of its kind in the world. Many parliaments that do not have these benefits are establishing similar services. For example, the Japanese National Diet's Library has a Research and Legislative Reference Department half the size of CRS, modeled on this Library's Legislative Reference Service in 1948. Members of parliaments of other countries, visiting CRS from time to time, express enthusiasm and admiration when they learn of the kinds of assistance that are available to the Congress through the Congressional Research Service. But perhaps the driving motivation of most CRS staff derives from the realization that through its collective effort it can assist the Congress in effectively fulfilling its constitutional role; whatever dearth there may be of time or tranquility there is no dearth of challenge in applying intelligence to the problems of today's world.

3

The
Reference
Department

Five of the 15 divisions of the Reference Department celebrated 75th anniversaries during 1973. On July 1, 1897, Congress established in the Library of Congress new "departments" of periodicals, maps and charts, music, graphic arts, and manuscripts. However, these antecedents of the present Serial, Geography and Map, Music, Prints and Photographs, and Manuscript Divisions began functioning only after November 1, 1897, when the new Library building opened to the public. The origins of a sixth specialized division, the Division for the Blind and Physically Handicapped, can also be traced to November 1, 1897, for on that day the Library began operating the first reading room for the blind in a major American library. The intervening 75 years are notable not only for the enormous growth of the collections within the department but, more importantly, for the steady expansion of the reference, research, and bibliographic services based on those collections and reflected in the activities described in this chapter.

50

Significant trends during fiscal 1973 included the following:

□ A continuation of the active departmental program for publishing such specialized bibliographies and resource guides as *French-Speaking West Africa: A Guide to Official Publications in American Libraries.*

□ Success in acquiring unique items of Americana, among them the earliest known photographs of the Capitol and the White House, but an inability to attract major new literary collections because of the unfavorable provisions of the Tax Reform Act of 1969.

□ Increased use of the specialized reading rooms, particularly the Microform, Rare Book, Local History and Genealogy, Prints and Photographs, and Science and Technology Reading Rooms.

□ Publication of an exceptional number of pamphlets describing the department's varied collections and services, for example, *The National Union Catalog: Reference and Related Services.*

REFERENCE DEPARTMENT OFFICE

Acquisitions, processing, and preservation activities of the various Reference Department divisions and liaison between those divisions and other departments of the Library centers in the departmental office. In fiscal 1973, measurable progress was made in bringing the Library's stated acquisitions policies into conformity with its present needs and practices. With the aid of the department's area studies specialists and in consultation with the Law Library and the Processing Department, seven new or revised acquisitions policy statements were drafted and approved by the Acquisitions Committee and the Librarian. They concern legal materials, international organizations, and official publications of foreign countries and of U.S. cities and towns. In its continuing effort to ensure the protection and future usefulness of the Library's resources, the office surveyed the cartographic, manuscript, newspaper, sound recording, motion picture, pictorial, and rare monographic collections to assist the Preservation Office in planning an effective preservation program. The first issue of *Foreign Newspaper Report* was published. This newsletter, which will appear three times a year, is intended to keep research libraries informed about current developments in matters related to the acquisition and microfilming of foreign newspapers.

Reference uses of the MARC data base are coordinated in the Reference Department Office. During the year, several new current-awareness services in specialized subject fields were established, including a monthly printout of catalog records of books on library and information science.

THE GENERAL COLLECTIONS

Direct service to Congress is the dominant activity of the Loan Division. During the fiscal year the division charged over 73,000 items to congressional borrowers; of these, more than 8,000 came from the congressional waiting list, which is maintained to fill, by special purchase if necessary, requests for materials not readily available from the Library's collections. Topics of greatest interest included taxes, drugs, psychiatry, the careers of recent Presidents and, toward the end of the year, the energy crisis. The Senate Book Room was transferred from the Loan Division to the Congressional Research Service, which had taken over responsibility for the book room in the Rayburn House Office Building in 1971.

In April there was a demonstration of a prototype of a new system for automating the central charge file, the Library's master record of books in circulation or assigned to special collections. Using a screen similar to those seen in airline terminals, the system is designed to charge and discharge materials and to search the files for several types of entries. Plans are under way for its development and implementation.

The Stack and Reader Division, which is responsible for custody and service of the general classified collections, reported a decline in use of the Main Reading Room and the Thomas Jefferson Room; by contrast, use of the Microform Reading Room (which changed its name from Microfilm Reading Room during the year to reflect more accurately the scope of its holdings) rose a dramatic 33 percent. Microform holdings very nearly reached the million mark. Evening hours of service were expanded to include Wednesdays as well as Tuesdays and Thursdays, and Saturday use continued to be very heavy. Special study facilities administered by the Stack and Reader Division were used to capacity; revised editions of the brochures *Information for Readers in the Library of Congress* and *Special Facilities for Research in the Library of Congress* were issued.

Shelf space for books remained the primary problem; seven classes representing nearly 2 million volumes were relocated or shifted so as to relieve the desperately overcrowded conditions in some stack areas. Priority 4 material, a large collection of partially cataloged publications, was

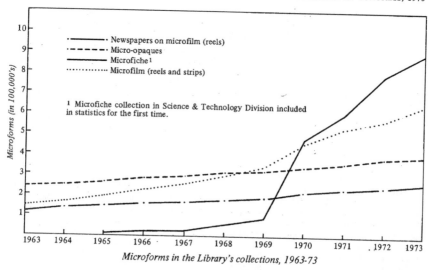

Microforms in the Library's collections, 1963-73

placed in storage in the Library's Pickett Street Annex, from which needed items can be retrieved on request. Several more major moves were scheduled for fiscal 1974 which should result in the shelving of most of the volumes now on the floor. The long-range forecast, however, is that all parts of the general collections will be severely cramped before the Madison Building is ready for occupancy, and that further moves will be required. In March a pilot project for an automated book paging system got under way with a terminal at the Main Reading Room issue desk relaying information to a similar terminal on Deck 42, where a call slip was printed out. The experiment, still in progress at the year's end, demonstrated that such a method is indeed feasible. Further research is needed on means of permitting readers, rather than Library staff, to input the data and of tying this system in with other bibliographic and circulation control systems throughout the Library.

Development of a computerized book catalog of the Main Reading Room's reference collection has for several years been a major undertaking of

the Public Reference Section of the General Reference and Bibliography Division (GR&B). The catalog data base now contains approximately 11,500 monographic and 2,400 serial titles. This catalog and its future cumulations or supplements are expected to be a notable contribution to reference service everywhere; in the meantime, the several parts of the preliminary book catalog are proving to be useful within the Library.

Inquiries handled by the Public Reference Section and the Bibliography and Reference Correspondence Section included the origin of the word "watergate," American presidential campaign funds, presidential impeachment and resignation, the kinds of wild animals in the woods of England in the 15th century, representations of Hercules on Etruscan vases, and biographical information on a friend of Walt Whitman. Scholarly interest in two broad subjects, the American Negro and the American Revolution, remained at a high level.

Robert W. Schaaf, head of the Union Catalog and International Organizations Reference Section, combined attendance at a United Nations-sponsored Symposium on Intergovernmental Documents in Geneva, Switzerland, with fruitful acquisitions visits to key international agencies in Rome, Paris, and Brussels. The section found that union catalog inquiries decreased slightly due to the availability of more volumes of the *National Union Catalog, Pre-1956 Imprints* and to its own efforts to restrict replies to those for which local or regional library resources are known to be insufficient. This means that only the more difficult and time-consuming inquiries are likely to come to the Library of Congress. A 33-page guide and instruction manual, *The National Union Catalog: Reference and Related Services*, was issued in April and is proving to be most helpful to inquirers.

Because of the discontinuation of support from its sponsors, the Arms Control and Disarmament Agency, the GR&B Arms Control and Disarmament Section was abolished at the end of fiscal 1973. The section came into existence in the spring of 1964 and published the first issue of its *Arms Control and Disarmament* (Winter 1964/65) in January 1965. For nearly nine years this quarterly provided researchers with an annotated and indexed survey of the literature on arms control, disarmament, and related political, military, economic, and social developments. The last issue of the periodical was that for spring 1973 (volume 9, number 2); in all, a total of 15,241 entries were published. In addition, 960 abstracts were prepared in a "Disarmament Digest" series and 20 special bibliographic studies were compiled. The small staff of the section, in establishing bibliographic control over a specialized field of knowledge during a crucial period, did credit to the Library of Congress.

The Children's Book Section celebrated its 10th anniversary on March 5, 1973, with a lecture by Erik Haugaard and a discussion with the speaker the next morning. The anniversary was highlighted in the *Quarterly Journal* for April 1973, which was devoted to children's literature at the Library, and in an article by Paul Heins, editor of *Horn Book* magazine, published in April in *The Calendar*, the widely distributed quarterly of the Children's Book Council. New

publications prepared by the section included *Children's Books—1972*, the ninth in the series; *Creating Independence, 1763-1789*, a selected annotated bibliography; and the first supplement to *Children's Literature* (1967).

Reader services in the Newspaper and Current Periodical Reading Room of the Serial Division continued their upward trend. In particular, the increased use of domestic newspapers appears to indicate their greater research value as source material, despite the removal of bound domestic newspapers to the Duke Street Annex to join the foreign volumes as a necessary space-saving measure. Unfortunately, these volumes require 48 hours' advance notice for retrieval for reader use.

Significant progress was made in organizing the collections of unbound newspapers and periodicals for use by readers. A major contributing factor was the decision to transfer custody of congressional documents and bills to the Law Library beginning with the convening of the 93d Congress in January 1973; at that time some 61,000 pieces were removed from the division. In advance of the move, the division completed the collation of the bills for the 92d Congress—about 123,000 pieces—and disposed of the duplicate issues. Among the notable receipts were the following newspapers on microfilm:

Russian provincial newspapers for the post-World War II period; substantially complete files for 68 titles from 19 cities.

Rhodesian Herald (Salisbury, Rhodesia), January 1927 to May 1950.

La Vanguardia (Buenos Aires, Argentina), 1894-1944.

O Estado ·de São Paulo (São Paulo, Brazil), 1875-1939. The Library now has complete holdings of this major Brazilian newspaper for 1875 through 1972.

In all, over 14,000 reels of foreign and domestic newspapers on microfilm were added to the collections.

A program of exhibiting rare and interesting

materials in the custody of the Serial Division
was inaugurated. The first exhibit, "The Declaration of Independence in the Domestic and Foreign Press," displayed the text of the Declaration
as it was presented in three newspapers of the
period.

Reference service to readers in the Rare Book
Division jumped 44 percent over the previous
year. Consultations, tours, special requests from
the Congressional Research Service, projects for
television, and a variety of activities new to the
division are included in this figure. Much of the
energy of the new chief, William Matheson,
appointed on July 10, 1972, was devoted to an
indepth analysis of the division's collections and
acquisitions policies. Many of his conclusions are
outlined in his article about the Rare Book Division in the July 1973 issue of the *Quarterly Journal.* Collection development was also a topic of
major concern on Mr. Matheson's four-week survey of leading antiquarian bookdealers and selected major libraries in Paris, Geneva, Brussels,
Zurich, London, and other parts of England.

Shifts within the stacks of the division created
a limited amount of additional space, and special
efforts were made to clean and rearrange these
and other book storage areas. Processing activities were eyed critically and new procedures
instituted wherever desirable. For example, the
division began bookplating and embossing its
own receipts, functions previously performed
elsewhere in the Library. This change in routine
has resulted in more efficient service to readers
and improved control over newly acquired items.
Accessibility to one specialized collection was
improved with the publication of the catalog to
the division's broadsides collection by G. K. Hall
& Co.

The mission of the Federal Research Division is
to provide support to other government agencies
by making use of the collections and facilities of
the Library of Congress. Continuing projects for
the Department of Defense, NASA, and the
National Institutes of Health resulted in scholarly
studies, parts of studies for incorporation into
major papers produced by others, background
papers, and a continuous flow of abstracts from
foreign publications.

AREA STUDIES

Four administrative units within the Reference
Department are specifically concerned with area
studies: the African Section of GR&B, the Latin
American, Portuguese, and Spanish Division, the
Orientalia Division, and the Slavic and Central
European Division. The activities of the language
and subject specialists within these units are
focused on developing and utilizing the Library's
extensive resources for the study of foreign cultures and societies.

One of the best methods of making the Library's collections more widely known and hence
more useful is through the publication of bibliographies based primarily on those collections.
A good example was the appearance in 1973 of
the African Section's *French-Speaking Central
Africa: A Guide to Official Publications in American Libraries.* Compiled by Julian W. Witherell,
section head, the 314-page publication is the
largest in the section's series of guides to official
publications of African nations or regions. It was
as favorably reviewed by Africanists as its predecessors. These bibliographic guides have played a
large part in establishing the African Section's
reputation as, in the words of a grateful reader,
"an important documentation centre for African
studies." The high level of interest in Africa
shown by scholars, government officials, and the
general public was reflected in a considerable
increase in reference correspondence and telephone inquiries to the section during the past
year.

Similarly, there was an increase in the number
of readers who used the Hispanic Society Room,
the reading room for the Latin American, Portuguese, and Spanish Division (LAPS). Known until
last year as the Hispanic Foundation, LAPS
serves as a center for the pursuit of studies in the
cultures of Latin America, the Iberian Peninsula,
and those areas were the influence of the Iberian
Peninsula has been significant. The appearance of
a new information brochure describing the division's principal activities helped to publicize its
services and publications.

To strengthen and improve the Library collections concerning the Iberian Peninsula, a special

55

survey was initiated to evaluate the collections on Spain and Portugal. The survey, which began in the autumn of 1972 and was conducted with the assistance of scholars from the academic community, has two objectives: to describe in the form of bibliographical essays the strengths of the Library's collections on Spain and Portugal for the benefit of scholars and to identify important gaps in the literature so that the collections may be augmented. An acquisition trip to the Caribbean in April by Earl J. Pariseau, acting chief, resulted in the strengthening of the collections from Jamaica, Haiti, the Dominican Republic, and Trinidad. The demise of the Latin American Cooperative Acquisitions Program (LACAP) on January 1, 1973, necessitated the establishment of new methods of acquiring many important research materials.

Volume 34 (Humanities) of the *Handbook of Latin American Studies*, edited by Donald E. J. Stewart, was published in April 1973 by the University of Florida Press. Part of the continuing bibliographic program of LAPS, the *Handbook*, regarded as one of the most important bibliographic tools for Latin American studies, utilizes the efforts of over 80 specialists, who prepare annotated references to the most

significant monographs and periodical articles about Latin America published anywhere in the world.

A long-term bibliographic project in the Orientalia Division was brought to fruition in fiscal 1973 with the publication by G. K. Hall & Co. of the *Southeast Asia Subject Catalog*. The catalog, which contains reproductions of over 65,000 cards representing a wide variety of monographs, periodical articles, pamphlets, dissertations, and materials on microform dealing with Southeast Asia, was published in six volumes. It represents the culmination of 28 years of work by Cecil Hobbs, who retired in early 1972 from his post as head of the Southern Asia Section. A major effort was made in the Southern Asia Section during the past year to analyze groups of materials received under the Library's Public Law 480 and NPAC programs, which generate most of the section's receipts. These detailed reviews help agents in the field in their selection of materials and provide useful information for other libraries whose collections complement and supplement those of the Library of Congress.

During the fiscal year the Chinese and Korean Section in the Orientalia Division added over 10,000 volumes to its collections, which now

Growth of the Orientalia collections, 1968-73

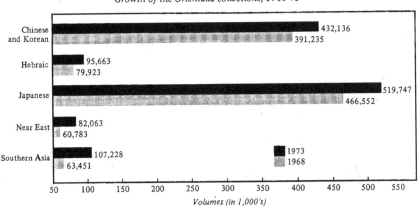

total over 430,000 volumes. The annual increase, considerably larger than in past years, is attributed to improved acquisition arrangements made with the Library's blanket-order dealers in Taiwan, Hong Kong, and Seoul. The section reports that acquisitions from the People's Republic of China are increasing slowly. One result of the 1972 visit of Chi Wang, assistant section head, to the People's Republic of China was an agreement whereby the Library has received a reprint of 202 volumes of the monumental 15th-century compendium entitled *Yung-lo ta tien.* The Japanese collection in the Orientalia Division now has an estimated total of 405,000 monographic titles in 519,000 volumes. Of this total, 76,000 titles in 107,000 volumes are represented by LC printed cards; this collection has grown rapidly since the Library's NPAC acquisitions program began in Tokyo in March 1968. The decline in the number of currently published Japanese trade monographs purchased by the Library in fiscal 1973 was due primarily to the devaluation of the American dollar and the inflationary trend of the Japanese economy. Congressional requests for translations and reference services by the Japanese Section doubled in fiscal 1973, a reflection of the nation's constantly increasing interest in the Far East.

Queries on the following matters were among the reference questions answered by the Hebraic Section: the Rosetta Stone, Massadah, Ethiopic manuscripts, the Khazars, the biblical city of Luz, the Jewish calendar, Australian doctoral dissertations in Semitics, sociomedical problems in Israel, the disposition of the papers of Chaim Weizmann, and the location of publications in the Judeo-Tat dialect. The Near East Section reported questions emphasizing primarily the current political situation in the Middle East. A highlight of the year was the acquisitions trip made by George Atiyeh, section head, to Turkey, Iran, Kuwait, Iraq, Lebanon, Jordan, Saudi Arabia, and Bahrain, the first survey by a head of the Near East Section to that area and one that resulted immediately in the addition of approximately 800 new titles to the collections and the filling of many gaps among the Turkish, Arabic, and Persian serials.

Personal contacts between specialists from the Slavic and Central European Division and their counterparts in libraries, publishing firms, and government agencies in Czechoslovakia, Austria, Yugoslavia, Finland, and Greece also enhanced the Library's Slavic and East European collections. These contacts, along with the review by recommending officers of national bibliographies, exchange offerings, and lists from book-dealers, are important methods by which the Slavic Division aids in the Library's acquisitions function. In fiscal 1973 the division's specialists recommended nearly 34,000 items for addition to the collections.

Bibliographic and reference activities of the Slavic Division also had a noticeable impact on acquisitions. For example, in January 1973 the division assumed responsibility for compiling the *American Bibliography of Slavic and East European Studies for 1973.* This annual bibliography, sponsored by the American Association for the Advancement of Slavic Studies, lists current publications on Slavic and East European subjects written primarily by North American authors. Its compilation brought to light a number of English-language titles missing from the Library's collections. The extensive surveys of the Library's collections on East Central and Southeastern Europe, undertaken as a contribution to the American Council of Learned Society's forthcoming handbook of library and research resources in those areas, pinpointed areas of strength as well as of weakness and prompted action to remedy the deficiencies. Finally, questions from readers often serve the same function. For example, a query about the women's rights movement in the Russian Empire revealed a gap in the collections that the division is endeavoring to fill by a number of recommendations for both book and microfilm material.

SUBJECT-ORIENTED DIVISIONS

Noise pollution, the metric system, and geothermal energy were three of 20 subjects covered in the *LC Science Tracer Bullet* series in fiscal 1973. Issued by the Science and Technology Division, these brief guides to published sources about specialized topics proved to be enormously popular. The heavy demand for the first *Tracer Bullet*, on acupuncture, prompted the preparation of a form letter updating the references in it. In all, the division's total direct reference services—in person, by telephone, and by correspondence—increased 13 percent from the previous year.

The number of requests answered by the division's National Referral Center, which directs those who have scientific or technical questions to organizations or individuals with specialized knowledge in the appropriate subjects, rose to an alltime high of over 4,000. As part of a project to revise the NRC general directories of information resources, new editions of *Biological Sciences* and *Social Sciences* were published in September 1972 and July 1973, respectively. The first was a 577-page revision of one of the fields covered in the center's first directory, published in 1965 under the subtitle *Physical Sciences, Biological Sciences, Engineering*. The new *Social Sciences* directory updates and extends the coverage of its predecessor with the same subtitle, published in 1965. Both revised directories were produced by a computer-based photocomposition system. During the year, substantial progress was made toward a completely automated data base for the division's many bibliographic projects; eventually that will be used to produce bibliographies and book catalogs and for a variety of searching operations.

The cartographic collections of the Geography and Map Division now exceed 3,500,000 pieces. Of the 1973 receipts, which totaled almost 117,000 maps and over 2,000 atlases, 67 percent were transferred from other U.S. government agencies. A gift of more than 1,000 pictorial maps collected by Ethel M. Fair is to be retained as a collection. Several noteworthy retrospective items were acquired by purchase, among them a crude sketch map of Franklin D. Roosevelt's properties at Hyde Park, N.Y., drawn by the former President around 1930, and three 19th-century Japanese woodblock maps.

Although the number of readers visiting the division remained fairly constant, Saturday morning use increased and mail and telephone inquiries rose significantly. Among the requests was that of a Congressman for information on rainfall patterns in his state, and a distinguished historian's query was answered with the title of the "earliest map which named the United States." A German geographer, on a year's leave in the United States, studied maps showing colonial settlement patterns in Maryland, Pennsylvania, and Virginia.

In 1968 the division received a grant from the Council on Library Resources in support of a project to devise computerized map cataloging procedures. Developed in cooperation with the Information Systems Office and the MARC Development Office, MARC Map has since become fully operational and an active and productive component of the Library's automation program. The versatility of MARC Map was demonstrated in 1973 through the generation of computer-produced bibliographies from MARC Map bases, via the MARC retriever. They included a printout of catalog descriptions of all Revolutionary War maps in MARC Map, citations of 804 maps and 64 atlases for the division's annual contribution to *Bibliographie cartographique internationale*, and a list of maps of early railroads in the United States. The distribution of MARC Map tapes through the Library's Card Division started in April 1973.

Clara Egli LeGear completed 11 years of service as the Library's honorary consultant in historical cartography, a period of voluntary service preceded by 47 years of full-time employment. Mrs. LeGear's continuous association with the Library for 58 years is believed to be unequaled in the Library's history. In her successive capacities as bibliographer (1950-61) and honorary consultant (1961-72), Mrs. LeGear compiled three supplementary volumes to Philip Lee Phillips' monumental four-volume *List of Geographical Atlases in the Library of Congress* (1909-20). Volume 7, which lists American atlases acquired by the Library between 1920 and 1969, was published as fiscal year 1973 came to an end.

Since its establishment on July 1, 1897, the holdings of the Music Division have grown from under 200,000 items to over 4 million, making the division the most comprehensive music li-

58

REPORT OF THE LIBRARIAN OF CONGRESS, 1973

brary in the world. The 75th anniversary was observed with an exhibition of manuscripts selected from categories in which the division particularly excels. Among composers' manuscripts, those of Schumann's "Spring" Symphony, Bach's Cantata No. 10, and Prokofiev's String Quartet, Op. 50, were representative of the holographs of the great masters in the collections, while Ethelbert Nevin's "The Rosary" marked the beginning of the systematic effort to acquire the manuscripts of American composers. Rare and early imprints, the activities of the Recorded Sound Section and Archive of Folk Song, the chamber music concerts, and new commissioned works were also represented in the exhibit.

The most notable gift of the year came from Mrs. Robert Littell and consisted of items that had belonged to her father, the late Walter Damrosch. It includes autograph scores and sketches by Franz Liszt and Richard Wagner, plus an album presented to Mr. Damrosch on his 80th birthday by fellow members of the National Institute of Arts and Letters and the American Academy of Arts and Letters. Included in it are autograph inscriptions by Stephen Vincent Benét, Ernest Bloch, John Alden Carpenter, Willa Cather, John Erskine, and Sinclair Lewis.

With the microfilming of over 4,000 librettos from the Schatz collection, the end of this large-scale preservation project is finally in sight; it is expected that within another year the entire collection of 12,500 librettos will be on microfilm. Valuable autograph manuscripts of Samuel Barber, Leonard Bernstein, Aaron Copland, and Henry Cowell were also microfilmed.

SPECIAL FORMAT COLLECTIONS

Last year this report noted legislation making it possible to register claims to U.S. copyright in sound recordings and requiring that two copies of each published sound recording be sent to the Library of Congress. The impact of this law on the Library was felt in fiscal 1973, when the Recorded Sound Section of the Music Division added approximately 10,000 copyrighted phonorecords to its collections. The deposits also include cassettes, filmstrips, and a variety of

training pamphlets or brochures. The handling of these diverse items naturally poses a technical and custodial challenge to the division, which is developing new selection policies and procedures. The Recorded Sound Section also received, for the Archive of Folk Song collection, about 3,000 early cylinders that add to the Library's already impressive accumulation of American Indian music. Of these, approximately 2,000 were recorded by various scholars for the Navaho Museum of Ceremonial Art in Santa Fe; the remainder, mostly devoted to the Acoma Pueblo ritual, were acquired from the School of American Research in the same city. The section's preservation program kept pace with previous years' progress: some 2,300 acetate discs, 90 cylinders, and 1,200 acetate tape recordings were rerecorded on polyester magnetic tapes.

Volunteers began assisting the Archive of Folk Song in the organization of the voluminous ex-slave narrative materials that were gathered by the WPA Federal Writers' Project. The Archive issued a new two-disc LP recording, *Music of Morocco*, edited by Paul Bowles from material he recorded for the Archive in 1959. The album features a wide variety of music, from that of the mountain-dwelling Berbers and the Sephardic Jewish traditions to the Andaluz "classical" music of the country.

Bestselling Records from the Library of Congress Recording Laboratory, 1962-72

American Fiddle Tunes
Negro Ballads and Hollers
Railroad Songs and Ballads
Songs from the Iroquois Longhouse
Anglo-American Shanties, Lyric Songs, and Spirituals

One of the prize acquisitions by the Prints and Photographs Division in fiscal 1973 was a set of six daguerreotypes taken about 1846, which include the earliest known photographic images of the Capitol and White House, along with views of the Patent Office (now the National Portrait Gallery), the General Post Office Building (now the Tariff Commission), and the Battle Monument in Baltimore. Attributed to John Plumbe, Jr., these unique pictures are without question the finest early photographic items received by the Library of Congress in many decades. Other notable photographs acquired during the year included an album by J. Leroy French, showing the construction of the additions to the U.S. Capitol in the 1860's, and two views of the inauguration of Abraham Lincoln in 1861.

The Library's holdings of prints from the American Revolutionary period were expanded by the acquisition of. 16 French engravings of events in the colonies at the end of the 18th century and two Dutch political cartoons of the period. Six rare aquatints by Abner Reed depicting Stafford Springs, Conn., a popular 19th-century New England health resort, a woodblock by Leonard Baskin after Ben Shahn's drawing *Beatitudes,* and 24 Jean Charlot lithographs were noteworthy additions to the graphic collections. The poster collections were enhanced by the addition of a series for the Munich Olympics, 200 German exhibit and political posters, Polish film posters, and works by Lucian Bernhard and Frank Hazenplug.

Edgar Breitenbach retired on June 30, 1973, after a 17-year tenure as division chief. Dr. Breitenbach will continue to serve the Library as honorary consultant in graphic arts and cinema. It is anticipated that he will continue his deep interests in the development of the pictorial collections and in the motion picture acquisition and preservation programs. Alan Fern, assistant chief since 1964, was appointed as the new chief.

One of Dr. Breitenbach's numerous contributions to the division was the expansion and upgrading of the Motion Picture Section into a major national center for film preservation and cinema scholarship. That section continued its steady growth in 1973, enlarging the collections through large gifts from Columbia Pictures, the American Film Institute, and other donors. Noteworthy feature and television films that were added ranged from *L'Enfant Sauvage* to *All in the Family.* The Motion Picture Laboratory produced more than 3 million feet of preservation film, and the major portion of an exchange preservation program with German film companies

was concluded. Two public motion picture programs were held: a screening of *Bolero,* the first motion picture produced under a public media grant from the National Endowment for the Arts, and a program of experimental films by the noted American surrealist Ian Hugo. Use of the motion picture collection increased considerably. In March, for example, a record 170 readers were served.

More scholars, students, and members of the public also used the Prints and Photographs Reading Room; in fact, the total number of researchers using the division's facilities was 16 percent higher than in the previous year. Virginia Daiker, reference specialist in architecture, received an award from the National Trust for Historic Preservation recognizing her long service to the Library and her personal efforts on behalf of the American architectural heritage.

"I do not choose to run for President in nineteen twenty eight." A holograph draft of Calvin Coolidge's famous statement was one of the more interesting items added to the Manuscript Division's vast collections this past year. In addition to other important presidential documents and letters, the division acquired major new collections in the fields of law, science, and cultural history. Once again, however, the adverse effects of the Tax Reform Act of 1969 prevented the donation of any major new literary collections.

The papers of Hugo L. Black, Associate Justice of the U.S. Supreme Court from 1937 to 1971, enriched the division's political-legal history collections. American 20th-century source materials were further augmented by the papers of Agnes Meyer, noted publisher and humanitarian. The purchase of a sizable group of papers of Mrs. Edward MacDowell, wife of the American composer, enhanced the American cultural history collections. Notable American scientists whose papers were received in the division include physicist and scientific adviser Merle Tuve, inventor Edward G. Acheson, and Nobel Prize recipient in medicine Georg von Békésy. The papers of Thomas O. Paine, engineer and former NASA Administrator, were also donated to the Library. Significant additions were made to the Sigmund Freud collection.

The Preparation Section completed the processing of the magnificent Reid Family archive, a collection especially important for the study of American journalism. The organization and description of other massive collections, notably the records of the NAACP and the National Urban League, continued apace during the year, and the first volume of the register of the NAACP records was published. Publication of the guide to the Nelson Aldrich papers marked the debut of the combined register-index as a finding aid. The final part of the index to the vital statistics of the Russian Orthodox Greek Catholic Church records was also produced, and 10 large collections totaling nearly 40,000 items were prepared for microfilming. Fifty-six collections were reported to the *National Union Catalog of Manuscript Collections*. The indexes to the Woodrow Wilson papers went to press during fiscal 1973 and completion of work on the index and microfilm of the James A. Garfield papers finished 22 of the 23 collections in the Presidential Papers program, leaving only the Jefferson papers index and microfilm to be prepared.

The Master Record II, a bibliographic and administrative device for the control of the collection's, was developed and put into partial operation during the year. A total of 356 collections containing over 800,000 items was cataloged and entered into the new data base. A cumulative index of descriptive terms was an important product of the new system.

Assistance to scholars in the field of Afro-American history was strengthened by the appointment of Sylvia Lyons Render as a·manuscript historian. The security system in the reading room was improved to ensure the maximum safety of the division's incomparable collections. Major exhibits displayed in the room included manuscripts of various writers of the "Harlem Renaissance" of the 1920's and representative items tracing the history of the division in commemoration of its 75th anniversary.

CONCERTS AND LITERARY PROGRAMS

In its 48th concert season, the Library presented 29 programs in 39 chamber music concerts in the

Coolidge Auditorium; of these, seven were sponsored by the Elizabeth Sprague Coolidge Foundation, 26 by the Gertrude Clarke Whittall Foundation, and six by the McKim Fund. The Coolidge Foundation concerts offered several compositions rarely heard and world premieres of works by Alec Wilder and Stanislaw Skrowaczewski. The Juilliard String Quartet presented 20 of the concerts sponsored by the Whittall Foundation, performing some works of great interest and difficulty. Three of the McKim programs premiered new works commissioned by the fund: *Sounds Remembered* (1971) by Leslie Bassett, played by Charles Treger, violin, and Samuel Sanders, piano; *Night Music* (1972) by Ned Rorem, played by Earl Carlyss, violin, and Ann Schein, piano; Sonata No. 2 (1973) by Benjamin Lees, played by Rafael Druian, violin, and Ilse von Alpenheim, piano. All of the chamber music programs were broadcast locally on WETA-FM, and, through the Katie and Walter Louchheim Fund, were also heard on radio stations in 16 other cities.

A 30th program, presented under the auspices of the Norman P. Scala Memorial Fund on October 6, 1972, was hailed with delight. The well-known conductor Frederick Fennell gave an illustrated lecture entitled "American Band Music 100 Years Ago," and some 20 musicians played contemporary music on instruments borrowed from the collections of the Smithsonian Institution.

The Serge Koussevitzky Music Foundation voted to proffer commissions to six composers to write new works, three for symphony orchestra and three for chamber ensemble.

Nine literary programs plus a two-day conference on teaching creative writing were presented during the 1972-73 season. The poetry readings and discussions, sponsored by the Gertrude Clarke Whittall Poetry and Literature Fund, featured poets X. J. Kennedy, Anne Sexton, Samuel Allen (Paul Vesey), Ned O'Gorman, Ian Hamilton, Lucille Clifton, Owen Dodson, Donald Justice, and Carolyn Kizer. Josephine Jacobsen, completing her second year as the Library's consultant in poetry in English, moderated four of the programs. Mrs. Jacobsen also gave two poetry readings during the year and a lecture, "The Instant of Knowing." Daniel Hoffman, poet and professor of English at the University of Pennsylvania, has been appointed consultant in poetry for the 1973-74 term.

Attended by over 500 persons, the Conference on Teaching Creative Writing, held January 29-30, 1973, under the sponsorship of the Gertrude Clarke Whittall Poetry and Literature Fund, proved one of the highlights of the year. Elliott Coleman, Paul Engle, Wallace Stegner, and John Ciardi moderated the four panel discussions, and 14 other distinguished American men and women of letters served as panelists and read from their writings.

A complete listing of all concerts and literary programs is found in the appendixes.

SERVICES TO THE BLIND AND PHYSICALLY HANDICAPPED

In the belief that reading is truly for everyone, the Library of Congress produces and distributes special reading materials for blind and physically handicapped readers who cannot read conventional print. Under this program, the Division for the Blind and Physically Handicapped (DBPH) works with 51 cooperating regional libraries and, through them, with over 72 local public libraries in the United States in circulating books and magazines in braille or recorded on discs or cassettes. In fiscal 1973, DBPH provided braille or recorded books to approximately 400,000 readers, nearly an 18 percent increase over 1972.

Robert S. Bray, chief of the division since May 1957, retired on December 11, 1972. In the past decade, Mr. Bray received awards from the American Foundation for the Blind, the American Optometric Association, and the American Library Association's Round Table on Library Service to the Blind for his remarkable contributions to the Library's national program for the blind and physically handicapped. At the end of the fiscal year, it was announced that Frank Kurt Cylke, an experienced administrator of national and local library programs, had been appointed as the new chief. Mr. Cylke has been with the Library of Congress since January 1970 as executive secretary of the Federal Library Committee and, since April 1972, also as chairman of the U.S. National Libraries Task Force on Cooperative Activities.

An era in the Library's service to blind and physically handicapped readers in the District of Columbia came to an end in April 1973, when the service was transferred from the division to the newly established regional library at the District of Columbia Public Library. The Library of Congress had served as a regional library for the District since the national program began in 1931. The new regional library supplies talking books and magazines to eligible District readers and maintains a reading room of braille reference and recorded materials in its Special Services Division. With this transfer of services, the former Regional Library Unit of DBPH was reorganized to become the Library Services Unit, responsible for all support services to regional, subregional, and institutional libraries, including tape duplication.

Adoption of automated techniques to assist in the production and control of books for the blind and physically handicapped came one step closer to reality with the approval and completion of programing support for the first phase of an automated system. This system will allow each regional library to select the number of copies needed for titles produced by the program, will facilitate the production of catalog cards and bibliographic information, will enable the division to monitor all phases of book production, and can eventually provide a data base giving the availability and location of any title produced for the blind and physically handicapped.

A total of 700 talking books, 300 braille books, and 125 books in cassettes were selected for production in 1973. The recording of all disc talking books at 8 1/3 rpm began in January 1973 and, at the end of the fiscal year, plans were under way to record cassette books at 15/16 ips. Use of these low recording speeds makes it possible to include almost twice as much material as previously on each disc or cassette tape and thus to increase the number of copies issued for each title selected. Readers will benefit through reduced waiting periods for books and by having fewer records or cassettes to handle. Arthur Hailey's *Wheels* was experimentally recorded in a series of low-cost flexible discs bound as a volume. Favorable readers' comments led to the production of *The Man Who Loved Cat Dancing* in the same format. Because of the popularity of book-record combinations for juveniles, it was decided to apply this approach, on a test basis, to Richard Bach's *Jonathan Livingston Seagull* for the benefit of adult readers with sufficient vision to enjoy the illustrations.

Collection development, a responsibility of the National Collections Section, focused on the areas of occupational material, self-help literature, consumer information, and current affairs. Over 3,000 titles, in cassette or handcopied braille and supplemental to the national distribution program, were added to the National Collections. The braille collections were systematically weeded, providing sufficient space for storing new materials for at least the next three years. The section also worked on plans for a reliable union catalog, sponsored a biweekly book discussion group for adults, and conducted tours for nearly 600 division visitors.

The first three braille music titles produced with the aid of a computer were made available for loan. Work on this project is being completed under a contract with the American Printing House for the Blind. The approximately 6,400 users of the music program currently have access to more than 24,000 volumes of musical instruc-

tion. An important recent addition is *The Recorded Aid for Beginning Piano*, a series of volumes containing cassette instruction in how to read braille music, a teacher's guide in print, and examples of braille notation. Another first for the division was the production of a printed supplement to the *New Braille Musician* for use by sighted instructors and others who work with blind music students and musicians. In addition, a new brochure entitled *Music Services for the Blind and Physically Handicapped* rounded out the information made available on the music services provided by the division.

During fiscal 1973, the Reference and Information Section received an average of 1,000 reference questions a month. Of this total, approximately one-fifth required individual research while the remainder were in the category of quick reference. Several new reference tools were developed and have proven to be very useful. An index to articles that appeared in *Talking Book Topics* and *Braille Book Review* during 1971-72 was produced and distributed to the division staff and cooperating libraries. Because of the favorable reaction from users, this index will be issued annually. A new edition of the *Directory of Library Resources for the Blind and Physically Handicapped*, published during the year, reflects the growing number of cooperating libraries. Reference circulars compiled and issued during the year include *Aids for Handicapped Readers*, *Large Type Sources*, *Cassette Sources*, and *Magazines in Special Formats*.

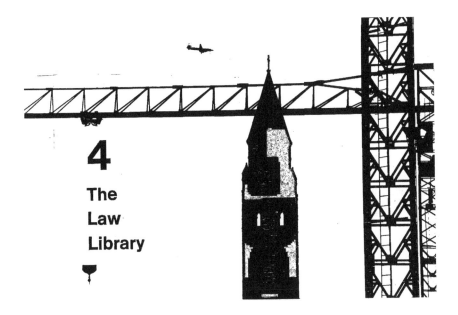

4

The
Law
Library

To provide authoritative responses to incoming reference and research inquiries within the shortest possible time was the overriding goal of the Law Library during fiscal 1973. To aid in accomplishing this objective, an operations plan that called for the inauguration of new programs and the intensification of ongoing ones was implemented. The plan was aimed primarily at ensuring the inclusion in the collections of the most comprehensive and up-to-date legal sources available and improving the accessibility of these materials to the staff.

Specific goals receiving heightened attention during the fiscal year included:

□ Ensuring prompt receipt after publication of the primary sources and upkeep materials crucial to authoritative responses

□ Rounding out the collections by systematic acquisition of missing items

□ Expanding staff indexing and bibliographic activities

□ Increasing the use of microreproductions for both the addition of new titles and the preservation of materials already in the collections

□ Improving the physical condition of the collections by binding, rebinding, filming, and phased preservation operations

□ Creating maximum accessibility to the collections by shelf review, reorganization, systematic weeding, and storage of less-frequently used materials

Also receiving attention under the operations plan was the continuous upgrading of the skills of the Law Library staff, particularly those responsible for the day-to-day maintenance of the collection and those providing editorial and

63

translation assistance to the specialists in foreign and international law.

The success of the operations plan was evidenced by the staff's ability to meet an increased demand for its services. Oral and written responses to reference and research inquiries increased by more than 6 percent over the previous fiscal year, numbering 168,200 in 1973 as opposed to 158,000 in 1972. On the basis of a seven-day week, the Law Library staff was handling an average of 465 requests daily, excluding holidays. Further evidence of the plan's success was the 30-percent reduction in the number of instances in which the staff was unable to locate a piece of material for a reader.

READER SERVICES

The Law Library is a service organization. While Congress is always accorded preeminence among the users of the Law Library's services, its clientele also includes the executive and judicial branches of the federal government, academic institutions, legal practitioners and scholars, law librarians, students, representatives of foreign governments, and the general public. To fulfill the disparate needs of its patrons, the Law Library offers a wide range of services, from providing a cited volume to giving a legal opinion involving foreign law. Many a lawyer enters practice with perhaps not-so-fond memories of hours spent in the Anglo-American Law Reading Room trying to absorb law reports and journals which he could locate only in the collections of the Law Library. For such a patron it may be necessary only to point out where the materials he wants are located. On the other hand, the Social Security Administration may forward a Jordanian birth certificate whose authenticity is crucial to the determination of whether or not the petitioner will receive benefits. In this case, the Law Library staff will provide a translation of the document and an opinion on its probable validity. A congressional staff member may phone to inquire which nations, if any, mete out the death penalty for a particular crime involving drugs. Response to this request involves an expeditious checking of relevant legislation of as many nations as possible. Another congressional staff member may request a selective annotated bibliography of English-language sources on labor insurance legislation in Latin America.

It is the provision of indepth research services to certain of its patrons that distinguishes the Law Library, and the quality of these services is the ultimate test of its overall performance. In the preparation of a special study all the diverse skills and functions of the Law Library staff converge.

The law of every nation is in a constant state of flux, with almost daily issuances of new statutes, regulations, court decisions, decrees, and proclamations. The authoritativeness of a legal study prepared by the Law Library hence is dependent first of all upon the completeness and currentness of its collections. The materials themselves are useless, however, if the legal specialist or research assistant does not have the bibliographic tools which lead him to those materials. For many foreign legal systems, the staff member himself must prepare the indexes, bibliographies, and other finding aids which guide him to relevant information.

To reflect accurately the state of the law and its applicability to the question or set of facts involved, the legal report must be succinctly and precisely written. The specialist must take care in his translation, analysis, and writing to respect the bounds of the law, indicating clearly what is given and what is not, discussing problematic and unsettled areas, and explicitly identifying the assumptions and speculative aspects of his statements. The usefulness of the study often hinges upon the ability of the specialist and the supportive editorial staff to render foreign legal terms and concepts into English that is intelligible to a reader either unversed in law or versed only in American law. A report, therefore, often requires not only aptness of phrase but also discussion of the legal, economic, political, and social background of a particular provision. Although the specialist relies heavily upon primary sources whenever possible, he must also consult secondary legal sources and nonlegal materials to give weight to his analysis. Transcription of his edited draft must be done painstakingly, for a single typographical error may change the significance of a provision crucial to an important decision.

In seeking optimum responsiveness to its patrons' needs, the Law Library attempts to strike the proper balance between depth and speed. Particularly in the case of complex requests and those involving the law of a multitude of nations, striking this balance requires a high degree of coordination among the various components of the staff.

Reference and Research Service to Congress

With the exception of congressional inquiries involving research in American public law, which are handled by the American Law Division of the Congressional Research Service, the Law Library is responsible for proper disposition of all requests for legal reference and research services from Members of Congress and congressional committees. The demand from congressional sources for research services in foreign, comparative, and international law during fiscal 1973 was the largest in the history of the Law Library. The staff prepared 490 special studies totaling 20,201 pages, 79 translations, and 12 bibliographies, representing an increase of better than 5 percent over fiscal 1972.

Although each congressional request for the Law Library's research service is unique and requires a singular response, one can group these requests into three broad and often overlapping categories: those involving topical legal issues receiving congressional attention, those for a survey of the law of as many nations as possible on a particular subject, and those involving a specific aspect of the law of a single country or region.

In anticipation of congressional requests, the legal specialists of the Law Library devote considerable attention to keeping abreast of topical issues involving foreign and international law which might become the object of the legislators' interest. Topics of special studies prepared during fiscal 1973 included the following:

Exit fees, emigration taxes, work permits, and other barriers to the free external movements of

citizens, especially those required by East European countries

Regulation of multinational companies in municipal law, especially in countries with differing social, economic, and legal structures

Adherence by the Soviet Union to the Universal Copyright Convention, particularly with regard to its effect on publication outside the USSR of works by dissident Soviet writers

Legal aspects of trade and commercial affairs affecting the U.S. relationship with Japan

Various features of foreign election laws and regulations, such as mandatory voting, campaign financing and practices, public opinion polls, and dates of elections

Surveys of the law of a multitude of nations on a particular problem are of great value to congressional sponsors and drafters of proposed legislation, for each provides a wealth of information on the distinctive approaches adopted by other countries in their attempts to resolve the problem in question through legislative or other official action. The frequent congressional requests for multinational surveys received during 1973 can be exemplified by the following:

Laws and regulations aimed at controlling pollution of the air and water, specifically pollution caused by pesticides, radiation, solid wastes, noise, and automobile gaseous emissions

Financial disclosure requirements for government officials

Tax laws as they relate to repatriated profits from foreign subsidiaries

Legislation on validation procedures for the determination of coastal boundaries separating publicly and privately owned lands

Laws concerning secured interests in goods sold by U.S. exporters

Development of the public domain through private concessions and like methods

Collection, maintenance, and dissemination of criminal arrest and conviction records

Laws and decisions relating to the privilege of newspapers and journalists against divulging sources of information

Ocean dumping and oil spillage laws

Laws and regulations on inflammatory literature in penal institutions

Representative of special studies prepared in answer to congressional requests·for information on a narrowly defined subject in the law of a single country or region were these:

Financial contributions by the central government to the budgets of Scandinavian cities

Right of an author, artist, or his beneficiaries under French law to collect from the dealer the proceeds from the sale of a work by public auction, regardless of transfer of the original work

Rehabilitation of criminals in European systems through innovations in correctional methods and stricter control or expunction of criminal records

Taxation in Europe of automobiles according to weight or horsepower

Requirements for the sale of agricultural products in the Bahamas

Territorial waters of the Republic of Vietnam

Limitation of damages in civil actions in Cambodia

Divorce under the Islamic Shari'ah law courts

Customary law of the Tiv tribes of Nigeria

Investment and mining legislation of the Congo

Law of negligence in Syria

Legal status of Chinese concubines and their children in Macao

Some of the information appearing in Law Library special studies prepared for congressional inquirers appeared in the *Congressional Record* and in committee prints.

To improve the access of Members and their staffs to the legal periodicals in greatest demand, the American-British Law Division established a reserve collection for congressional use only. Service was further augmented by the transfer of current congressional documents from the Serial Division to the Law Library gallery, thereby bringing all such documents together in one location for the convenience of users of these materials. A library technician who had worked with these documents in the Serial Division was transferred to the Law Library staff, making it possible to extend hours of service.

Other Reference and Research Services

Research and reference services provided to noncongressional users of the Law Library during 1973 showed a marked growth. The estimated number of readers using the facilities and materials of the various reading rooms of the Law Library rose from 84,000 in 1972 to 89,000 in 1973. Noncongressional telephone inquiries from various sources, including government agencies, rose by almost 12 percent over the previous fiscal year, and the number of letters sent as part of the Law Library's correspondence service increased by 30 percent. The 286 special studies prepared for government agencies contained nearly three times the total number of pages in such studies in 1972. Similarly, the number of special studies prepared for noncongressional and nongovernmental inquirers rose ·from 302 in 1972 to 613 in 1973.

As in previous years, many of the special studies prepared for government agencies dealt with the law of foreign nations on such personal status questions as marriage, divorce, adoption, legitimation, and guardianship. The action of various U.S. government agencies upon petitions submitted by aliens or naturalized U.S. citizens often depends upon the legality of certain of their actions in the country of their former or present citizenship, and the agency can make no decision until it has authoritative information on the foreign law involved. In these cases, the Law Library often is the most ready source of such information and frequently the only feasible source in view of the prohibitively high cost of maintaining collections and counsel on foreign law in each agency or hiring private organizations to perform the service.

Topics of special studies dealing with questions other than personal status included statutory protection of artistic works and objects valuable to anthropological studies in Honduras, Spanish colonial land grants, practice of law in the Seychelles, extraterritorial rights in Morocco, trusts under Jordanian law, Malaysian patent law, Canadian pardon procedures, investment by American companies in East Europe, and third-party liability for damages resulting from the use of nuclear energy in Europe.

During the year several staff members testified on foreign law as expert witnesses on behalf of the U.S. Department of Justice. In two such instances, land titles in the Virgin Islands were at issue; a third dealt with Cuban law.

To reduce the time a reader must wait to receive from the stacks an item requested in the Anglo-American Law Reading Room, an intercom system and an answering service were installed, as well as additional telephones on various decks.

Indexes, Other Bibliographic Tools, and Publications

The volume of legal publications in almost every jurisdiction is massive. The official ones are issued piecemeal with a view toward making them available to potential users as quickly as possible and with little consideration given to subsequent ease of identification and location. A legal study, however, carries little weight unless the official material cited is both the most pertinent and the most current of its kind. Although

for advanced nations location of the materials that will be most authoritative still presents difficulty to legal practitioners and scholars, various complex and sophisticated but reliable systems for gaining access to relevant documents and writings have been developed. Such is not the case with the legal publications of a large number of the less advanced nations. To make optimum use of much of the foreign legal material in the collection, the staff of the Law Library must devote considerable time to preparing indexes, index-digests, bibliographies, and other finding aids for its own use and, in some instances, for wider use through publication. During the past fiscal year, for example, the staff was indexing the legislation of 59 countries.

The Hispanic Law Division has received considerable acclaim for the ongoing publication *Index to Latin American Legislation*, an index-digest to statutory material from 20 Latin American official gazettes. In 1973 the staff completed the final editing of the entries for the period 1966-1970; these soon will be photographed and published by G. K. Hall & Co. as the second supplement to the bound *Index*. The staff of the Hispanic Law Division also prepares an index to Hispanic legal periodicals, covering over 600 periodicals dealing wholly or in part with Hispanic law, and an index-digest to Mexican Supreme Court decisions, both in card form. The division also completed the final editing and indexing of *A Revised Guide to the Law and Legal Literature of Mexico*, which was published by the Library in a 463-page volume shortly after the close of the fiscal year.

The Near Eastern and African Law Division is indexing and digesting the legislation from 1970 to date of the countries under its jurisdiction. Working during this and previous fiscal years, its staff has put into index-digest form the statutory materials issued since 1970 by over one-half of the states in its area—19 French- and Italian-language countries in Sub-Saharan Africa, six English-language African countries, and four Arabic-language countries of the Near East, as well as the states of Algeria, Egypt, Iran, Libya, Morocco, Turkey, and Tunisia.

Compiled by Paul Ho of the Far Eastern Law

Division, *The People's Republic of China and International Law: A Bibliography of Chinese Sources*, was issued as a Library of Congress publication. Partially annotated, it covers monographic materials and articles in periodicals and newspapers published in the Chinese language in the People's Republic of China. By the end of the fiscal year, approximately 500 copies had been distributed.

Members of the staff of the Far Eastern Law Division both index the legislation of Burma, Korea, and Thailand, and prepare entries from Chinese, Korean, and Japanese law journals for the *Index to Foreign Legal Periodicals*, a publication of the American Association of Law Libraries. Entries for Ukrainian legal periodicals were prepared for the *Index* by the staff of the European Law Division, which in addition worked during fiscal 1973 on the compilation of a bibliography of English translations of legislative and administrative enactments of European countries.

Various members of the Law Library staff continued the compilation of bibliographies of Japanese writings on Communist Chinese law, North Korean legal literature, Communist Chinese newspaper legal literature, and monographs on Turkish law during the last quarter century published either in Turkish or in Western languages. Also under preparation were a survey of criminal legislation of the French- and Italian-language countries of Africa, and compilation of documents dealing with the legal aspects of Uganda's expulsion of its Asians, and an annotated guide to Iranian legal periodicals in Persian and Western languages.

A further development in the Law Library's effort to make the results of its research known to a wider audience and to publicize the richness of its holdings of legal materials was the inauguration in fiscal 1973 of a series of Law Library Research Reports. The first issuance, "The Constitution of the Hungarian People's Republic," combined the original Hungarian text of this document with an English translation prepared by William Sólyom-Fekete, senior legal specialist of the European Law Division. Through this series of reports the Law Library from time to time will provide the Congress with substantial discussion of selected legal questions in anticipation of its possible concern with them and also make available to a limited audience certain of its previously prepared special studies chosen for their topical interest, scholarly substance, or basic research value.

During the year the staff issued several manuals designed to aid readers in locating materials in the collection and to guide the staff in servicing reference problems and preparing legal research reports. They included a guide to the various collections and reference services available to the user of the Anglo-American Law Reading Room, describing in detail the organization and maintenance, processing procedures, and circulation policies of appellate briefs, and another explaining the internal procedures of the department's branch in the Capitol and the reference services it offers.

Aimed in part at standardizing various technical aspects of the department's special studies, a revised research and uniform style manual describes policies and procedures related to the proper disposition of incoming legal inquiries. The manual will be supplemented by divisional uniform citation handbooks.

Exhibits

Through exhibits in the foyer of the Anglo-American Law Reading Room the Law Library acquaints viewers with many unusual and valuable items in its unequaled collection. The brochure prepared for each exhibit provides information on the publications displayed and on the Law Library's holdings of similar works. Various newspapers in the area and elsewhere have printed feature articles on the exhibits, a testimony to their popularity.

The Friends of the Law Library of Congress assisted in the preparation of an exhibit on early American legal imprints and an accompanying brochure for the annual meeting of the American Bar Association, held in Washington, D.C., shortly after the close of the fiscal year. Officers of the Friends of the Law Library of Congress, all from the District of Columbia, are Robert N. Anderson, president; James Oliver Murdock and John K. Pickens, vice presidents; J. Thomas Rouland, secretary; and L. Alton Denslow, treasurer.

COLLECTION DEVELOPMENT

The quality of service rendered by the Law Library is directly dependent upon the adequacy and the organization of its collections. Although the department receives many materials through the worldwide acquisition programs administered by the Processing Department on behalf of the Library as a whole, it is the continuing responsibility of the Law Library to ensure the systematic development of its resources, both current and retrospective. The staff also retains primary responsibility for keeping this distinguished collection in condition for use through proper processing, organization, maintenance, and preservation activities.

Bound volumes added to the collections during fiscal 1973 totaled 40,000. Some 27,000 of these volumes of books, serials, and briefs were processed by the Law Library, 11,000 by the Class K Project, and 2,000 by the Serial Record Division of the Processing Department. The Law Library staff weeded over 11,000 volumes from the collection through continued review in preparation for classification, leaving a net addition of some 29,000 volumes to the permanent collection. Thus at the end of the fiscal year there were 1,274,000 volumes in the direct custody of the Law Library. The addition of over 1,500 items to the microtext collection brought the total holdings to almost 5,000 reels of microfilm and 108,000 microcards and pieces of microfiche.

Selection and Acquisition

Acquisition activities centered on the formulation of a defined acquisition policy statement for law and on participating in the revision of the LC acquisition policy statements for foreign provinces, cities, and other jurisdictions and for

United States local jurisdictions.

An extensive study by the European Law Division of its receipt of Scandinavian materials through blanket-order dealers resulted in amendments to the Order Division's instructions to the dealers involved to ensure a more effective purchasing program. The Hispanic Law Division also devoted considerable attention to the selection of effective blanket-order dealers for Latin American legal publications to replace the defunct Latin American Cooperative Acquisitions Program (LACAP).

The staff made detailed examinations of holdings for several nations to identify gaps in important retrospective materials. The major targets were Greece, the various states of Latin America, and countries without an organized book trade. Efforts were made to obtain missing issues and volumes of legal periodicals and government publications and to improve receipt and review of national and commercial bibliographies from these countries. Receipts of official gazettes from all nations by direct airmail were continuously scrutinized to evaluate the effectiveness of this procedure.

Southeast Asia is another area in which an undeveloped book trade and adverse political, economic, and military conditions hamper acquisition activities. In a effort to improve Law Library holdings from this area, Mya Saw Shin of the Far Eastern Law Division took advantage of a visit to Burma and Thailand to acquire almost 270 monographs and serial pieces.

In relation to 1972, the number of lists and offers scanned for desirable titles increased 15 percent in 1973, and 21 percent more items were recommended for acquisition. In addition to what has become an annual growth in the number of serial pieces received routinely, several special additions were made to the Law Library collection. Some 16,500 U.S. appellate briefs were acquired—6,800 from the Supreme Court and 9,700 from the courts of appeals. The U.S. Supreme Court also transferred 450 boxes of state reports, the contents of which were checked against the Law Library's holdings to fill gaps in the collections and to replace volumes in poor condition. An additional 60,000 serial pieces were acquired and processed as a result of the transfer to the Law Library of current congressional documents and all of the current Latin American official gazettes received by the Library of Congress.

Several significant individual items were acquired during the year. These include *Das behmische Lanndrecht oder Lanndsbrdnung deutsch* (1572), a manuscript on Bohemian law in force in 1564; *Covstvmés* [sic] *generales dv bailliage dv Bassigny* (Av Pont-a-Movsson, 1607), a record of the customs of Bassigny, France, during the second part of the 16th century; and *Fihrist-i Maqālāt-i Huqūqī* [Index to Persian Articles on Law], covering 13 Iranian law periodicals from 1305 to 1345 A.H. (A.D. 1926-67). The Law Library also acquired seven reels of microfilm containing various issues of 15 pre-1949 gazettes of National Chinese government and Kuomintang party organs at the central level and the first Communist Chinese legal monograph to be added to the collection of some years, *Shui lu huo wu yùn shu kuei tse* [Regulations Governing the Transport of Commodities by Water], compiled by the Ministry of Transportation and published by the People's Transportation Press in February 1972.

Organization and Maintenance of Collections

Efficient organization and maintenance activities facilitate the staff's reference and research work and the optimum use of limited shelf space. In recent years the staff has increased its attention to these activities in preparation for the extended application of Class K to legal materials and for the anticipated move to the James Madison Memorial Building.

As part of its general objective of responding expeditiously to reference and research inquiries, the Law Library intensified its efforts to develop procedures for processing and shelving incoming materials as quickly as possible. The staff gave special attention to integrating the operations of the departmental Processing Section with those of the divisions. Critical evaluations were made of shelflisting procedures and the sorting, posting, and claiming of serials.

The shelflisting work of the Law Library increased in 1973 despite the fact that the Class K Project has taken over the processing of current English legal publications and both current and retrospective American legal materials. Some 28,000 volumes were shelflisted in the Law Library in 1973, as opposed to 21,000 in 1972, an increase of 33 percent. There was a 57-percent growth in the number of items prepared for shelving by perforation, plating, lettering, labeling, and marking. Entries were made in the visible files for some 36,000 items, 35 percent more than in the previous fiscal year.

The staff worked on a number of special processing projects during 1973, including replacing temporary cards in the Law Library shelflist with printed cards and incorporating into the collection much retrospective English material that had not been previously processed. A sizable backlog of incoming Japanese materials resulting from a six-month vacancy in the processing assistant's position was completely eliminated, and the processing of the Japanese materials already on the shelves was brought into conformity with standard Law Library form by an assistant from the Shared Cataloging Division detailed to the Law Library on a part-time basis.

Each division named a representative to the reconstituted departmental Coordinating Committee on Processing Activities, which has as its chairman the head of the Processing Section. Among the problems considered by the committee during the year were receipt of official gazettes by direct airmail, uniform recording of serial receipts in visible files, procedures for preparing material for microfilming and inspection of the resulting films, routing and distribution of incoming material, preparation of purchase recommendations for regular and subscription orders, revision of the statistical forms used in the Law Library, retention policies for brittle books, and disposal of unwanted materials.

The branch collection in the Law Library in the Capitol was thoroughly evaluated, reorganized, and shifted, and the filing of its backlog of looseleaf services was completed. In addition, a card catalog was provided and broader coverage via microtext material begun. The Hispanic Law

Division prepared a shelflist inventory of approximately 500 rare and uncataloged books and broadsides in its case collection. To facilitate use of the Law Library public and shelflist catalogs, which are utilized increasingly by both readers and staff, additional sections were added, necessitating a shifting and relabeling of the trays.

Preservation

A Binding and Preservation Unit was established in the departmental Processing Section to work systematically with the divisions, and almost 14,000 monographs and serials were bound or rebound in 1973, twice as many as in 1972. In addition, over 1,100 rare and valuable books were boxed, reshelflisted, and labeled as the first stage of a phased restoration project, and 500 volumes of congressional bills and resolutions were placed in slip cases.

Through initial acquisition, the Law Library microfilming program, or transfer from the Microfilm Reading Room of the Reference Department, the collection in the Law Library Microtext Reading Room was increased by 2,300 reels of microfilm and 400 microfiche. Notable additions included: *Official Gazettes of the Mexican States; Takvim-i Vakai* [Ottoman Official Gazette], 1835-1922; *Official Records of the Case Involving the U.S. Against General Tomoyuki Yamashita: Proceedings and Exhibits* (1945); *U.S. Emergency Court of Appeals Briefs* (Part 1); *U.S. Supreme Court Records and Briefs,* 1832-96; *Buletinul Oficial* [Romanian Gazette], 1913-49; and *French Impressions,* 1963-68.

PERSONNEL

The Law Library staff participated in a wide range of activities during the fiscal year designed to improve on-the-job performance, ensure effective communication, and enhance prospects for advancement. Several staff members also made admirable contributions to legal scholarship and the professions of law and law librarianship. To make the most effective use of human resources,

the Office of the Law Librarian devoted considerable attention to staffing matters.

Thirty-three members of the Law Library staff spent a total of 360 hours attending eight Library of Congress inservice courses, while 92 employees attended some 500 hours of courses and programs conducted by the Law Library itself, including legal research, service and maintenance of legal materials, and Law Library orientation. Twenty-three staff members were allotted financial aid to spend some 650 hours in 20 courses, mainly library science, editing, and management.

Although 84 positions are budgeted for the Law Library, several of these remained unfilled during the year due to financial reasons. Two new positions—preservation specialist and stack service section supervisor—were established, and promotion plans were set up for reference librarians and legal research assistants. The Law Library participated in the public service careers program by hiring a worker-trainee, and a law student and library science student were enrolled in the Law Library intern program.

Professional Activities

Staff members engaged in the usual range of professional activities in fiscal 1973. Some served as officers, committee chairmen, or members of the Law Librarians' Society of Washington, D.C., Federal Bar Association, American Bar Association, American Association of Law Libraries, Association for Asian Studies, American Society of International Law, Women's Bar Association, District of Columbia Bar, and the International Association of Law Libraries. Some served as consultants to various law libraries, and others presented lectures or conducted courses at library schools, law library meetings and institutes, international symposia, and commemorative sessions. Among other professional activities were book reviewing, translating and digesting articles for journals, and editing various types of publications. William Sólyom-Fekete's article, "The Golden Bull of Hungary, 1222-1972," was published in the October 1972 issue of the *Quarterly*

Journal of the Library of Congress. Tao-tai Hsia and Kathryn Haun of the Far Eastern Law Division coauthored a study of laws of the People's Republic of China on industrial and intellectual property for publication in *Law and Policy in International Business,* a journal of the Georgetown University Law School. Another member. of the Far Eastern Law Division staff, Sung Yoon Cho, contributed the article "Law and Justice in North Korea" to the *Journal of Korean Affairs* for January 1973. Several staff members visited other law libraries to review collections and to discuss common problems and interests.

The American Association of Law Libraries and the American Bar Association maintained their concern with the services and development of the Law Library through the perpetuation of their special committees on the Law Library. The AALL Committee on Liaison with the Library of Congress was made up of Viola A. Bird, chairwoman, University of Washington Law Library; Jane L. Hammond, Villanova University Law Library; Dan F. Henke, Hastings College of Law Library; Charlotte B. Stillwell, Cook County Law Library; Erwin C. Surrency, Temple University Law Library; and Carleton W. Kenyon, ex officio member. The ABA Standing Committee on the Law Library, under the chairmanship of George C. Freeman, Jr., Richmond, Va., consisted of Catherine Anagnost, Chicago, Ill.; Charlotte C. Dunnebacke, Michigan State Library; Maurice H. Merrill, Norman, Okla.; Charles S. Murphy, Washington, D.C.; and John T. Subak, Philadelphia, Pa.

5

The Administrative Department

Continuing growth and continuing change within the Library environment must perforce mean continuing adaptation of the Administrative Department's organization and programs.

Early in the fiscal year the responsibility for the administration of the Library's employee health program was transferred from the Employee Relations Office to the Health Services Office—both units of the Personnel Office. This organizational change was concurrent with the employment of a physician as health services officer with responsibility for development and administration of a comprehensive medical program, embracing numerous aspects of occupational and preventive medicine.

Particular attention was given throughout the year to improving the Library's personnel management programs. High priority was given to equal employment opportunity. Regulations were changed to implement the Equal Employment Opportunity Act of 1972 (Public Law 92-261) and to strengthen the system for pro-

cessing discrimination complaints. In establishing procedures and placing responsibilities, the principle of equal opportunity for all was treated as an essential, integral, and continuing part of the total personnel program. The position of assistant director of personnel for equality programs was established and assigned the immediate responsibility for developing, overseeing, and evaluating the Equal Employment Opportunity Plan of Affirmative Action.

AUTOMATION ACTIVITIES

In the Library's use of computers during the fiscal year, the emphasis in essentially all cases was on extending human capability through use of online techniques. Greater capabilities were obtained in the central computer facility and improvements, extensions, and expansions of user systems continued.

73

Computer Applications

Expansion of the application of the computer in support of the Congressional Research Service was significant. Capabilities for retrieval from bibliographic files were substantially improved; this led to a fourfold increase in the production of demand bibliographies for Members of Congress, committees, and CRS researchers. Other improvements have reduced the manual effort required for adding or changing data in the *Bill Digest* file. A new method was developed for computerized page makeup of the subject index of the *Bill Digest* requiring less manual effort while introducing a more usable format. Online access to a file of bibliographic citations to literature on current events was realized. A new system for the collection and reporting of statistics on congressional inquiries was implemented as the first phase of the effort to develop a comprehensive automated resource-management system for CRS.

In the Reference Department the first experimental phase of the book paging system that communicates book request data was developed and operational testing begun. The prototype consists of a communications network between reading room issue desks and a deck area housing one part of the collection. Subsequent phases will include expansion of the network to additional decks, direct reader input to the system, and management control. A system was developed for handling orders for materials required by the Division for the Blind and Physically Handicapped and testing was begun. When fully operational, it will provide online input and retrieval of information on the status of materials being produced for the division.

Automation activities in the Copyright Office included the implementation of a system for the generation of copyright catalog cards for sound recordings (Class N). This is the predecessor of a cataloging system for all copyright classes and features online cataloging and weekly production of new catalog cards. Building on the experience derived from the Class N operation and making use of new software capabilities, a complete up-to-date system is being designed to capture in machine-readable form accounting and registration data. Eventually, the system will generate copyright catalog cards and a format for the micropublishing of the *Catalog of Copyright Entries*. It will also produce, as a valuable by-product, statistical information for more effective management control.

Efforts continued to promote Library use of generalized software. The generalized bibliographic system (BIBSYS) was used in an expanding number of applications, for example, the preparation of a Library of Congress bibliography of the Arab world and of the Antarctic bibliography for the National Science Foundation. The commercial Display Management System (DMS) and the Customer Information Control System (CICS) were used heavily in projects for the Personnel Office, the Accounting Office, and the Division for the Blind and Physically Handicapped. A new retrieval language backed by programs and called SPECOL was obtained and installed. It has been used to extract data for special reports from the personnel data file and the existing copyright catalog file and is expected to be extensively used in the future. Activities involving online storage and retrieval of legislative and bibliographic citations for CRS and the Reference Department continue to require the expansion of a set of algorithms referred to collectively as the logic library. This library of subroutines, which has been developed by the Computer Applications Office, is used extensively in programs for the *Bill Digest* subject index and file reorganization.

Central Computer System Operations

The increase in applications supported by the central computer facility made necessary closer monitoring of the system's performance so that its capabilities might be utilized effectively. The change from two central processing units to one and the upgrading of disc, tape, and terminal equipment demanded close coordination for efficient operation.

The system was upgraded to take advantage of the advanced technology available. A disc-storage-management plan was developed and implemented for allocation and utilization of high-speed, large-capacity magnetic disc units. Tape storage management schemes were devised to take advantage of the new automatic-loading, high-speed, high-density magnetic tape units, and a software component was added to manage transfer of data into and out of the central processing unit more efficiently.

A programing, accounting, control, and evaluation system was installed which provides a detailed account of the use of the computer system. Results enable present and future workloads to be assessed more accurately.

The expanding workload and wide dispersion of elements of the computer system focused concern on reliability and availability. Effort was devoted to devising strategies for backing up equipment and for providing alternate means of processing in case of failure. Recovery procedures for critical data sets and computer programs were strengthened. Copies of important files and computer programs were systematically stored at a remote location under LC control in the event that the files or programs were damaged or destroyed at the central computer facility.

Many new online computer applications were added to the LC data communications systems. The online text-editing capabilities of the Administrative Terminal System (ATS) were extended to 20 additional terminals. The Customer Information Control System, providing the basic environment for LC online information storage and retrieval, was upgraded significantly and a comprehensive guide to help programmers use CICS was distributed. More than 30 CRT display terminals, which can be linked with printers, were added to the system.

The extensive changes in equipment and software technology required many revisions to the *Library of Congress Automation Standards Manual* and the *Library of Congress Automation Resources Manual,* which document the principles and practices considered to be best adapted to the LC automation environment. In addition, more than 30 technical seminars and training courses were conducted.

MANAGEMENT SERVICES

The most pressing problem of the past year for the several divisions under the assistant director for management services was what to do about space or, rather, the lack thereof. As the Library awaits the completion of the James Madison Memorial Building, the space problem becomes more acute daily. The acquisition of space through the General Services Administration, the planning to utilize available space to the greatest degree possible, the internal moves required, and finally the provision of services to relocated operations kept the staff in a continuous problem-solving status. Unfortunately, space difficulties will get worse before they get better.

The management analysts completed a number of reports recommending solutions to various problems. A study of the Training Office was completed and the establishment of a training data and status control system recommended. Material handling by the Division for the Blind and Physically Handicapped was reviewed. The keying and verification of data for the position skills file was accomplished. Among the studies under way at the close of the fiscal year was one on binding-procedure workflow and, for the Congressional Research Service, one on a word-processing system.

**Buildings Management and
Space Planning and Utilization**

There were significant developments in acquisition and utilization of space in three categories.

First, the GSA assigned to the Library 42,300 square feet of warehouse space on the third floor of the Navy Yard Annex, Building 159. This space was partially renovated for a full-scale Training Office with classrooms and self-help areas and for the Procurement and Supply Division offices. The remaining space was used for storage.

Second, the Buildings Management Office planned and supervised about 20 space adjustments. Of the moves completed, the majority were made in the Congressional Research Service and the Administrative Department.

Third, the Architect of the Capitol made a number of essential building improvements.

The following major space moves and improvements were accomplished during fiscal 1973:

The move of the Special Reference Section of the Congressional Reference Division to G-147, basement, allowed for the relocation of the Inquiries Unit to 115E and the renovation of the director's office and expansion of his staff.

Rearrangement of shelving in the Reading Room Gallery made additional work locations available for the American Law Division. Part of the Information Systems Section of the Congressional Reference Division was relocated to one bay of that space, leaving approximately 25 work locations for the American Law Division. The Environmental Policy Division then was assigned the space vacated by the Information Systems Section on the second floor.

Relocation of a portion of the Education and Public Welfare Division to Deck E resulted in approximately 12 additional work locations. Before moving this division to Deck E, it was necessary to relocate nearly half of the desks of the study facilities on Deck E to Decks C and D.

Removal of the Procurement and Supply Division, indicated above, to the Navy Yard Annex, allowed the relocation and expansion of the Equal Opportunity Office on the ground floor of the Main Building.

The long-needed renovation of the area occupied by the Photoduplication Service Microphotographic Section in the Annex subbasement.

Expansion of the snack bar concession in the Annex Building and the changeover to a self-service facility increased the seating capacity. Additional improvements to the remaining area were made early in fiscal 1974.

Disestablishment of the Special Police Office and Locker Room in the Annex and consolidation of the functions with the Main Building facilities

left space free for the relocation of the Federal Credit Union.

Renovation of the Basement Octagon, Main Building, provided space for the Office of the Assistant Director for Personnel. This move in turn allowed space for growth of the Placement and Classification Office.

Although by statute the structural and mechanical maintenance of the Library buildings is the responsibility of the Architect of the Capitol, the Library maintains close coordination with his staff in planning and scheduling repairs, alterations, and improvements. It maintains similar relations with the General Services Administration with respect to rented buildings.

During the year, the Architect of the Capitol began improvement of the illumination in the Annex bookstacks. After extensive testing, lighting fixtures were selected; installation was completed by September 1973. A combination freight-passenger elevator in one of the empty elevator shafts in the east lobby of the Annex Building was completed shortly after the close of the fiscal year. The badly needed air-conditioning system for the subbasement floor on the east side of the Annex Building was installed before the close of calendar 1973 and a system for the west side is under way.

The steam radiators on Decks A and B have been removed and new fan coil units will be installed to improve air-conditioning in these areas. Modifications to the control systems of the book carriers were accomplished, reducing nuisance system stoppages. All fire alarm and burglar alarm systems were consolidated into new central annunciator panels in the Special Police Office. Work was completed on the emergency power system for the elevators in both buildings.

The daily maintenance and police protection of the buildings is considered routine and is therefore not subject to detailed reporting; however, the improved appearance of the buildings and the increased professionalism of the Special Police Force has been a topic of comment by visitors as well as a source of considerable pride to the institution.

THE ADMINISTRATIVE DEPARTMENT

James Madison Memorial Building

The seed for the Library of Congress James Madison Memorial Building, which was planted in May 1971 with the beginning of excavation on Square 732, finally took root and by June 30, 1973, had grown approximately 40 feet as branches of concrete and steel columns sprouted above grade level on the northeast side of the main stem. Thus there is now visible evidence of a third Library building becoming a reality.

Phase I, which included excavation of the site, the pouring of the concrete base mat, and the four side walls up to grade level was officially completed in January.

As of the close of the fiscal year, 18 months after the award of the Phase II contract for the quarrying and fabrication of exterior stone, 75,000 cubic feet or 52 percent of the stone had been delivered to the Poplar Point storage yard in southeast Washington. The erection or application of the exterior stone is included in the Phase III construction.

Invitations for bids for the superstructure of the building were issued by the Architect of the Capitol under the date of September 6, 1972. Bids were opened November 28 and on December 7, 1972, the Architect of the Capitol awarded the Phase III contract for the superstructure in the amount of $24,789,000. The official contract time of 840 calendar days began on January 23, 1973, and accordingly, the work is due for completion on May 12, 1975. Basically the superstructure work includes the pouring of steel reinforced concrete structural columns and floor slabs, construction of the shell of the building, setting of exterior stone, and the construction of two tunnels from the Madison Building—one under Independence Avenue to the Library's Main Building and the second under First Street to the Cannon House Office Building. The cutting and relocation of trees and shrubs and the erection of a fence around the southeast corner of the Main Building grounds in preparation for the Independence Avenue tunnel excavation started on January 29 and was the first noticeable sign of the Phase III work. At the close of the fiscal year, excavation and the relocation of utilities had been completed and forms were in place to receive concrete for the first stage of the three-stage tunnel construction. And, at the main construction site, all of the basement floor slab and most of the ground floor slab had been completed, and columns for the northeast quadrant of the first floor slab had been poured.

Phase IV, the final phase of construction, will include all mechanical work and the interior finishes. It is estimated that this will be the most time consuming and the most costly of the four phases. Preliminary contract drawings and specifications for the fourth phase of construction were submitted by the Associate Architects to the Architect of the Capitol and to the Building Planning Office for review in April and May 1973. The drawings and specifications, in varying stages of completion, were still under review at the close of the fiscal year.

The test area at the Pickett Street Annex, which consists of four 25- by 25-foot bays, each with columns and ceiling heights dimensioned to simulate physical conditions within typical bays in the Madison Building, was completed by mid-year. Following the installation of four different designs of one- by four-foot light fixtures, tests were made to determine which design provided the light comfort most desirable for both work and collection areas. The design features of the fixtures selected have now been incorporated in the Phase IV drawings and specifications. Movable metal partitions, some floor-to-ceiling and some low-bank, have been installed in the test area to form four of the most popular size and type offices, a secretarial-receptionist area, and two open-work areas, one of which will be used for testing various components of typical reading room furniture. Carpet from a variety of mills and in various colors has been installed in each office and in two of the three areas mentioned above. Furniture which will be used for evaluation purposes has been ordered for each office and for the clerical and reading room areas.

Design drawings and specifications for the compact shelving mockup were completed in 1972, and two 24-foot-long double-faced ranges were installed and operated under test conditions at the Pickett Street Annex by March 1973.

By the end of the year semifinal furniture and equipment layouts for all areas of the building had been completed and approved by the appropriate officials of the departments involved. As had been anticipated, during the preparation of these layouts it was necessary to adjust the configuration and location of some partitions and doors, and to change some floor assignments to accommodate organizational changes, revised staffing figures, workflow, and improved traffic circulation. As this work progressed, special staff work stations and readers stations were designed, and reader stations for bound newspapers, microforms, and maps have been ordered for test purposes. The hardware, door, and surveillance schedule was also completed by midyear.

Assistance was also given to the exhibits officer in assembling information, photographs, architectural renderings, and related items for a Madison Building exhibit, which was installed on the first floor of the Main Building in December.

Financial Management

During the year the Library received $79,104,450 from direct appropriations, working fund advances and transfers, and gift, trust, and service fee funds. Appropriations to the Architect of the Capitol for use in support of the Library amounted to $1,531,400. Included in the above figures were two supplemental appropriations,

one for $150,000 for one-half year funding of a new affirmative personnel management program and a second one for $663,000, for increased costs resulting from the January 1973 pay increase. The Library was able to absorb $618,000 or 48 percent of the pay increase cost for the year.

A detailed statement of the funds appropriated for fiscal year 1973 is given below.

A summary of financial statistics and a detailed report of the gift and trust funds are found in the appendixes.

Materiel Management and Support

Severe space limitations made it necessary to move the Procurement and Supply Division to the Navy Yard Annex. The first phase of this move was accomplished on February 28, when the division office was moved. As the year closed, plans were being completed to move much of the contents of the supply storeroom and the bulk storage to the same location. Simultaneously with this move, a supply of highly repetitive items will be established in the Main Building to meet immediate requirements for office supplies.

The first permanent chief of the Procurement and Supply Division was appointed in the latter half of the fiscal year. The appointment marked a significant milestone in the reorganization plan

Salaries and Expenses, Library of Congress		$37,181,000
Copyright Office		4,911,500
Congressional Research Service		9,155,000
Distribution of catalog cards		10,193,000
Books for the general collections		1,118,650
Books for the Law Library		181,500
Books for the blind and physically handicapped		8,905,500
Public Law 480:		
U.S.-owned foreign currency	$2,627,000	
U.S. currency	276,000	2,903,000
Furniture and furnishings		4,435,300
Hinds' and Cannon's *Precedents*		120,000
TOTAL		$79,104,450

initiated in the spring of 1971. As a part of this plan, the handling of nonpersonal service contracts were transferred to this division from the Financial Management Office and responsibility for the Library space at the Federal Depot warehouse at Middle River, Md., where less-used bulk material is stored, was transferred from the Collections Maintenance Office.

During the year a program to provide better utilization of storage space and the maintenance and safeguarding of supplies and equipment in storage was initiated. A start was also made on an asset control system.

Central Administrative Services

On November 1, 1972, the Main Building of the Library of Congress was 75 years old. The Central Services Division, under several different titles, first as the Chief Clerk's Office and then as the Secretary's Office, has served the Library in its essential housekeeping operations during the entire 75-year period. Although the functions it performs have increased enormously in volume and sophistication and processes have been modernized by the application of new techniques and equipment, the division continues to receive and deliver the mail, operate an inhouse printing plant, maintain the central files, control and design forms, and provide many other similar services.

On the other hand, some of the methods used today were neither dreamed of nor needed at the turn of the century. For example, in fiscal 1973, the coldtype word-processing system produced more than 2,500 pages of camera-ready copy and the Printing Unit produced over 43 million impressions, nearly 18 million of which were for the Congressional Research Service.

Service rendered to congressional offices in establishing records-management systems increased substantially. A total of 123 visits were made during the year to 61 offices.

PERSONNEL

The enactment of the Equal Employment Opportunity Act of 1972 added a new dimension to the activities of the Personnel Office, namely, the development of policies, programs, and procedures aimed at affirmative actions in the broadest areas of personnel management and complaint investigation. Of the 17 positions sought from and granted by Congress, 14 were assigned to the Personnel Office. Eleven of these positions were made available in 1973 to plan and to carry out affirmative equal employment opportunity efforts. These additions of staff were instrumental in enabling the Personnel Office to effect significant portions of the Library's Affirmative Action Plan for fiscal year 1973 in such areas as training for lower-paid employees and pertinent supervisory orientation and instruction.

The involvement of the director of personnel and key principals of the Personnel Office in issues and cases growing out of complaints, grievances, appeals, hearings, and federal court cases consumed a disproportionate amount of time and energy and severely taxed the resources of top management as well as the Personnel Office.

A total of 390 supervisors participated in a mandatory supervisory training program during fiscal 1973, and a new management techniques course was added. A tuition support program, mainly for nonsupervisory personnel, was activated during the last six months of the fiscal year, 140 staff members receiving a total of $16,074 to aid in their further education.

The Placement and Classification Office instituted the first Public Service Careers Program for the Library. This program, which was approved in January 1973, provided the Library with a $74,000 Department of Labor-Civil Service Commission fund to pay a part of the cost of training participants in basic occupations through the end of fiscal year 1974. The Library has enrolled 83 current employees and 30 new employees in a generally effective and well-received "upward bound" program.

The appointment of a physician as the Library's first full-time health services officer gave impetus to the Library's overall health program by vigorous action in the areas of preventive medicine, mental health, hypertension, drug abuse, and alcoholism.

The Library's long-established Intern Program,

formerly called the Special Recruit Program, was suspended for the year due to unusually severe budget constraints.

Statistically, the Placement and Classification Office received over 1,700 Personnel Action Recommendations, processed over 15,000 applications for employment, and reviewed 1,750 positions for proper pay classification through individual and maintenance reviews of organization positions and functional needs.

Overall, the year yielded impressive personnel statistics—personnel actions processed during fiscal year 1973 increased by 15 percent to a total of 9,000; there was a 5-percent rise in the number of appointments; separations were up 7 percent; and Personnel Action Recommendations increased by 27 percent over the previous fiscal year.

PRESERVATION AND RESTORATION OF COLLECTIONS

The Library's preservation program developed in several important directions during fiscal year 1973. The Binding Office processed more volumes—215,000—than in any previous year. Furthermore, revised specifications have resulted in the Library's obtaining the highest quality binding now available from commercial sources.

The Collections Maintenance Office planned and supervised the relocation of almost 3 million volumes, cleaned and reshelved more than half a million volumes, inspected over 180,000 reels of nitrate motion picture film, and serviced 34,000 volumes from the Duke Street Annex and Middle River storage facilities.

Preservation microfilming of the Library's deteriorating general collections made good progress, with more than 5.7 million pages prepared for microfilming during the year. This is more than a 400-percent increase over 1968 figures and represents an expenditure of $195,000. Both the Photoduplication Service and the Preservation Microfilming Office are watching with interest the development of new, high-speed machines which may bring down microfilming costs and thus hasten the process of saving the Library's millions of deteriorating books.

One of the stumbling blocks in the preservation of many types of library materials has been a lack of fundamental knowledge about the causes and cures of paper deterioration. The Preservation Research and Testing Office, established two years ago to study the problems of preservation, made advances in certain problem areas, most significant of which was the search for a method for gaseous deacidification of books. The laboratory continued its testing and evaluation of deacidification processes—an evaluation much needed by conservators—and expects to be able to publish the results in 1974. Efforts to develop a process which will not only deacidify but also restore lost strength to brittle sheets met with some success and will be continued during fiscal 1974. A major undertaking of the Preservation Research and Testing Office during the past fiscal year was an investigation into methods of salvaging materials damaged by floods, fires, and other catastrophes. This work, most of which is now completed, will eventually result in a major report on the salvage of water-damaged materials.

The Restoration Office, too, played a major role in helping libraries salvage materials damaged in the floods caused by Hurricane Agnes and in the fire damage suffered by the Temple University Law Library. More than 2,000 copies of the preliminary version of a pamphlet on emergency procedures for salvaging flood or water-damaged library materials had been distributed by the end of the year, and numerous unfilled requests are on hand. This pamphlet, under revision at the close of fiscal 1973, will be published by the Library when it is completed.

The serious shortage of binders of rare books forced the Restoration Office to initiate an in-house training program in this area. Fortunately, several new employees with good basic skills were recruited who have demonstrated that they have the potential to meet this pressing need.

In addition to the routine restoration of items from the various custodial divisions, special attention was given to the development of a program to stabilize the deterioration of 8,000 rare volumes in the collection of the European Law Division. This program will be expanded during fiscal 1974.

PHOTODUPLICATION SERVICES

The first phase of the photo laboratory renovation program was completed and work began on the second phase, scheduled for completion during 1974. Renovation will provide acoustical ceilings, improved air-conditioning capabilities, and semiprivate work stations for microphotographers.

Continuing the series of microfilming specifications begun last fiscal year, *Specifications for the Microfilming of Books and Pamphlets in the Library of Congress* was written during the year and will be published by the Library in the fall of 1973.

After a careful cost analysis and an examination of all factors involved in the various services offered, a new rate schedule was developed and put into effect on October 1, 1972. It included the provision that, effective July 1, 1973, official and general rates correspond. As has been the case historically, the rate change did not immediately halt the recurring monthly deficits; however, at the end of the fiscal year, it did appear that increased revenues would allow the Service to reach the break-even point.

To meet the heavy demand, two additional coin-operated copiers were purchased and installed for public use. For patron convenience, dollar-bill changers were also installed near the coin-operated copiers in the Main Building and Annex catalog areas.

Equipment was leased to make hardcopy prints from roll film. This method is especially useful in satisfying orders for scattered newspaper prints. A camera was purchased during the year to produce microfiche.

Increased funds for the LC preservation microfilming program resulted in a total negative exposure count of over 3.4 million, an increase of more than 8 percent over the last year.

During the past year, the editing of the negative microfilm of the papers of Presidents Wilson, Taft, and Garfield was completed and the six-volume *Index to the William Howard Taft Papers* was published.

The microfilming of selected newspapers, periodicals, and gazettes of India, Pakistan, Bang-

ladesh, Sri Lanka, Nepal, and Indonesia in New Delhi reached an alltime high with 646 reels sent to the Photoduplication Service for processing and editing.

Filming of the House and Senate bills and resolutions for the Third Session of the 45th Congress, which was inadvertently omitted at the time of original filming, was begun. The microfilming of the bills and resolutions of the 92d Congress, 1971-72, was completed during the year and it is anticipated that editing will be completed by the end of July 1973.

The retention of negatives produced for generating hardcopy prints on continuous electrostatic copiers was initiated for those works filmed in their entirety. The use of these negatives for future orders will help to preserve the Library's collection by obviating the need to film a volume or set more than once. This collection now consists of 2,000 reels of film.

Specialized Library card files filmed for G. K. Hall & Co., which specializes in the production of book catalogs, were the *Catalog of Broadsides in the Rare Book Division* and the first supplement to *Africa South of the Sahara: Index to Periodical Literature, 1900-1970* from the African Section. At the end of the fiscal year, filming of the Geography and Map Division's *Bibliography of Cartography* was approximately one-half completed.

The Copyright Preservation Program reached a milestone during the past year: the microfilming of all bound volumes was completed. The filming of application cards, 1898-1937 (Books A) was also concluded during the year and work began on application cards, 1898-1937 (Music E). It is now anticipated that the program will be completed in approximately a year and a half.

The production of out-of-print LC catalog cards through continuous electrostatic copying is now in its fifth year, and the negative exposure count climbed 37 percent, to 7 million. This major increase was realized during the early part of the year. The second half of fiscal 1973 saw a steady decline in this work volume.

The economic problems faced by large research libraries resulted in other decreases in demand for services provided by the Photoduplication

Service. This fact, coupled with the substantial drop in the Card Division's reproduction program, led to a slight staff dislocation. Staff strength was down, primarily through attrition, to 152 full-time persons, a 5 percent drop from last fiscal year. On the brighter side, however, 36 staff members or 22 percent of the total staff achieved promotions during the past year.

6

The Copyright Office

Some activity on the bill for the revision of the copyright law, a general increase in the workload, significant administrative changes in the Copyright Office, and important progress ·on the international scene—these were the major developments in the copyright field during fiscal 1973.

GENERAL REVISION OF THE COPYRIGHT LAW

The bill for the general revision of the copyright law was put before the 93d Congress with the introduction of S. 1361 on March 26, 1973, by Senator John L. McClellan, chairman of the Subcommittee on Patents, Trademarks, and Copyrights of the Senate Judiciary Committee. Except for certain technical changes, the new bill was identical with the measure introduced in the 92d Congress and was similar, other than for some few amendments, to the bill in the 91st Congress

that was approved by the subcommittee in December 1969. A similar bill had been passed by the House of Representatives in April 1967.

Senator McClellan stated, in introducing the new bill, that the cable television issue had precluded progress on general revision and that another major issue, the photocopying of copyrighted works, was at present the subject of considerable attention. While expressing reservations about the value of further hearings, he indicated that the subcommittee would hear supplementary presentations on issues that might have been affected by recent developments. And, as the fiscal year ended, hearings were announced for July 31 and August 1, 1973, on library photocopying, general educational exemptions, the cable television royalty schedule, carriage of sporting events by cable television, and an exemption for recording religious music for broadcasts.

H.R. 8186, a bill for the general revision of the copyright law, identical with its Senate counterpart, was introduced on May 29, 1973, by Representative Bertram L. Podell. No action was taken by the House on this bill during the fiscal year.

ADMINISTRATIVE DEVELOPMENTS

George D. Cary retired as register of copyrights in March 1973 after 35 years of government service, 26 of them in the Copyright Office. He had been deputy register of copyrights from 1961 until his appointment as register in September 1971.

The Librarian of Congress announced the appointment of Barbara A. Ringer as register of copyrights on September 7, 1973. Miss Ringer, an employee of the Copyright Office for more than 20 years and assistant register of copyrights from 1966 to 1972, was serving as director of the Copyright Division of UNESCO in Paris at the time of her appointment as register. She is expected to assume her duties as register in November 1973.

Abe A. Goldman, general counsel of the Copyright Office, has served as acting register of copyrights in the interval.

L. Clark Hamilton was named assistant register of copyrights in February 1973. Mr. Hamilton has had broad experience in legal work, in management, and in computer systems, both in private industry and in the government. Before assuming his new position, he was chief of the Library's Computer Applications Office.

While the uncertain future of copyright revision continues to hamper long-range planning in the Copyright Office, significant advances were made on two fronts in fiscal 1973.

Early in the fiscal year a management consulting firm began a study of the Copyright Office aimed at identifying areas where better methods could be used and proposing specific improvements. The firm submitted a report containing its recommendations, and steps have already been taken to implement a number of them. It is believed that these changes, and others that may follow, will allow the office to perform its functions more effectively and more quickly.

Further steps were taken toward automation

of cataloging routines, an area where considerable progress had already been made in dealing with the registrations for sound recording. Detailed studies by the Library's Information Systems Office and the Copyright Office of the requirements for other classes of materials had begun before the fiscal year ended.

THE YEAR'S COPYRIGHT BUSINESS

Total copyright registrations for fiscal year 1973 amounted to almost 354,000, an alltime high. This is an increase of 3 percent over the previous year and 33 percent over the total figure a decade ago.

The class with the highest percentage of increase this year was sound recordings, which totaled almost 7,000. This category of material, which first became subject to statutory copyright protection on February 15, 1972, consists of sound recordings fixed and published on or after that date with the prescribed copyright notice. The total for fiscal 1973 was almost five times the number registered in the four and a half months of eligibility in fiscal 1972.

There was also a significant increase in registrations for periodicals, the total being 88,500, a gain of 5 percent over the previous year. Registrations for books, the largest single class, amounted to 104,500, an increase over last year of one percent.

Although music registrations decreased by 2 percent as against last fiscal year, the number of registrations for musical compositions since July 1, 1909, topped 3 million. It is appropriate at this point to note from the yearly registration statistics the ratio of published to unpublished music since statutory copyright first became available for unpublished musical works by the act of 1909. As the accompanying table reveals, the yearly totals for published music have gradually diminished, and the overall growth in music is attributable entirely to the growth in the number of registrations for unpublished works.

Among the smaller categories, there were increases in registrations of contributions to periodicals, dramas, maps, works of art, technical

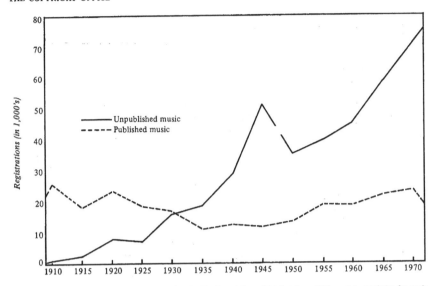

This graph is based primarily on information in the Catalog of Copyright Entries, which contain statistics for each calendar year. The graph shows the totals at·five-year intervals.

Copyright registration of published and unpublished music, calendar years, 1909-72

drawings, photographs, commercial prints and labels, and motion pictures other than photoplays; there were decreases in lectures, reproductions of works of art, prints and pictorial illustrations, and motion picture photoplays. There were more than 6,000 registrations for artistic designs embodied in useful articles, a drop of almost 3 percent; this kind of material constitutes at present 38 percent of the registrations in the art classes. Foreign registrations increased by more than 8 percent. And renewal registrations decreased by less than one percent.

Notices of Intention To Use decreased by 7 percent from the recordbreaking total of fiscal 1972 but remained extraordinarily high, almost 18,000 being recorded. There was also an 8-percent drop in Notices of Use. Assignments and related documents showed a slight increase.

Fees earned for copyright services during the fiscal year amounted to over $2.2 million. More than 127,000 separate remittances were scheduled, and almost 2,000 others were withheld from deposit for various reasons and returned to the remitter. A total of 453,000 pieces of incoming mail were processed, and 436,000 pieces of outgoing mail were dispatched.

The Copyright Office handled 397,000 applications for registration and documents submitted for recordation. Of these, 86 percent were accepted without correspondence; over 2 percent were rejected; and almost 12 percent were accepted after correspondence.

A total of over 2.6 million catalog cards were prepared. More than a million of these were added to the copyright card catalog, a record number for a single year; 61,000 were used by other departments of the Library of Congress; 244,000 were supplied to subscribers to the

Cooperative Card Service; and the rest were used in the preparation of the *Catalog of Copyright Entries.*

The Public Information Office received some 41,000 telephone calls, an increase of more than 30 percent over the previous fiscal year and double the number five years ago; it also answered 32,000 letters, an increase of 3 percent over last year. In addition, almost 5,000 visitors came to the Public Information Office, the largest number since 1969, when the Copyright Office was moved to the Crystal Mall Annex.

OFFICIAL PUBLICATIONS

Thirteen semiannual issues of the *Catalog of Copyright Entries* were published during the fiscal year. In addition, two of the parts, *Periodicals* (Third Series, Volume 25, Part 2, January-December 1971) and *Commercial Prints and Labels* (Third Series, Volume 26, Part 11B, January-December 1972), were published as annual accumulations. Also, during the year the Regulations of the Copyright Office were amended, as permitted by law, to increase the subscription price for all parts of the *Catalog,* effective with Volume 27, to $75; and the prices of the individual parts were raised accordingly.

Among the new pamphlets issued during the year was Circular 91, *Copyright Law of the United States of America,* which for the first time in recent decades provides the public with a free publication containing the full text of the current copyright statute.

COPYRIGHT CONTRIBUTIONS TO THE LIBRARY OF CONGRESS

Almost 571,000 articles were deposited in the Copyright Office in fiscal 1973. Of this number some 353,000, or 62 percent, were transferred to other departments of the Library of Congress, where they were available for accession to its collections or for shipment to other institutions in accordance with the Library's various exchange and gift programs.

LEGISLATIVE DEVELOPMENTS

Apart from the activity on the revision bill, the most significant legislative action during the fiscal year was the enactment of Public Law 92-566. Approved by President Nixon on October 25, 1972, this act, together with seven earlier acts of a similar nature, extends to the end of 1974 the second term of all copyrights in which the total regular term of 56 years would otherwise have expired between September 19, 1962, and December 31, 1974. The purpose of this series of enactments is to give the benefits of the extended term of protection contemplated in the revision bill to those works whose second terms would otherwise expire while the bill is under prolonged consideration.

Following announcement of the adherence by the Soviet Union to the Universal Copyright Convention, Senator McClellan, on March 26, 1973, introduced S. 1359, a bill to amend the copyright law by providing that a copyright secured to citizens or subjects of foreign nations, and the right to secure such copyright, shall vest in the author of the work, his executors or administrators, or his voluntary assigns, and that any such copyright or right to secure copyright shall remain their property "regardless of any law, decree or other act of a foreign state or nation which purports to divest the author or said other persons of the United States copyright in his work, or the right to secure it." In introducing the bill Senator McClellan stated that concern had been expressed that the Soviet adherence to the convention could be used to restrict publication in the United States of "works by Russian authors considered anti-Soviet," and that before "this legislation is processed by the Congress it will obviously be desirable to secure clarification of the intentions of the Soviet Government." Two bills identical with S. 1359 were also introduced in the House of Representatives—H.R. 6214 by Representative Jonathan B. Bingham on March 28, 1973, and H.R. 6418 by Representative Mario Biaggi on April 2, 1973.

Also on March 26 Senator McClellan introduced S. 1360, a bill to provide a remedy for postal interruptions in patent, trademark, and copyright cases. The part relating to copyright would amend title 17 of the United States Code to provide that in any case in which the register of copyrights determines that material to be delivered to the Copyright Office by a particular date would have been received in due time "except for a general disruption or suspension of postal or other transportation or communications services, the actual receipt of such material in the Copyright Office within one month after the date on which the register determines that the disruption or suspension of such service has terminated, shall be considered timely."

S. 1 and S. 1400, bills to revise the criminal laws of the United States, would both make certain changes in the criminal provisions of the copyright statute. The most important such amendment in S. 1 would provide that criminal actions instituted under the copyright law must be filed within one year from the time the crime was committed; the present law specifies that such actions must be started within three years after the cause of action arose. The most significant change in title 17 of the United States Code provided by S. 1400 would be to increase the penalties for criminal infringement of copyrighted sound recordings.

On February 27, 1973, Representative Ogden R. Reid introduced H.R. 4850, a bill to establish a commission to study and make recommendations on methods for compensating authors for the use of their books by libraries. The bill proposes establishment of a commission composed of the Librarian of Congress and 10 other members, who would report their findings to Congress and the President; the bill also proposes that "lending royalties," if found appropriate by the commission, would be provided by the federal government.

Bills for the taxation of sums received from the transfer of rights in literary, musical, and artistic property at capital gain rates have been introduced in each of the past several Congresses. Another such bill, H.R. 696, was introduced in the 93d Congress by Representative Edward I. Koch on January 3, 1973.

On that same date Representative Koch also introduced H.R. 697, to amend the Internal

Revenue Code so as to permit a deduction at fair market value for charitable contributions of literary, musical, or artistic compositions, or similar property, by their creators. Similar bills have been introduced to permit a deduction for such contributions at 50 percent of fair market value (H.R. 3152 by Representative Wilbur D. Mills on January 29, 1973, and S. 1367 by Senator Frank Church on March 26, 1973), at 75 percent (H.R. 6764 by Representative John Brademas and S. 1510 by Senator Jacob K. Javits, both on April 10, 1973), or at 100 percent (S. 1613 by Senator Lee Metcalf on April 17, 1973).

Another bill introduced by Senator Javits on January 11, 1973, S. 320, would amend the Social Security Act to exclude from excess earnings the gain derived by the creator from sale or other disposition of literary, musical, or artistic compositions, or similar property.

H.R. 3483, introduced by Representative Reid on January 31, 1973, would exempt from taxation the income received by a nonresident alien who is a citizen of a developing country from his literary, artistic, or musical works. This exemption would expire after five years unless the developing country had meanwhile granted an equivalent exemption for citizens of the United States.

JUDICIAL DEVELOPMENTS

For the first time in several years no litigation was either begun or pending against the Register of Copyrights during fiscal 1973. In other respects, copyright litigation gave little evidence of waning. Among legal disputes attracting more than passing attention were those involving cable antenna television systems and the constitutional status of state laws designed to prevent the unauthorized duplication of sound recordings.

Subject Matter and Scope of Copyright Protection

A copyrighted sales contract agreement was the subject of an action for infringement and unfair competition in *Donald* v. *Uarco Business Forms,*

478 F.2d 764 (8th Cir. 1973). Affirming a judgment for the defendant on grounds that the
wording of the contract agreement lacked sufficient originality for a valid copyright, the Court
of Appeals observed that for the most part the
form was "phrased in standard legal language,"
and moreover, in any event, the plaintiff "had
knowledge of, and drew upon, legal forms which
already existed in the public domain when he
drafted his form." As to the copyright status of
the form, a comment in a footnote was made
that a "copyright certificate will be issued
through a registration procedure in which the
validity of the copyright is not examined," and
that "such a certificate will not remain in force if
the subject matter, which it purports to cover, is
in the public domain."

A television service contract form containing
three paragraphs of printed text was held un-
copyrightable and the copyright claim invalid for
lack of originality in *M. M. Business Forms Corp.
v. Uarco, Inc.,* 347 F.Supp. 419 (S.D. Ohio
1972). Comparing the plaintiff's service contract
with other previously published forms that were
available to the author of the disputed form, the
court stated that it was unable to find a distin-
guishable variation that was not merely trivial.
The form was characterized as a "common gar-
den variety chattel mortgage" containing "no
creative and meaningful original work" capable
of distinguishing a "simplistic legal arrangement
from that which is presently subsisting in the
public domain."

The point of contention in *Alberto-Culver
Company v. Andrea Dumon, Inc.,* 466 F.2d 705
(7th Cir. 1972) was a commercial label for deodorant spray. Conceding that the label "as a
pictorial composition" was copyrightable, the
lower court had upheld copyright in the phrase
"most personal sort of deodorant," but the judge
reversed this ruling because such words constitute no more than "a 'short phrase' or expression'
which hardly qualifies as an 'appreciable amount
of original text.' " Referring to approximately 30
words of text on the plaintiff's label, the court
quoted approvingly the district judge's statement
that "the textual part of a label generally requires different treatment than the pictorial as-

pects of the label," and that, if "the text is
merely descriptive matter that does not aid or
augment the pictorial illustration, it is not subject to copyright."

In an action for infringement concerning wall
maps—*Champion Map Corp. v. Twin Printing
Co.,* 350 F.Supp. 1332 (E.D.N.C. 1971)—the
defense argued that the plaintiff should have obtained a separate copyright for a folding map
which was similar to the plaintiff's wall map,
except for its reduced scale and some deletions.
The court overruled the argument, pointing out
that the folding map was not entitled to separate
registration, and noting the pertinent observation
of another judge in a case on which defendant
relied, that the "reduction in size by the use of a
mechanical instrument is not an original idea.
The omission of towns, highways or other mark-
ings superfluous for . . . [the mapmaker's] purpose is not an indication of originality."

The distinction between a general idea and its
specific embodiment was stressed by the court in
dismissing a complaint for the infringement of
copyrighted buff-colored plastic statues of children in *Grossman Designs, Inc. v. Bortin,* 177
USPQ 627 (N.D. Ill. 1973). Holding that "only
specific expressions of an idea may be copyrighted," the opinion noted that others "may
utilize the same idea, plot or theme, but may not
copy the specific expressions or portions thereof." Observing that the dolls of both plaintiff
and defendant embodied the same basic theme or
idea, the judge commented that "these are three
universal child poses or activities which artists
have been depicting for centuries. Plaintiff obviously has no monopoly on the representation of
little boys on hobby horses, little girls standing in
nightgowns or standing in nightgowns holding
stuffed toys." Even if the plaintiff had been the
first one to portray these ideas, "she would not
secure a monopoly on them . . . by her copyright
she obtained a monopoly only on her specific
expression of these ideas."

The right of a courtroom reporter to profit
from the sale of his transcripts was the issue in
Lipman v. Commonwealth of Massachusetts, 175
F.2d 565 (1st Cir. 1973), a controversy growing
out of the judicial inquest into the Kopechne

drowning at Chappaquiddick Island, Mass., on the night of July 18, 1969. The earlier judgment dismissing-the reporter's complaint was vacated on the grounds that plaintiff had a legitimate property right in the transcripts. However, the court rejected plaintiff's claim of a common law copyright, with a significant observation about the nature of the authorship employed by a skilled stenotypist transcribing testimony: "Since transcription is by definition a verbatim recording of other persons' statements, there can be no originality in the reporter's product . . . ."

Publication

In an action for the infringement of common law rights in architectural drawings, judgment for the defendant was upheld on appeal because the plaintiff had distributed a series of more than 40 drawings to personnel of a construction firm for use in building a housing project, *Ballard H. T. Kirk & Associates, Inc.* v. *Poston,* 33 Ohio App.2d 117, 177 USPQ 92 (Ct. App. 1972). According to the opinion, the drawings were distributed without "any express restrictions, reservations or other limitations by means of an agreement, annotation on the plans, or otherwise, concerning the use and dissemination of such plans."

A different view was expressed in *Nucor Corp.* v. *Tennessee Forging Steel Service, Inc.,* 176 F.2d 386 (8th Cir. 1973), which was also an action for infringement of common law rights in construction plans. Reversing the lower court ruling that plaintiff had published its plans, the opinion declared that "a distribution of plans to potential contractors and subcontractors for bidding purposes does not constitute general publication" despite the fact that "the plans are not marked confidential, are not required to be returned, and can be obtained without paying a deposit." The court commented further on another aspect of the same issue: "We do not believe that displaying a building during or after construction, or publishing photographs of it, can be said to be the equivalent of publishing the building plans." Basically, a structure is the result of plans, and not a copy of them.

The issue of publication also arose in *Jones* v. *Spindel,* 196 S.E. 2d 22, 178 USPQ 303 (Ga. Ct. App. 1973), a suit for conversion of unpublished building plans for prefabricated houses. Affirming a judgment for plaintiff, the court held that the "filing of plans with a governmental authority to secure official approval was a publication for a limited purpose which did not cause loss of common law copyright."

In an action for infringement of copyrighted catalogs and pictorial prints, *National Council of Young Israel, Inc.* v. *Feit Company, Inc.,* 347 F. Supp.1293 (S.D.N.Y. 1972), the defendant claimed that the copyrights were forfeited because the plaintiff had licensed the printing and publishing of copies that were published without notice of copyright, although affixation of a proper notice had been made a condition of the permission to publish. The court found that there had been no abandonment and that the failure to police the licensee who published without notice did not indicate a purpose to surrender its copyrights.

The question of whether the sale of phonograph records of otherwise unpublished musical compositions constitutes a sufficient publication to divest the author of common law rights was presented to the court in *Rosette* v. *Rainbo Record Manufacturing Corp.,* 354 F. Supp. 1183 (S.D.N.Y. 1973), an action for infringement by the manufacture and sale of recordings containing children's songs and rhymes. The court pointed out that the common law protection reserved by §2 of the copyright law applied to unpublished works, including music, where no mechanical recordings have been made.

Observing that the "conditions for use of the musical composition on phonograph records are so well defined in the . . . Act of 1909 that it is unlikely that the Congress intended that contradictory principles of State law should survive," the judge was led to conclude "that the use of phonograph records without compliance with the Copyright Act bars claims for infringement, not because the record is a copy or a publication in the copyright sense, but because any other interpretation leads to conflict with the Federal statutory scheme."

90   REPORT OF THE LIBRARIAN OF CONGRESS, 1973

Nevertheless, noted the opinion, "the failure to file notice of use does not bar the copyright owner forever." The position of the court was further clarified:

I hold that the sale of phonograph records is not a divestment of common law rights [in unpublished music] by publication but that it does inhibit suit against infringers until the statutory copyright is obtained and the notice of use is filed. Thereafter . . . the statutory copyright owner may sue for subsequent infringement.

Notice of Copyright

In *L & L White Metal Casting Corp.* v. *Cornell Metal Specialties Corp.*, 353 F.Supp. 1170 (E.D.N.Y. 1972), an action for infringement of copyrighted metal castings used for pedestals, lamps, fixtures, and furniture, the court considered the question of whether the letters "L & L WMC" in the notice of copyright satisfied the requirements of section 19 of the statute (Title 17, U.S.C.) regarding the "name" of the copyright proprietor. The judge upheld the plaintiff's copyright, explaining that:

White Metal has existed as either a company or a corporation for over 35 years in an industry in which there are apparently relatively few established manufacturers [between 30 and 40 manufacturers of castings]. In addition, L & L WMC is a registered trademark, White Metal has filed a state certificate permitting it to do business under these letters and the letters appear on all of its advertising brochures. Substantial compliance with the statute has been established.

Three-dimensional "wire and polyethylene plastic sculptured reproductions of tea roses," published and copyrighted in 1967, were the subject of a suit for infringement in *First American Artificial Flowers, Inc.* v. *Joseph Markovits, Inc.*, 342 F.Supp. 178 (S.D.N.Y. 1972). Copies of the work were marketed in 1969 with a notice containing a "1969" date. The court ruled that the discrepancy in dates was "not a significant deviation for present purposes" and that the copyright had not been forfeited. Moreover, there had been no prejudicial reliance on the erroneous date by innocent third parties.

The defendant's failure to be "misled or prejudiced" by an error in date in the notice on copyrighted rubber squeeze-toy dolls moved the court to award plaintiff a preliminary injunction in *Uneeda Doll Co., Inc.* v. *Regent Baby Products Corp.*, 355 F.Supp. 438 (E.D.N.Y. 1972). The difference in dates was apparently less than a year.

Registration

Plaintiff, in *Coca Cola Co.* v. *Gemini Rising, Inc.*, 346 F.Supp. 1183 (E.D.N.Y. 1972), sued for an injunction against the sale or distribution of a poster consisting of an enlarged reproduction of its registered trademark with the words altered so as to read: "Enjoy cocaine." The defendant relied upon its registered claim to copyright in the poster as a defense. In granting the injunction, the court noted that, notwithstanding the registration in Class K, the offending poster was "of questionable validity on its face under the Rules and Regulations of the Register of Copyrights." Having observed the prohibition in section 202.1(a) of the Regulations against the registration of words, short phrases, slogans, and the like, the judge took particular note of section 202.14(c) of the Regulations: "A claim to copyright cannot be registered in a print or label consisting solely of trademark subject matter and lacking copyrightable matter . . . . registration of a claim to copyright does not give the claimant rights available by trademark registrations at the Patent Office."

A certificate of copyright registration was held to establish "prima facie evidence" not only of "the validity of the copyright, ownership by the registrant, and initial publication with notice" but also of "originality" in the previously mentioned case of *Champion Map Corp.* v. *Twin Printing Co.* Granting the plaintiff's motion for summary judgment, the court commented that a "prima facie case is not overcome by a mere denial."

Ownership and Transfer of Rights

The ownership of rights in copyrighted music

was the principal issue in *Royalty Control Corp. v. Sanco, Inc.*, 175 USPQ 641 (N.D. Calif. 1972). The court denied defendant's motion to dismiss for lack of federal jurisdiction despite the fact that the suit presented no proper claim for infringement, pointing out that "Section 26 creates a rebuttable presumption of copyright in the employer." Noting further that the determination of ownership under section 26 raises the question of renewal rights under section 24, the opinion continued: "Where a work is made for hire, all renewal rights are in the employer-proprietor, not the employee-author."

Since "a substantial issue" existed concerning the employment relation of both parties, the determination of which would affect ownership as well as renewal rights, the court found an adequate basis for federal jurisdiction.

The question of jurisdiction also arose in *Hill & Range Songs, Inc. v. Fred Rose Music, Inc.*, 58 F.R.D. 185 (S.D.N.Y. 1972), an action for declaratory judgment to determine ownership of renewal copyrights in musical compositions of a deceased composer, the rights of the contending parties deriving respectively from the son and alleged widow of the composer. Denying the defendant's motion to dismiss (while granting its motion for change of venue), the judge ruled that federal jurisdiction is sustained because the controversy depends upon a determination of whether one of the assignors of rights is a "widow" within the meaning of section 24 of the copyright law. "The right to obtain a renewal copyright and the renewal copyright itself exist by reason of the Act and are derived solely and directly from it." This remains true even though marital status and the content of an assignment contract may be determined by state rather than federal law.

Infringement and Remedies

Columbia Broadcasting System, Inc. v. Teleprompter Corp., 176 F.2d 338 (2d Cir. 1973), an appeal from a judgment dismissing the complaint in an action for copyright infringement of television programs, the issue concerned whether the defendant's CATV systems "perform" the copyrighted works they carry within the meaning of subsections 1(c) and 1(d) of the statute. The court, which affirmed in part and reversed and remanded in part, cited *Fortnightly Corp. v. United Artists, Inc.*, 392 U.S. 390 (1968), for the view that "a CATV reception service that receives broadcast signals off-the-air from an antenna or other receiving equipment erected within or adjacent to the community it serves, and distributes the programming received to subscribers, does not 'perform' the programs and, thus, is not subject to copyright liability, even though the subscriber could not otherwise receive the programs without the aid of CATV."

In formulating its decision, the court made a distinction:

We hold that when a CATV system imports distant signals, it is no longer within the ambit of the Fortnightly doctrine, and there is then no reason to treat it differently from any other person who, without license, displays a copyrighted work to an audience who would not otherwise receive it. For this reason, we conclude that the CATV system is a 'performer' of whatever programs from these distant signals that it distributes to its subscribers.

According to the opinion, there is "no reason to attach legal significance, in terms of copyright liability, to the decision to utilize microwave links," since microwave is "merely an alternative" to cable transmission.

On the other hand, although "a precise judicial definition of a distant signal is not possible," in the absence of a contrary showing, a signal should be presumptively deemed distant "when initially received by the CATV system on an antenna or other receiving device located between the originating community and the CATV community." Moreover, "the distances we envision here are small, and . . . any system that locates its antenna more than a few miles from the CATV community should bear the burden of showing that the signals it receives and distributes are not in fact distant signals."

The compulsory license provisions of sections 1(e) and 101(e) of the statute were interpreted to support plaintiff's motion for preliminary injunction in *Fame Publishing Co., Inc. v. S & S*

Distributors, Inc., 177 USPQ 358 (N.D. Ala. 1973), an action against an unauthorized duplicator of sound recordings for infringement of copyrighted musical compositions. Citing *Duchess Music Corp.* v. *Stern,* 458 F.2d 1305 (9th Cir. 1972); *cert. denied,* 409 U.S. 847 (1972), the court ruled that defendant's compliance with the compulsory license provisions "was of no force or effect" because the use made of plaintiff's music "is not a 'similar use' as the term is used in 17 U.S.C. §1(e), but is an 'identical use' . . . not sanctioned by §1(e). A compulsory licensee acquires no right to duplicate or reproduce the recordings of another. Anyone who seeks to rely on the compulsory license premium must hire some musicians, take them into a studio and make his own recording."

A contrary view was held in *Jondora Music Publishing Co.* v. *Melody Recordings, Inc.,* 351 F.Supp. 572 (D.N.J. 1972), a suit involving the mechanical rights in copyrighted music, where the judge granted the defendant's motion to vacate a writ of seizure and dissolve the injunction, commenting that the opinion in the above mentioned *Duchess Music* case does not state the law.

The judge said that the prohibition against unauthorized copying of recordings "clearly was not the law when Duchess was decided. Neither performance nor recording was copyrightable. It might have been unethical, . . . to 'steal' a recording of a performance and thereafter sell it as your own. But clearly the licensee-manufacturer had no claim under the Copyright Act." As far as congressional intent is concerned in Public Law 92-140 regarding application of the compulsory license provisions to duplicators, the opinion explained it this way:

Congress could have simply amended §1(e) by excluding from the benefits thereof those making an 'exact' or 'identical' copy of a preexisting recording. Thus, if Congress had desired to make all duplicators immediately liable for infringement of musical composition copyrights, it easily could have done so by restricting the compulsory license privilege in some fashion.

Dismissal of a suit against sound recording duplicators for infringement of copyrighted music was put on antitrust grounds in *Edward B. Marks Music Corp.* v. *Colorado Magnetics, Inc.,* 357 F.Supp. 280 (W.D. Okla. 1973). The court found that the plaintiff's marketing and pooling arrangements were "an abuse and misuse" of its copyright monopoly, amounting to an attempt to deny the defendant the right to take advantage of the compulsory license provisions of the law. Holding that the defendant had not infringed the plaintiff's music, and, by filing its Notices of Intention to Use and tendering royalty payments accordingly, had fully complied with sections 1(e) and 101(e) of the statute, the court berated the plaintiff's conduct "in using its copyright monopoly for the purpose of advancing unfounded accusations of copyright infringement and threats of infringement litigation. . . ."

In *C. M. Paula Co.* v. *Logan,* 355 F.Supp. 189 (N.D. Tex. 1973), designs on copyrighted greeting cards and note paper purchased at retail prices by defendant were transferred to ceramic plaques for sale. Each plaque received its design from a separately purchased copy of the work. Denying injunctive relief, the judge explained that "without copying there can be no infringement of copyright." The defendant's process "results in the use of the original image on a ceramic plaque; . . . [it] is not a 'reproduction or duplication.' " The opinion further observed that once the copyright owner has sold or otherwise disposed of copies of his work, the law " 'gives him no further right of control over the use or disposition of the individual copies. . . .' "

The previously mentioned case of *First American Artificial Flowers, Inc.* v. *Joseph Markovits, Inc.,* concerning the alleged infringement of three-dimensional plastic reproductions of tea roses, confronted the court with the question of what inferences should be drawn from an allegation of access and similarity. Denying plaintiff's motion for preliminary injunction, the judge cautioned that "any two devices purporting to represent a natural prototype or archetype are likely to be similar, quite apart from any copying. Thus, a copyright on a work which bears practically a photographic likeness to the natural article, as here, is likely to prove a relatively weak copyright. This is not to say that, as a matter of law, infringement of such a copyright cannot be inferred from mere similarity of appearance, but only that the plaintiff's burden will be that much more difficult to sustain because of the intrinsic similarities of the copyrighted and accused works."

A suit for infringement of a squeeze-toy doll occasioned the enunciation of different criteria in the aforementioned case of *Uneeda Doll Co., Inc.* v. *Regent Baby Products Corp.* Saying that the fact of copying was plain, the court awarded plaintiff a preliminary injunction even though "the aesthetic impression [made by the copies] is not the same," and despite the fact that the "differences in the two dolls are plain enough and . . . one would not be mistaken for the other." Although the infringer "has not copied the whole, . . . [nor] sought by his differences to disguise or hide the fact of copying," the opinion continued,

observation of the two dolls together would convince an observer that one depends on the other, not merely unimportant features but the purposive combination of features that characterizes the body of the doll and comprises a considerable part of its character and appeal.

The exemption in section 104 of the statute for performances "given for charitable or educational purposes and not for profit" was a basic issue in *Robert Stigwood Group Limited* v. *O'Reilly*, 346 F.Supp. 376 (D. Conn. 1972), an action for infringement of the copyrighted dramatico-musical rock opera *Jesus Christ Superstar*. Granting plaintiff's motion for preliminary injunction, the court observed: "The mere fact that the many professional performers [employed by defendant's rock company] are under the direction of a few priests cannot turn a professional touring company into a church choir." Nor is the group "a vocal society since the lay performers are professionals selected for their singing and musical abilities, and not because of homogeneous beliefs, charitable motives or religious affiliation." The court observed that section 104 "includes within its boundaries an opera or a rock opera."

Another defense raised was the right to the free exercise of religious beliefs under the first

amendment of the Constitution, to which the court responded that "the 'free exercise' does not include the wholesale appropriation of another's literary, artistic and musical works. In the balance must be weighed the constitutional right of authors to have 'the exclusive right' to their 'writings.' "

In *Twentieth Century Music Corp.* v. *Aiken*, 356 F.Supp. 271 (W.D. Pa. 1973), an action for copyright infringement was brought against a restaurant for the unauthorized playing of background music by means of a single radio set connected to five separate speakers located in various areas used by customers as well as part of the premises occupied by employees. Noting that at least one of the performing rights societies did not require a license as a matter of policy where a single standard radio set is used in small commercial establishments, the court awarded judgment to the plaintiff on grounds that there had been "a performance for 'profit,' " explaining that the decision would be fully supported regardless of whether the background music is designed to facilitate employee performance and efficiency or to give pleasure to customers.

A preliminary injunction was granted on motion in an action for copyright infringement of the characters in narrative cartoon comics, including "Mickey Mouse," in *Walt Disney Productions* v. *The Air Pirates*, 345 F.Supp. 108 (N.D. Calif. 1972). Addressing the question of whether a cartoon character really constitutes the story being told, the court said:

After all, the character is graphically represented many, many times, in the course of each series of panels [drawings]. The facial expressions, position and movements represented may convey far more than the words set out as dialogue in the 'balloon' hovering over the character's head, or the explanatory material appended. It is not simply one particular drawing, in one isolated cartoon 'panel' for which plaintiff seeks protection, but rather it is the common features of all of the drawings of that character appearing in the copyrighted work.

Unfair Competition and Other Theories of Protection

The constitutionality of a California statute making the unauthorized duplication of sound recordings a criminal offense arose on a writ of certiorari in *Goldstein* v. *California*, 412 U.S. 546 (1973). Neither the source of the original recordings nor the manufacturer of the tapes had been misrepresented. Upholding the state statute and affirming the petitioners' conviction in a 5-to-4 decision, Chief Justice Warren E. Burger, speaking for the majority, explained that the court's prior decisions in *Sears, Roebuck & Co.* v. *Stiffel Co.*, 376 U.S. 225 (1964) and *Compco Corp.* v. *Day-Brite Lighting*, 376 U.S. 234 (1964) "have no application in the present case, since Congress has indicated neither that it wishes to protect, nor to free from protection, recordings of musical performances fixed prior to February 15, 1972." Indeed, "[u]ntil and unless Congress takes further action with respect to recordings fixed prior to February 15, 1972, the California statute may be enforced against acts of piracy such as those which occurred in the present case." . "In regard to mechanical configurations," observed Chief Justice Burger,

Congress had balanced the need to encourage innovation and originality of invention against the need to insure competition in the sale of identical or substantially identical products. The standards established for . . . patent protection . . . indicated not only which articles . . . Congress wished to protect, but which configurations it wished to remain free. The application of state law in these cases . . . disturbed the careful balance . . . drawn and . . . gave way under the Supremacy Clause of the Constitution. No comparable conflict . . . arises in the case of recordings of musical performances. In regard to this category . . . Congress has drawn no balance; rather, they have left the area unattended, and no reason exists why the State should not be free to act.

Both dissenting opinions stressed the monopolistic implications of allowing state protection in perpetuity in derogation of a uniform and exclusive federal preemption. This view was summarized by Justice Thurgood Marshall:

The business of record piracy is not an attractive one; persons in the business capitalize on the talents of others without needing to assess independently the prospect of public acceptance of a performance. But . . . [s]uch people do provide low-cost reproductions that may well benefit the public. In light of the presumption of *Sears* and *Compco* that congressional silence betokens a determination that the benefits of competition

outweigh the impediments placed on creativity by the lack of copyright protection, and in the absence of a congressional determination that the opposite is true, we should not let our distaste for 'pirates' interfere with our interpretation of the copyright laws. I would therefore hold that, as to sound recordings fixed before February 15, 1972, the States may not enforce laws limiting reproduction.

A result contrary to that prevailing in the Supreme Court's decision in the *Goldstein* case had been reached a few weeks earlier in *Columbia Broadcasting System, Inc.* v. *Melody Recordings, Inc.*, 124 N.J. Super. 322, 306 A.2d 493 (1973), a class action brought by CBS on behalf of itself and "all other recording companies that produce, manufacture and sell musical performances on records and tapes." Granting the defendant's motion for summary judgment, the court concluded that the *Sears* and *Compco* cases are "controlling and dispositive" in making clear the "federal intendment" that "in the absence of patent . . . or copyright protection exact copies or duplicates [of pre-February 15, 1972, recordings] may be made by anyone."

INTERNATIONAL COPYRIGHT DEVELOPMENTS

The Union of Soviet Socialist Republics became the 64th adherent to the 1952 version of the Universal Copyright Convention, effective May 27, 1973. This was a historic event, since the Soviet Union had theretofore declined to adhere to any multilateral copyright treaty and had eschewed copyright relations with most of the other nations of the world.

On September 18, 1972, the United States deposited its instrument of ratification of the Universal Copyright Convention as Revised at Paris on July 24, 1971. The convention will come into force after 12 countries have adhered. The revised convention, in which the revisions deal primarily with the enumeration of the basic rights of authors and with special exceptions for developing countries, requires no implementing legislation in the United States, since the U.S. copyright law is already in conformity with it. The Senate, on August 14, 1972, had advised and consented to ratification of the revised convention. Algeria, Cameroon, France, Hungary, and Sweden acceded to the revised Universal Copyright Convention during the fiscal year, bringing the total number of adherents to seven. The United Kingdom, the first adherent to the revised convention, had deposited its instrument of ratification in the previous fiscal year.

In acceding to the revised convention, Cameroon and Algeria also adhered to the 1952 version of the convention. Thus Cameroon became the 63d member of the 1952 convention, effective May 1, 1973, and Algeria becomes the 65th member, effective August 28, 1973. As a member of the U.S. delegation, Mr. Goldman, acting register of copyrights, participated in the meeting of the Third Committee of Governmental Experts on Problems in the Field of Copyright and the Protection of Performers, Producers of Phonograms, and Broadcasting Organizations Raised by Transmission via Space Satellites. As a result of the meeting, which was held at Nairobi, Kenya, in July 1973, a new draft Convention Relating to the Distribution of Programme-Carrying Signals Transmitted by Satellite was prepared, and a resolution was adopted recommending that a diplomatic conference be convened in 1974 for the purpose of concluding an international convention on this subject.

On April 11, 1973, President Nixon transmitted to the Senate, for ratification, the Convention for the Protection of Producers of Phonograms Against Unauthorized Duplication of Their Phonograms, which was concluded at Geneva on October 29, 1971. Under the terms of this convention, adhering countries would provide international protection against the making or importation of unauthorized duplicates of phonograms (sound recordings) for distribution to the public. The President's message to the Senate recommended favorable consideration. This convention entered into force on April 18, 1973, among the five countries that had adhered to it by that date. It will become effective for later adherents three months after notification of the deposit of their instruments of adherence.

Respectfully submitted,

ABE A. GOLDMAN
Acting Register of Copyrights

International Copyright Relations of the United States as of June 30, 1973

Code: UCC Party to the Universal Copyright Convention, as is the United States. The effective date is given for each country. The effective date for the United States was September 16, 1955.

BAC Party to the Buenos Aires Convention of 1910, as is the United States.

Bilateral Bilateral copyright relations with the United States by virtue of a proclamation or treaty. 1

Unclear Became independent since 1943. Has not established copyright relations with the United States, but may be honoring obligations incurred under former political status.

None No copyright relations with the United States.

Country	Status of copyright relations	Country	Status of copyright relations
Afghanistan	None	Egypt	None
Albania	None	El Salvador	Bilateral by virtue of Mexico
Algeria	Unclear		City Convention, 1902
Andorra	UCC Sept. 16, 1955	Equatorial Guinea . .	Unclear
Argentina	UCC Feb. 13, 1958; BAC;	Ethiopia	None
	Bilateral	Fiji 3	UCC Oct. 10, 1970
Australia	UCC May 1, 1969; Bilateral	Finland	UCC April 16, 1963; Bilateral
Austria	UCC July 2, 1957; Bilateral	France	UCC Jan. 14, 1956; Bilateral
Bahrain	None	Gabon	Unclear
Bangladesh	Unclear	Gambia	Unclear
Barbados	Unclear	Germany 4	Bilateral; UCC with Federal
Belgium	UCC Aug. 31, 1960; Bilateral		Republic of Germany,
Bhutan	None		. Sept. 16, 1955
Bolivia	BAC	Ghana	UCC Aug. 22, 1962
Botswana	Unclear	Greece	UCC Aug. 24, 1963; Bilateral
Brazil	UCC Jan. 13, 1960; BAC;	Guatemala	UCC Oct. 28, 1964; BAC
	Bilateral	Guinea	Unclear,
Bulgaria	None	Guyana	Unclear
Burma	Unclear	Haiti	UCC Sept. 16, 1955; BAC
Burundi	Unclear	Holy See	UCC Oct. 5, 1955
Cambodia	UCC Sept. 16, 1955	Honduras	BAC
Cameroon	UCC May 1, 1973	Hungary	UCC Jan. 23, 1971; Bilateral
Canada	UCC Aug. 10, 1962; Bilateral	Iceland	UCC Dec. 18, 1956
Central African		India	UCC Jan. 21, 1958; Bilateral
Republic	Unclear	Indonesia	Unclear
Chad	Unclear	Iran	None
Chile	UCC Sept. 16, 1955; BAC;	Iraq	None
	Bilateral	Ireland	UCC Jan. 20, 1959; Bilateral
China 2	Bilateral	Israel	UCC Sept. 16, 1955; Bilateral
Colombia	BAC	Italy	UCC Jan. 24, 1957; Bilateral
Congo	Unclear	Ivory Coast	Unclear
Costa Rica	UCC Sept. 16, 1955; BAC;	Jamaica	Unclear
	Bilateral	Japan	UCC April 28, 1956
Cuba	UCC June 18, 1957; Bilateral	Jordan	Unclear
Cyprus	Unclear	Kenya	UCC Sept. 7, 1966
Czechoslovakia . . .	UCC Jan. 6, 1960; Bilateral	Korea	Unclear
Dahomey	Unclear	Kuwait	Unclear
Denmark	UCC Feb. 9, 1962; Bilateral	Laos	UCC Sept. 16, 1955
Dominican Republic .	BAC	Lebanon	UCC Oct. 17, 1959
Ecuador	UCC June 5, 1957; BAC	Lesotho	Unclear

Country	Status of copyright relations	Country	Status of copyright relations
Liberia	UCC July 27, 1956	Romania	Bilateral
Libya	Unclear	Rwanda	Unclear
Liechtenstein	UCC Jan. 22, 1959	San Marino	None
Luxembourg	UCC Oct. 15, 1955; Bilateral	Saudi Arabia	None
Madagascar	Unclear	Senegal	Unclear
Malawi	UCC Oct. 26, 1965	Sierra Leone	Unclear
Malaysia	Unclear	Singapore	Unclear
Maldives Islands . . .	Unclear	Somalia	Unclear
Mali	Unclear	South Africa	Bilateral
Malta	UCC Nov. 19, 1968	Soviet Union	UCC May 27, 1973
Mauritania	Unclear	Spain	UCC Sept. 16, 1955; Bilateral
Mauritius 5	UCC Mar. 12, 1968	Sri Lanka (Ceylon) . .	Unclear
Mexico	UCC May 12, 1957; BAC; Bilateral	Sudan	Unclear
		Swaziland	Unclear
Monaco	UCC Sept. 16, 1955; Bilateral	Sweden	UCC July 1, 1961; Bilateral
Morocco	UCC May 8, 1972	Switzerland	UCC Mar. 30, 1956; Bilateral
Nauru	Unclear	Syria	Unclear
Nepal	None .	Tanzania	Unclear
Netherlands	UCC June 22, 1967; Bilateral	Thailand	Bilateral
New Zealand	UCC Sept. 11, 1964; Bilateral	Togo	Unclear
Nicaragua	UCC Aug. 16, 1961; BAC	Tonga	None
Niger	Unclear	Trinidad and Tobago .	Unclear
Nigeria	UCC Feb. 14, 1962	Tunisia	UCC June 19, 1969
Norway	UCC Jan. 23, 1963; Bilateral	Turkey	None
Oman	None	Uganda	Unclear
Pakistan	UCC Sept. 16, 1955	United Arab Emirates	None
Panama	UCC Oct. 17, 1962; BAC	United Kingdom . . .	UCC Sept. 27, 1957; Bilateral
Paraguay	UCC Mar. 11, 1962; BAC	Upper Volta	Unclear
Peru	UCC Oct. 16, 1963; BAC	Uruguay	BAC
Philippines	Bilateral; UCC status undetermined by UNESCO (Copyright Office considers that UCC relations do not exist.)	Venezuela	UCC Sept. 30, 1966
		Vietnam	Unclear
		Western Samoa . . .	Unclear
		Yemen (Aden) . . .	Unclear
		Yemen (San'a) . . .	None
Poland	Bilateral	Yugoslavia	UCC May 11, 1966
Portugal	UCC Dec. 25, 1956; Bilateral	Zaire	Unclear
Qatar	None	Zambia	UCC June 1, 1965

1 Foreign sound recordings fixed and published on or after February 15, 1972, with the special notice of copyright prescribed by law (e.g., ℗ 1973 Doe Records, Inc.), may be entitled to U.S. copyright protection only if the author is a citizen of one of the countries with which the United States maintains bilateral relations as indicated above. Circular 56 offers further information on sound recordings.
2 A citizen of China domiciled on Formosa (Nationalist China) or on the mainland (Red China) may secure U.S. copyright. Applications for registration must state that the author is a citizen of "China" or 'Nationalist China."
3 On December 13, 1971, Fiji notified UNESCO that it considers itself bound by the UCC from October 10, 1970.
4 UCC relations are with the Federal Republic of Germany only. A citizen of Germany may secure U.S. copyright, regardless of whether or not he is domiciled in the Federal Republic of Germany. However, applications for registration must state that the author is a citizen of "Germany," "West Germany," "German Federal Republic," or the "Federal Republic of Germany."
5 On August 20, Mauritius notified UNESCO that it considers itself bound by the UCC from March 12, 1968.

Number of Registrations by Subject Matter Class, Fiscal Years 1969-73

Class	Subject matter of copyright	1969	1970	1971	1972	1973
A	Books, including pamphlets, leaflets, etc. . . .	83,603	88,432	96,124	103,231	104,523
B	Periodicals (issues)	80,706	83,862	84,491	84,686	88,553
	(BB) Contributions to newspapers and periodicals	1,676	1,943	1,884	2,004	2,074
C	Lectures, sermons, addresses	1,155	1,669	1,855	1,940	1,714
D	Dramatic or dramatico-musical compositions .	3,213	3,352	3,553	3,838	3,980
E	Musical compositions	83,608	88,949	95,202	97,482	95,296
F	Maps	2,024	1,921	1,677	1,633	1,914
G	Works of art, models, or designs	5,630	6,807	7,916	7,901	8,621
H	Reproductions of works of art	2,489	3,036	3,047	3,434	3,190
I	Drawings or plastic works of a scientific or technical character	552	835	924	1,059	1,114
J	Photographs	936	1,171	1,160	1,140	1,354
K	Prints and pictorial illustrations	2,837	3,373	4,209	4,524	4,441
	(KK) Commercial prints and labels . . .	4,798	5,255	4,424	4,118	4,216
L	Motion-picture photoplays	1,066	1,244	1,169	1,816	1,449
M	Motion pictures not photoplays	1,298	1,301	1,226	1,388	1,420
N	Sound recordings				1,141	6,718
R	Renewals of all classes	25,667	23,316	20,835	23,239	23,071
	Total	301,258	316,466	329,696	344,574	353,648

Number of Articles Deposited, Fiscal Years 1969-73

Class	Subject matter of copyright	1969	1970	1971	1972	1973
A	Books, including pamphlets, leaflets, etc. . . .	164,958	174,519	189,887	203,875	206,671
B	Periodicals	160,707	166,976	168,114	168,463	176,142
	(BB) Contributions to newspapers and periodicals	1,676	1,943	1,884	2,004	2,074
C	Lectures, sermons, addresses	1,155	1,669	1,855	1,940	1,714
D	Dramatic or dramatico-musical compositions .	3,563	3,751	3,993	4,216	4,538
E	Musical compositions	103,164	110,010	116,537	117,425	114,378
F	Maps	4,047	3,840	3,352	3,264	3,786
G	Works of art, models, or designs	9,688	11,736	13,894	13,590	14,843
H	Reproductions of works of art	4,811	6,046	6,056	6,821	6,313
I	Drawings or plastic works of a scientific or technical character	839	1,267	1,419	1,614	1,873
J	Photographs	1,565	2,080	2,056	2,063	2,471
K	Prints and pictorial illustrations	5,671	6,740	8,417	9,036	8,873
	(KK) Commercial prints and labels . . .	9,595	10,510	8,846	8,235	8,408
L	Motion-picture photoplays	2,100	2,448	2,305	3,593	2,855
M	Motion pictures not photoplays	2,471	2,460	2,318	2,648	2,654
N	Sound recordings				2,282	13,388
	Total	476,010	505,995	530,933	551,069	570,981

Number of Articles Transferred to Other Departments of the Library of Congress [1]

Class	Subject matter of articles transferred	1969	1970	1971	1972	1973
A	Books, including pamphlets, leaflets, etc. . . .	90,435	92,664	107,468	115,242	[2] 120,452
B	Periodicals	169,671	175,301	176,259	176,161	183,755
	(BB) Contributions to newspapers and periodicals	1,676	1,943	1,884	2,004	2,074
C	Lectures, sermons, addresses	0	0	0	0	7
D	Dramatic or dramatico-musical compositions .	221	100	41	226	179
E	Musical compositions	25,021	25,235	25,567	21,275	22,517
F	Maps	4,102	3,946	3,352	3,264	3,796
G	Works of art, models, or designs	173	286	376	1,252	2,957
H	Reproductions of works of art	714	431	845	1,620	2,933
I	Drawings or plastic works of a scientific or technical character	2	0	0	0	10
J	Photographs	28	28	42	65	66
K	Prints and pictorial illustrations	819	370	614	499	52
	(KK) Commercial prints and labels . . .	350	98	409	220	38
L	Motion-picture photoplays	52	63	4	64	67
M	Motion pictures not photoplays	132	153	111	183	331
N	Sound recordings				2,282	13,405
	Total	293,396	300,618	316,972	324,357	352,639

[1] Extra copies received with deposits and gift copies are included in these figures. For some categories, the number of articles transferred may therefore exceed the number of articles deposited as shown in the preceding chart.
[2] Of this total, 29,400 copies were transferred to the Exchange and Gift Division for use in its programs.

Gross Cash Receipts, Fees, and Registrations, Fiscal Years 1969-73

	Gross receipts	Fees earned	Registrations	Increase or decrease in registrations
1969	$2,011,372.76	$1,879,831.30	301,258	-2,193
1970	2,049,308.99	1,956,441.37	316,466	+15,208
1971	2,089,620.19	2,045,457.52	329,696	+13,230
1972	2,313,638.14	2,177,064.86	344,574	+14,878
1973	2,413,179.43	2,226,540.96	353,648	+9,074
Total	10,877,119.51	10,285,336.01	1,645,642	

Summary of Copyright Business

Balance on hand July 1, 1972		$ 536,258.04
Gross receipts July 1, 1972, to June 30, 1973		2,413,179.43
Total to be accounted for		2,949,437.47
Refunded	$ 113,754.34	
Checks returned unpaid	5,511.15	
Deposited as earned fees	2,245,348.22	
Deposited as undeliverable checks	6,841.10	

Balance carried over July 1, 1973
Fees earned in June 1973 but not deposited until

July 1973	$183,675.56	
Unfinished business balance	100,718.22	
Deposit accounts balance	290,175.57	
Card service	3,413.31	
	577,982.66	
		2,949,437.47

	Registrations	Fees earned
Published domestic works at $6	230,628	$1,383,768.00
Published foreign works at $6	5,025	30,150.00
Unpublished works at $6	83,077	498,462.00
Renewals at $4	23,071	92,284.00
Total registrations for fee		2,004,664.00
Registrations made under provisions of law permitting registration without payment of fee for certain works of foreign origin	11,838	
Registrations made under Standard Reference Data Act, P.L. 90-396 (15 U.S.C. §290), for certain publications of U.S. government agencies for which fee has been waived	9	
Total registrations	353,648	
Fees for recording assignments		37,135.00
Fees for indexing assignments		18,534.50
Fees for recording notices of use		21,073.00
Fees for recording notices of intention to use		65,609.00
Fees for certified documents		6,622.00
Fees for searches made		63,520.00
Card Service		9,383.46
Total fees exclusive of registrations		221,876.96
Total fees earned		2,226,540.96

Appendix 1

LIBRARY OF CONGRESS
TRUST FUND BOARD

SUMMARY OF ANNUAL REPORT

MEMBERSHIP. Members of the Library of Congress Trust Fund Board at the end of fiscal year 1973 were:

Ex Officio

George P. Shultz, Secretary of the Treasury, Chairman; Lucien N. Nedzi, Chairman of the Joint Committee on the Library; and L. Quincy Mumford, Librarian of Congress, Secretary.

Appointive

Mrs. Charles William Engelhard, Jr. (term ends March 8, 1975). Walter S. Gubelmann was appointed to the board in October 1973. Mr. Gubelmann's term will end on March 9, 1978.

MEETINGS OF THE BOARD. The Trust Fund Board met on September 7, 1972. The report of the U.S. Treasury Department on the status of assets held by the board was reviewed, and poll

votes taken by the board since the last meeting were confirmed by unanimous vote. The board adopted resolutions to permit the deposit of securities held in the McKim Fund and the Katie and Walter Louchheim Fund with a bank or trust company in the District of Columbia for management on behalf of the funds. The secretary of the board was authorized to select, upon the advice and assistance of the U.S. Treasury Department, one bank or trust company on the basis of written proposals invited from the institutions that had expressed an interest in managing the funds. The American Security and Trust Company, 15th Street and Pennsylvania Avenue NW., Washington, D.C., was subsequently selected.

The board approved amendments to its bylaws concerning regular meetings, notice of meetings, and definition and reaffirmation of poll votes.

INCREASE IN INVESTMENTS. Contributions of $250 from John W. Auchincloss, $25 from Olin Dows, and $100 from Mrs. Joan F. Kahn

Summary of Income and Obligations [1]

	Permanent loan account [2]	Investment account	Total
Unobligated funds carried forward from fiscal 1972	$284,993.08	$115,403.79	$400,396.87
Income, fiscal 1973	209,949.08	59,953.27	269,902.35
Available for obligation, fiscal 1973	494,942.16	175,357.06	670,299.22
Obligations, fiscal 1973	215,544.19	58,087.65	273,631.84
Carried forward to fiscal 1974	279,397.97	117,269.41	396,667.38

1 See appendix 11 for a detailed statement on the trust funds.
2 For income and obligations from the Gertrude M. Hubbard bequest, see appendix 11.

101

102

were received to augment the endowment of the Friends of Music in the Library of Congress.

ACTIVITIES SUPPORTED BY FUNDS HELD BY THE BOARD. The income from these funds was used to strengthen the collections and services of the Library of Congress and to enhance the Library's cultural offerings to the community and the nation.

Among the acquisitions supported by this income were materials selected for addition to the Walt Whitman papers and the Alfred Whital Stern Collection of Lincolniana, Ira Gershwin manuscripts, a John Philip Sousa letter, band music, flute music, prints, Hispanic and Slavic materials, and photocopies of materials relating to America in European repositories.

Trust Fund income supported a variety of concerts and literary programs in the Coolidge Auditorium during the fiscal year, including a two-day conference on the teaching of creative writing. Several new musical compositions were commissioned and the Library's Stradivari instruments were repaired. Work continued on a catalog of the Lessing J. Rosenwald collection.

Assistance was provided in connection with the cataloging of maps and music and the acquisition of prints and other materials. Arrangements were made for blind persons to work on the braille music collection.

Income from the funds also provided consultant services related to various Library programs and assistance in indexing and publication activities. Support was provided for Library of Congress specialists to attend a number of scholarly meetings, and special activities connected with visits to the Library by noted scholars and other distinguished persons were made possible.

ACQUISITIONS
AND ACQUISITIONS WORK

THE COLLECTIONS OF THE LIBRARY

	Total pieces, June 30, 1972	Additions, 1973	Withdrawals, 1973	Total pieces, June 30, 1973
Volumes and pamphlets	1 16,064,837	402,068	6	16,466,899
Technical reports (hardcopy)	1,267,306	41,480	27,183	1,281,603
Bound newspaper volumes	115,933	90	5,009	111,014
Newspapers on microfilm (reels)	242,826	17,042		259,868
Manuscripts (pieces)	30,618,658	418,621	5,775	31,031,504
Maps	3,444,234	76,647	18,780	3,502,101
Micro-opaques	381,828	12,283		394,111
Microfiche	780,430	2 123,875	13	904,292
Microfilm (reels and strips)	569,688	76,045		645,733
Motion pictures (reels) . . . . :	167,753	15,449		183,202
Music (volumes and pieces)	3,373,825	10,353		3,384,178
Recordings				
Discs	312,590	29,984		342,574
Tapes and wires	31,413	9,755		41,168
Books for the blind and physically handicapped 3				
Volumes				
Books in raised characters	1,205,118	45,602	36,153	1,214,567
Books in large type	3,861	400	115	4,146
Recordings (containers)				
Talking books on discs	2,678,515	373,841	267,851	2,784,505
Talking books on tape	194,448	75,544	5,833	264,159
Other recorded aids	2,561	550		3,111
Prints and drawings (pieces)	176,482	309	2,379	174,412
Photographic negatives, prints, and slides	3 8,446,394	3,079	1,036	8,448,437
Posters	41,550	490		42,040
Other (broadsides, photocopies, nonpictorial material, photostats, etc.)	985,907	15,198	18,073	983,032
Total	1 71,106,427	1,748,705	388,206	72,466,926

1 Adjusted figure.
2 Includes 21,058 microfiche cards in the Public Reference Section, GR&B, not previously reported.
3 Includes books deposited in regional libraries for the blind and physically handicapped.

RECEIPTS BY SOURCE

	Pieces, 1972	Pieces, 1973
By purchase		
Funds appropriated to the Library of Congress		
Books for the blind and physically handicapped	7,807	12,295
Books for the Law Library	48,140	47,129
Books for the general collections	548,675	501,536
Copyright Office	4,295	1,933
Distribution of catalog cards	840	
Congressional Research Service	113,220	147,005
Preservation of motion pictures	39	5
Public Law 480	67,708	76,014
Salaries and expenses, Library of Congress		
Reprints and books for office use	3,176	3,488
Microfilm of deteriorating materials	49,951	41,965
NPAC	115,616	82,410
Funds transferred from other government agencies		
Federal Research Division	8,468	51,388
Other working funds	573	346
Gift funds		
American Council of Learned Societies		115
Babine Fund	1	
Carnegie Fund	5	
Feinberg Fund		14
Friends of Music		1
Gulbenkian Foundation	214	282
Heineman Foundation	30	6
Hubbard Fund	17	13
Huntington Fund	38	35
Lindberg Fund	17	
Loeb Fund	1	
Louisiana Colonial Records Project	825	
Mearns Fund	2	
Mellon Fund	303	273
Miller Fund	17	9

RECEIPTS BY SOURCE—Continued

	Pieces, 1972	Pieces, 1973
Pennell Fund	199	69
Porter Fund		1
Rizzuto Fund		5
Rosenwald Fund	29	8
Scala Fund	8	1
Stern Memorial	42	17
Whitman Collection	508	
Wilbur Fund	451	88
Total	971,215	966,451
By virtue of law		
Books for the blind and physically handicapped	260	608
Copyright	269,742	301,101
Public Printer	925,260	849,147
Total	1,195,262	1,150,856
By official donation		
Local agencies	4,762	3,848
State agencies	155,645	161,219
Federal agencies	2,016,318	2,011,048
Total	2,176,725	2,176,115
By exchange		
Domestic	57,115	29,547
International, including foreign governments	481,808	461,816
Total	538,923	491,363
By gift from individual and unofficial sources	[1] 6,400,671	1,662,838
Total receipts	[1] 11,282,796	6,447,623

[1] Adjusted figure based on official count of *Look* collection.

OUTGOING PIECES [1]

	1972	1973
By exchange	1,310,988	1,218,503
By transfer	420,265	351,950
By donation to institutions	399,736	499,128
By pulping	2,638,737	2,580,664
Total outgoing pieces	4,769,726	4,650,245

[1] Duplicates, other materials not needed for the Library collections, and depository sets and exchange copies of U.S. government publications are included.

ACQUISITIONS ACTIVITIES, LAW LIBRARY

	1972	1973
Lists and offers scanned	3,070	3,522
Items searched	18,969	16,946
Recommendations made for acquisitions	1,741	2,114
Items disposed of	1,513,937	1,304,118

ACQUISITIONS ACTIVITIES, REFERENCE DEPARTMENT

	1972	1973
Lists and offers scanned	48,062	55,850
Items searched	113,297	124,347
Items recommended for acquisition	[1] 116,605	154,310
Items accessioned	1,917,389	2,237,861
Items disposed of	1,649,348	2,081,213

[1] Adjusted figure.

CATALOGING AND MAINTENANCE
OF CATALOGS

CATALOGING AND CLASSIFICATION

	1972	1973
Descriptive cataloging stage		
Titles cataloged for which cards are printed	249,983	240,250
Titles recataloged or revised	19,510	16,195
Authority cards established	119,496	100,339
Subject cataloging stage		
Titles classified and subject headed	247,816	243,587
Titles shelflisted, classified collections	215,329	219,531
Volumes shelflisted, classified collections	303,904	312,801
Titles recataloged	18,611	16,285
Subject headings established	11,693	11,424
Class numbers established	6,002	9,811
Decimal classification stage		
Titles classified	80,463	80,474
Titles completed for printing of catalog cards	243,753	253,260

RECORDS IN THE MARC DATA BASE

	Total records, June 30, 1972	Additions, 1973	Total records, June 30, 1973
Books	271,379	82,380	353,759
Films	1,853	9,447	11,300
Maps	16,161	5,398	21,559
Total	289,393	97,225	386,618

SERIALS PROCESSING

	1972	1973
Pieces processed	1,425,361	1,335,916
Volumes added to classified collections	27,679	30,598

GROWTH OF LIBRARY OF CONGRESS GENERAL CATALOGS

	Cards in catalogs, June 30, 1972	New cards added, 1973	Cards in catalogs, June 30, 1973
Main Catalog	16,748,984	737,652	17,486,636
Official Catalog	19,218,982	951,395	20,170,377
Annex Catalog	13,970,245		13,970,245
Catalog of Children's Books [1]	176,040	14,794	190,834
Far Eastern Languages Catalog	371,565	58,105	429,670
Music Catalog	2,730,738	45,505	2,776,243
National Union Catalog of Manuscript Collections	55,023	2,990	58,013
Law Library Catalog	1,578,498	68,573	1,647,071
Total	54,850,07	1,879,014	56,729,089

[1] Previously reported as two catalogs.

GROWTH OF THE UNION CATALOG

	1972	1973
CARDS RECEIVED (Pre-1956 imprints)		
Library of Congress cards		
Printed main entry cards	10,302	16,076
Corrected and revised reprints for main entry cards	6,021	3,837
Printed added entry cards	4,578	4,776
Corrected and revised added entry cards	2,827	2,122
Total	23,728	26,811
Cards contributed by other libraries	484,571	513,637
Total cards received	508,299	540,448
CARDS RECEIVED (Post-1955 imprints)		
Library of Congress cards		
Printed main entry cards	240,414	258,833
Corrected and revised reprints for main entry cards	14,593	15,163
Printed added entry cards	102,969	66,823
Corrected and revised added entry cards	7,184	11,892
Printed cross-reference cards	41,641	67,033
Revised cross-reference cards	587	10
Total	407,388	419,754
Cards contributed by other libraries	2,626,104	2,801,083
Total cards received	3,033,492	3,220,837
CARDS IN AUXILIARY CATALOGS		
Chinese Union Catalog	336,470	333,470
Hebraic Union Catalog	291,965	340,765
Japanese Union Catalog	135,060	135,060
Korean Union Catalog	40,734	43,730
Near East Union Catalog	74,740	83,048
Slavic Union Catalog	396,834	404,699
South Asian Union Catalog	41,200	41,200
Southeast Asian Union Catalog	17,644	21,531
National Union Catalog: Pre-1956 imprints, supplement	691,040	964,790
National Union Catalog: Post-1955 imprints	5,175,248	5,854,094
Total cards in auxiliary catalogs	7,200,935	8,222,387

VOLUMES IN THE CLASSIFIED COLLECTIONS [1]

		Added, 1972		Added, 1973		Total volumes, June 30, 1973
		Titles	Volumes	Titles	Volumes	
A	Polygraphy	1,927	4,556	2,142	4,758	297,798
B-BJ	Philosophy	5,960	7,537	5,006	6,281	149,048
BL-BX	Religion	7,476	8,353	9,844	11,964	374,542
C	History, auxiliary sciences	2,207	3,476	2,488	3,758	138,721
D	History (except American)	18,820	23,842	19,948	25,369	661,228
E	American history	3,675	4,994	2,176	3,778	178,953
F	American history	3,907	5,272	4,068	5,137	262,878
G	Geography-anthropology	6,113	8,462	5,741	7,718	204,509
H	Social sciences	27,614	42,030	34,223	52,584	1,537,227
J	Political science	6,101	11,157	6,062	10,303	558,571
K	Law	6,960	23,951	6,396	21,904	122,491
L	Education	8,473	10,683	6,735	9,736	327,030
M	Music	6,987	10,368	7,934	12,053	446,782
N	Fine arts	9,142	10,419	7,977	9,546	224,350
P	Language and literature	43,945	50,469	49,819	58,108	1,352,756
Q	Science	16,923	21,333	14,020	18,566	624,212
R	Medicine	5,350	6,695	5,243	6,470	250,208
S	Agriculture	5,881	7,673	5,426	7,407	261,542
T	Technology	21,090	29,433	16,952	23,424	739,781
U	Military science	1,094	1,741	1,017	1,953	124,719
V	Naval science	749	1,215	716	1,355	71,093
Z	Bibliography	4,640	9,799	5,459	10,428	358,809
	Incunabula	295	446	139	201	1,498
	Total	215,329	303,904	219,531	312,801	9,268,746

[1] Totals do not include, among others, part of the Law collections, part of the Orientalia collections, and materials given preliminary cataloging and a broad classification.

CARD DISTRIBUTION

TOTAL INCOME FROM SALES OF CARDS AND TECHNICAL PUBLICATIONS

Sales	1972	1973
General	$6,180,527.00	$6,795,930.80
To U.S. government libraries	346,198.32	379,527.39
To foreign libraries	365,297.39	486,340.22
Total gross sales before credits and adjustments	6,892,022.71	7,661,798.41

ANALYSIS OF TOTAL INCOME

	1972	1973
Card sales (gross)	3,653,582.81	3,875,134.48
Technical publications	238,914.48	277,870.43
Nearprint publications	2,595.67	1,663.50
National Union Catalog, including *Motion Pictures and Filmstrips, Music and Phonorecords,* and *National Register of Microform Masters*	2,047,533.50	2,319,670.00
National Union Catalog of Manuscript Collections	43,970.00	43,415.00
Library of Congress Catalog—Books: Subjects	462,635.00	630,090.00
New Serial Titles	367,181.25	393,795.00
MARC tapes	75,610.00	120,160.00
Total gross sales before credits and adjustments	6,892,022.71	7,661,798.41

ADJUSTMENTS OF TOTAL SALES	Credit returns	U.S. government discount	
Cards	$44,218.24	$17,542.45	
Publications	1,371.35	1,382.90	
Subscriptions			
National Union Catalog	19,555.00	9,107.73	
National Union Catalog of Manuscript Collections	125.00	123.65	
Library of Congress Catalog—Books: Subjects	3,400.00	3,399.09	
New Serial Titles	665.00	2,330.47	
MARC tapes		329.09	
Total	$69,334.59	$34,215.38	(103,549.97)
Total net sales			$7,558,248.44

CARDS DISTRIBUTED

	1972	1973
Cards sold	72,002,908	73,599,751
Cards distributed without charge		
Library of Congress catalogs	17,091,168	16,927,359
Card Division catalogs	2,629,046	2,424,837
Depository libraries	27,318,064	21,480,287
Other no-charge accounts	3,447,645	1,999,825
Total	50,485,923	42,832,308
Total cards distributed	122,488,831	116,432,059

CARD SALES, 1964 TO 1973

Fiscal year	Cards sold	Gross revenue	Net revenue
1964	52,505,637	$3,117,322.47	$3,076,082.56
1965	61,489,201	3,703,565.96	3,652,483.51
1966	63,214,294	4,008,540.64	3,936,075.92
1967	74,503,175	4,934,906.25	4,852,670.71
1968	78,767,377	5,168,440.64	5,091,944.04
1969	63,404,123	4,172,402.93	4,101,695.31
1970	64,551,799	4,733,291.73	4,606,472.22
1971	74,474,002	4,470,172.86	4,334,833.07
1972	72,002,908	3,653,582.81	3,596,965.03
1973	73,599,751	3,875,134.48	3,813,375.15

PRINTING AND REPRINTING OF CATALOG CARDS

	1972	1973
New titles printed:		
Regular series	184,789	189,833
Cross-references	33,445	54,772
Film series	7,983	8,341
Sound recording series	2,984	2,256
Far Eastern languages series	10,853	17,099
Talking-book series	932	979
Manuscript series	1,364	2,286
Total	242,350	275,566
Titles reprinted by letterpress	23,399	19,372
Titles reprinted by offset	337,740	340,980

PHOTODUPLICATION

	LC orders		All other orders [1]		Total	
	1972	1973	1972	1973	1972	1973
Photostat exposures	15,101	7,600	24,672	21,277	39,773	28,877
Electrostatic prints Catalog cards	235,954	182,046	5,462,883	7,163,339	5,698,837	7,345,385
Other material (Photo- duplication Service) .	54,176	24,146	1,189,542	742,825	1,243,718	766,971
Other material (other divisions)	6,038,512	5,772,682			6,038,512	5,772,682
Negative microfilm exposures Catalog cards	2,086,019	1,958,131	306,091	657,255	2,392,110	2,615,386
Other material	[2] 2,136,716	[2] 1,367,127	14,703,978	10,910,681	16,840,694	12,277,808
Positive microfilm (in feet) .	23,084	3,490	5,295,145	5,896,630	5,318,229	5,900,120
Enlargement prints from microfilm	976	2,235	12,982	9,580	13,958	11,815
Photographic negatives (copy, line, and view) . . .	2,763	1,839	12,144	8,751	14,907	10,590
Photographic contact prints	4,860	3,618	23,566	19,579	28,426	23,197
Photographic projection prints . . . :	214	738	11,227	12,413	11,441	13,151
Slides and transparencies (including color)	490	316	1,858	1,752	2,348	2,068
Black line and blueprints (in square feet)	3,316	16	23,162	12,819	26,478	12,835
Dry mounting and laminating	456	1,274	40	861	496	2,135

1 Library of Congress preservation orders are included in this category.
2 Includes exposures made in New Delhi, India: 306,184 in 1972, 483,100 in 1973.

Appendix 6

READER SERVICES [1]

	Bibliographies prepared	
	Number	Number of entries [3]
Reference Department		
Division for the Blind and Physically Handicapped [2]	12	954
General Reference and Bibliography Division	9	26,149
Geography and Map Division	8	6,123
Latin American, Portuguese, and Spanish Division	72	51,638
Loan Division		
Manuscript Division		
Music Division		26
Orientalia Division	13	2,621
Prints and Photographs Division	1	384
Rare Book Division	5	176
Science and Technology Division		
Serial Division	2	7,947
Slavic and Central European Division	1	2,800
Stack and Reader Division	20	32,080
Total	143	130,898
Law Library		
Law Library in the Capitol	95	1,833
Processing Department		
Grand total—1973	238	132,731
Comparative totals—1972	179	133,440
1971	204	77,665
1970	267	96,321
1969	379	90,028

[1] Not included here are statistics for the Congressional Research Service, which answered 181,064 inquiries for Members and committees of Congress in fiscal 1973.
[2] See appendix 7 for additional DBPH statistics.
[3] Includes entries for continuing bibliographies.

APPENDIX 6

Circulation of Volumes and other units		Direct reference services			
For use within the Library	Outside loans 4	In person	By correspondence	By telephone	Total
		521	8,695	1,024	10,240
		98,908	63,135	51,542	213,585
49,297	1,375	4,970	3,733	4,269	12,972
5,773	5,550	6,431	4,429	16,233	27,093
	243,114	11,912	58,114	86,630	156,656
90,954	3,698	12,652	2,701	10,703	26,056
57,289	1,652	18,284	7,648	29,252	55,184
54,362	5,172	23,232	1,757	28,580	53,569
168,240	8,312	26,097	7,408	17,392	50,897
37,719	63	8,411	944	10,392	19,747
46,461	49	12,364	8,176	6,836	27,376
279,395	14,285	38,422	2,067	19,728	60,217
41,794	804	17,975	1,832	22,489	42,296
1,015,059	2,702	59,583	17,478	19,344	96,405
1,846,343	243,114	339,762	188,117	324,414	852,293
369,204	5,473	109,114	3,032	44,807	156,953
21,000	10,229	3,417		7,623	11,040
		100	14,536	135,155	149,791
2,236,547	253,343	452,393	205,685	511,999	1,170,077
2,122,105	250,793	449,046	200,184	507,205	1,156,435
2,165,660	242,417	442,958	178,285	440,942	1,062,185
2,421,720	257,438	5 466,590	166,816	480,046	5 1,113,452
2,486,753	257,378	458,781	5 169,082	424,293	5 1,052,156

4 All loans except those made by the Law Library in the Capitol are made by the Loan Division; figures for other divisions (shown in italics) represent materials selected for loan.

5 Adjusted figure.

Appendix 7

SERVICES TO THE BLIND
AND PHYSICALLY HANDICAPPED

NATIONAL COLLECTIONS IN THE LIBRARY OF CONGRESS

	1972	1973
Circulation		
Talking-book containers	63,800	100,800
Tape containers	19,300	17,500
Braille Volumes	56,900	46,600
Large-type Volumes	16,500	33,800
Total	156,500	198,700
Readers		
Talking-book	3,130	3,970
Tape	2,810	3,440
Braille	4,460	4,780
Large-type	220	70

NATIONAL PROGRAM

	1972	1973
Purchase of sound reproducers	45,000	42,500
Acquisitions		
Books		
Recorded titles, including music	860	819
Press-braille titles, including music	289	274
Handcopied-braille titles	410	565
Tape titles produced by volunteers	586	531
Commercial recordings (containers)	599	1,341
Thermoform braille volumes	1,598	697
Magazines		
Talking book titles, including music	24	26
Tape titles, including music	12	10
Press-braille titles, including music	21	23
Music scores		
Press-braille volumes	1,520	376
Handcopied-braille volumes	311	217
Large-type volumes	906	400
Large-type volumes produced by volunteers	220	2,952
Certification of volunteers		
Literary braille transcribers	562	479
Braille proofreaders	7	7
Braille music transcribers	8	8
Tape readers	61	46
Circulation (all regional libraries) [1]		
Talking-book containers [2]	7,844,300	9,416,300
Tape containers [2]	578,500	726,100
Braille volumes [2]	706,300	684,500
Large-type volumes	134,200	185,700
Readers (all regional libraries) [1]		
Talking-book	270,860	317,420
Tape	32,810	46,540
Braille	18,320	18,910
Large-type	7,310	8,700

[1] Includes National Collections.
[2] Includes direct circulation magazines.

PRESERVATION AND RESTORATION

	1972	1973
IN ORIGINAL FORM		
Books		
Volumes bound or rebound (commercial binding)	205,640	216,219
Rare books bound, rebound, restored, reconditioned, or otherwise treated . . .	5,180	10,671
Total volumes	210,820	226,890
Nonbook materials		
Manuscripts preserved or restored (individual sheets)	20,166	3,451
Maps preserved, restored, or otherwise treated	42,806	28,545
Prints and photographs preserved or restored	11,391	9,166
Total nonbook items	74,363	41,162
IN OTHER FORMS		
Brittle books and serials converted to microfilm (exposures)	2,888,553	2,897,406
Newspapers and periodicals converted to microfilm (exposures)		
Retrospective materials	1,026,863	882,895
Current materials	1,204,682	1,198,788
Nitrate still-picture negatives converted to safety-base negatives	5,400	2,436
Nitrate motion pictures replaced by or converted to safety-base film (feet)	1,571,535	4,335,545
Sound recordings		
Deteriorating discs converted to magnetic tape	7,728	2,808
Deteriorating tapes converted to magnetic tape [1]	200	[1] 1,156
Deteriorating cylinders, wire recordings, etc., converted to magnetic tape . . .	182	45

[1] Includes tape replacements received in exchange for duplicate publications.

EMPLOYMENT

	1972	1973		
		Paid from appropriations to the Library	Other funds	Total
	Total			
Office of the Librarian, including Audit, American Revolution Bicentennial, Exhibits, Information, and Publications Offices	59	57	12	69
Administrative Department	794	657	173	830
Copyright Office	350	350		350
Law Library	78	82		82
Congressional Research Service . . . . . . ·.	479	596		596
Processing Department				
General services	1,013	943	116	1,059
Distribution of catalog cards	534	563		563
Special foreign currency program (P.L. 480)	10	8		8
Total, Processing Department [1]	1,557	1,514	116	1,630
Reference Department				
General services	726	580	138	718
Books for the blind and physically handicapped . .	92	100		100
Total, Reference Department	818	680	138	818
Total, all departments [1]	4,135	3,936	439	4,375

[1] Does not include local personnel hired for overseas programs.

Appendix 10

LEGISLATION

Public Law 92-342 made appropriations for the legislative branch for the fiscal year ending June 30, 1973.

This act provided funds for the Library of Congress as follows:
Salaries and expenses
Library of Congress $36,170,000
Copyright Office 5,041,000
Congressional Research Service 9,155,000
Distribution of catalog cards 10,275,000
Books for the blind and physically handicapped 8,892,000
Revision of Hinds' and Cannon's *Precedents* 120,000
Books for the general collections 1,118,650
Books for the Law Library 181,500
Collection and distribution of library materials (special foreign currency program)
for carrying out the provisions of section 104(b) (5) of the Agricultural Trade
Development and Assistance Act of 1954 (P.L. 83-480), as amended (7 U.S.C.
1704):

U.S. currency 276,000
U.S.-owned foreign currency 2,627,000
Furniture and furnishings 4,435,300

This act also provided funds for the Architect of the Capitol to expend for the Library of
Congress buildings and grounds as follows:
Structural and mechanical care 1,531,400

Public Law 92-463 authorized the establishment of a system governing the creation and operation of
advisory committees in the executive branch of the federal government. Section 13 provided for
the filing with the Library of Congress of at least eight copies of each report made by every
advisory committee and, where appropriate, background papers prepared by consultants. The
Librarian of Congress is to establish a depository for such reports and papers, where they will be
available for public inspection and use.

Public Law 92-566 extended until December 31, 1974, all copyrights now in their second term that
would expire before that date.

Public Law 92-607, making supplemental appropriations for fiscal 1973, included a supplemental
appropriation of $150,000 under salaries and expenses, Library of Congress, to implement the
provisions of the Equal Employment Opportunity Act of 1972. Also included in this act, for
increased telephone and postage costs, were the following:

Salaries and expenses
Library of Congress . . . . [1] $109,000
Copyright Office . . . . [1] 20,500
Distribution of catalog cards . . . . [1] 11,000
Books for the blind and physically handicapped . . . . [1] 13,500

Public Law 93-50 made supplemental appropriations for the fiscal year ending June 30, 1973. Included is a supplemental appropriation for increased pay costs to the Library of Congress as follows:

Salaries and expenses
Library of Congress . . . . [2] $752,000
Distribution of catalog cards [3] . . . .

---

[1] To be derived from the reserve fund under salaries and expenses, distribution of catalog cards.

[2] Of which $89,000 was to be derived by transfer from the appropriation for salaries and expenses, Copyright Office, fiscal year 1973.

[3] $61,000 to be derived by transfer from the appropriation for salaries and expenses, Copyright Office, fiscal year 1973; in addition, the act authorized the use of $46,000 of the reserve fund of $200,000 under this head, fiscal year 1973, for increased pay costs.

Appendix 11

FINANCIAL STATISTICS

SUMMARY

	Unobligated balance from previous year	Appropriations or receipts, 1973
APPROPRIATED FUNDS		
Salaries and expenses, Library of Congress		$37,181,000.00
Salaries and expenses, Copyright Office		4,911,500.00
Salaries and expenses, revision of *Constitution Annotated* . . .	$50,302.44	
Salaries and expenses, Congressional Research Service		9,155,000.00
Salaries and expenses, distribution of catalog cards		10,193,000.00
Books for the general collections	31,754.12	1,118,650.00
Books for the Law Library	3,299.93	181,500.00
Books for the blind and physically handicapped		8,905,500.00
Collection and distribution of library materials, special foreign currency program	1,380,834.88	2,903,000.00
Indexing and microfilming the Russian Orthodox Greek Catholic Church records in Alaska	1,343.97	
Furniture and furnishings		4,435,300.00
Salaries and expenses, revision of Hinds' and Cannon's *Precedents*		120,000.00
Total annual appropriations	1,467,535.34	79,104,450.00
TRANSFERS FROM OTHER GOVERNMENT AGENCIES		
Consolidated working funds		
No-year	575,489.97	534,566.00
1973		2,395,298.00
1973-74		74,000.00
Total transfers from other government agencies	575,489.97	3,003,864.00
GIFT AND TRUST FUNDS [1]	2,809,478.65	4,820,395.32
Total, all funds	4,852,503.96	86,928,709.32

[1] The principal of $5,268,841.50 in the permanent loan and investment accounts consists of the following: $20,000 in the Gertrude M. Hubbard account, and a balance in the permanent loan account from the previous year of $5,248,466.50 to which $375.00 was added in 1973, making a total of $5,248,841.50. In addition, there are

Total available for obligation, 1973	Obligated, 1973	Unobligated balance not available	Unobligated balance forwarded to 1974
$37,181,000.00	$36,989,892.58	$191,107.42	
4,911,500.00	4,780,079.38	131,420.62	
50,302.44	45,330.48		$ 4,971.96
9,155,000.00	9,127,255.13	27,744.87	
10,193,000.00	10,188,212.16	4,787.84	
1,150,404.12	1,127,016.02		23,388.10
184,799.93	181,500.14		3,299.79
8,905,500.00	8,873,586.20	31,913.80	
4,283,834.88	2,296,139.23		1,987,695.65
1,343.97	244.88		1,099.09
4,435,300.00	562,865.26	5,931.51	3,866,503.23
120,000.00	85,936.32	34,063.68	
80,571,985.34	74,258,057.78	426,969.74	5,886,957.82
1,110,055.97	516,446.57		593,609.40
2,395,298.00	2,386,324.79	8,973.21	
74,000.00	10,015.00		63,985.00
3,579,353.97	2,912,786.36	8,973.21	657,594.40
7,629,873.97	4,634,422.05		2,995,451.92
91,781,213.28	81,805,266.19	435,942.95	9,540,004.14

investments valued at approximately $1,255,000 held by the Bank of New York under a provision made by the late Archer M. Huntington, from which the Library receives one-half of the income.

GIFT AND

Fund and donor	Purpose
Bequest of Gertrude M. Hubbard	Purchase of prints
Library of Congress Trust Fund, permanent loan account	
Babine, Alexis V., bequest	Purchase of Slavic material
Benjamin, William Evarts	Chair of American history, with surplus available for purchase and maintenance of materials for the historical collections of the Library
Bowker, R. R.	Bibliographical services
Carnegie Corporation of New York	Promotion and encouragement of an interest in and an understanding of fine arts in the United States
Coolidge (Elizabeth Sprague) Foundation, established by donation and bequest of Elizabeth Sprague Coolidge	Furtherance of musical research, composition, performance, and appreciation
Elson (Louis C.) Memorial Fund, established under bequest of Bertha L. Elson	Provision of one or more annual, free public lectures on music or its literature
	Encouragement of public interest in music or its literature
Feinberg (Lenore B. and Charles E.) Fund	Purchase of books, manuscripts, and other materials by and about Walt Whitman and other American writers
Friends of Music in the Library of Congress, established by the association	Enrichment of music collection
Guggenheim (Daniel) Fund for the Promotion of Aeronautics, Inc.	Chair of aeronautics
Hanks, Nymphus C., bequest	Furtherance of work for the blind, particularly the provision of books for the Library of Congress to make available to the blind
Huntington, Archer M. Donation	Purchase of Hispanic material
Donation	Consultant in Spanish and Portuguese literature
Bequest	Equipment and maintenance of the Hispanic Society Room and maintenance of a chair of English-language poetry
Koussevitzky (Serge) Music Foundation in the Library of Congress, established by the Koussevitzky Music Foundation, Inc.	Furtherance of the art of music composition

TRUST FUNDS

Cash in permanent loan [1]	Unobligated balance from previous year	Income or receipts, 1973	Total available for obligation	Obligated, 1973	Unobligated balance forwarded to 1974
[2] $20,000.00	$975.94	$800.00	$1,775.94	$1,068.91	$707.03
6,684.74	2,181.33	267.39	2,448.72	744.00	1,704.72
83,083.31	3,922.34	3,323.34	7,245.68	5,592.84	1,652.84
14,843.15	131.17	593.72	724.89		724.89
93,307.98	10,084.80	3,732.32	13,817.12	2,949.47	10,867.65
804,444.26	10,309.57	32,177.78	42,487.35	20,266.61	22,220.74
6,000.00	2,818.36	240.00	3,058.36		3,058.36
6,585.03	284.07	263.40	547.47	(44.00)	591.47
1,000.00	95.91	40.00	135.91		135.91
10,359.09	594.33	409.78	1,004.11	50.00	954.11
90,654.22	37,986.04	3,626.16	41,612.20		41,612.20
5,227.31	1,078.20	209.10	1,287.30		1,287.30
112,305.74	163.33	4,492.22	4,655.55	1,131.53	3,524.02
49,746.52	1,416.36	1,989.86	3,406.22	2,960.01	446.21
98,525.40	2,479.63	3,941.02	6,420.65	3,828.99	2,591.66
208,099.41	6,465.49	8,323.98	14,789.47	4,836.77	9,952.70

Fund and donor	Purpose
Library of Congress Trust Fund, permanent loan account—Continued	
Longworth (Nicholas) Foundation in the Library of Congress, established by the friends of the late Nicholas Longworth	Furtherance of music
Miller, Dayton C., bequest	Benefit of the Dayton C. Miller Collection of Flutes
National Library for the Blind, established by the National Library for the Blind, Inc.	Provision of reading matter for the blind and the employment of blind persons to provide library services for the blind
Pennell, Joseph, bequest	Purchase of materials in the fine arts for the Pennell Collection
Porter (Henry Kirke) Memorial Fund, established by Annie-May Hegeman	Maintenance of a consultantship or other appropriate purpose
Roberts Fund, established under bequest of Margaret A. Roberts	Benefit of the Library of Congress, its collections and services
Scala (Norman P.) Memorial Fund, established under bequest of Norman P. Scala	Arrangement, editing, and publication of materials in the Scala bequest
Sonneck Memorial Fund, established by the Beethoven Association	Aid and advancement of musical research
Stern (Alfred Whital) Memorial Fund, established by the family of the late Alfred Whital Stern	Maintenance of and addition to the Alfred Whital Stern Collection of Lincolniana, including the publication of guides and reproductions of parts of the collection
Whittall (Gertrude Clarke) Poetry and Literature Fund	Development of appreciation and understanding of good literature and poetry in this country, and for the presentation of literature in general
Whittall (Gertrude Clarke) Foundation, established by Gertrude Clarke Whittall	Maintenance of collection of Stradivari instruments and Tourte bows given by Mrs. Whittall, and presentation of programs in which those instruments are used
Wilbur, James B.	
Donation	Reproduction of manuscript sources on American history in European archives
Bequest	Establishment of a chair of geography
Bequest	Preservation of source materials for American history
Total, permanent loan account	

Cash in permanent loan [1]	Unobligated balance from previous year	Income or receipts, 1973	Total available for obligation	Obligated, 1973	Unobligated balance forwarded to 1974
$10,691.59	$690.22	$427.66	$1,117.88		$1,117.88
20,548.18	2,547.56	821.92	3,369.48	$128.01	3,241.47
36,015.00	1,252.22	1,440.60	2,692.82	1,890.11	802.71
303,250.46	3,104.43	12,130.02	15,234.45	15,232.42	2.03
290,500.00	54,252.07	11,620.00	65,872.07	22,396.67	43,475.40
62,703.75	38,241.63	2,508.16	40,749.79	13,383.49	27,366.30
92,228.85	14,204.93	3,689.15	17,894.08	8,123.11	9,770.97
12,088.13	8,014.34	483.52	8,497.86	15.32	8,482.54
27,548.58	108.41	1,101.94	1,210.35	800.00	410.35
957,977.79	37,531.43	38,319.10	75,850.53	47,091.71	28,758.82
1,538,609.44	12,477.17	61,544.38	74,021.55	47,892.08	26,129.47
192,671.36	30,326.71	7,706.86	38,033.57	11,842.88	26,190.69
81,856.92	51.66	3,274.28	3,325.94	1,507.33	1,818.61
31,285.29	2,179.37	1,251.42	3,430.79	2,924.84	505.95
5,248,841.50	284,993.08	209,949.08	494,942.16	215,544.19	279,397.97

Fund and donor	Purpose
Library of Congress Trust Fund, investment account	
Huntington, Archer M. [3]	Equipment and maintenance of the Hispanic Society Room, and maintenance of a chair of English-language poetry
McKim Fund, established under bequest of Mrs. W. Duncan McKim [4]	Support of the composition and performance of chamber music for violin and piano and of related activities
Sonneck Memorial Fund, established by the Beethoven Association	Aid and advancement of musical research
Total, investment account	
Library of Congress Gift Fund	
Ackerman, Carl W., estate of	Publication of a catalog of the Carl Ackerman Collection
American Association for the Advancement of Slavic Studies	Toward preparation of a bibliography of Slavic and East European studies
American Council of Learned Societies	Publication of a bibliographic guide to Yugoslavia
	Furtherance of a program for the acquisition of publications from Europe
American Film Institute	Support of the National Film Collection program
American Historical Association	Support of the conference on Latin American history
American Library Association	Editing the *National Union Catalog*
Archives of the American Psychological Association (Manuscript)	Furtherance of manuscript work
Bollingen Foundation, Inc.	Extension of the recording program and strengthening of the Library's Poetry Archive
Cafritz (Morris and Gwendolyn) Foundation	Symposia and related publications on the American Revolution
	Toward preparation of a directory of picture sources in the Washington, D.C., area
Canadian Defence Research Board	Toward preparation of the bibliography of aviation medicine

Cash in permanent loan 1	Unobligated balance from previous year	Income or receipts, 1973	Total available for obligation	Obligated, 1973	Unobligated balance forwarded to 1974
$32,865.86	$25,307.95	$58,173.81	$34,845.03	$23,328.78
82,453.25	34,645.32	117,098.57	23,157.94	93,940.63
	84.68		84.68	84.68	
115,403.79	59,953.27	175,357.06	58,087.65	117,269.41
	1,733.15		1,733.15	1,218.00	515.15
		6,500.00	6,500.00	4,873.11	1,626.89
	500.00		500.00		500.00
	3,200.00	500.00	3,700.00	1,416.33	2,283.67
	68,590.58	140,000.00	208,590.58	172,533.14	36,057.44
	1,325.42		1,325.42		1,325.42
	455.42	860,000.00	860,455.42	833,207.02	27,248.40
	1,231.49		1,231.49		1,231.49
	103.87		103.87	103.87	
	41,695.57		41,695.57	22,707.72	18,987.85
		9,186.00	9,186.00	0.20	9,185.80
	57.27		57.27	57.27	

Fund and donor	Purpose
Library of Congress Gift Fund–Continued	
Coolidge, Elizabeth Sprague	Furtherance of musical research, composition, performance, and appreciation
Council on Library Resources, Inc.	Continuation of the National Union Catalog of Manuscript Collections
	Distribution of cataloging information in machine-readable form
	Support of a feasibility study on conversion of the Library's cataloging records to machine-readable form
	Support of the Retrospective Conversion Pilot Project
	Purchase of equipment for the preservation research laboratory
Documents Expediting Project, Various contributors	Distribution of documents to participating libraries
Edwards (J. W.) Publishers, Inc.	Editing and preparation costs in connection with the publication of *Library of Congress Catalog–Books: Subjects*, 1965-69
	Editing and preparation costs in connection with the publication of *National Union Catalog*, 1968-72
Farnum, Henry M.	For disbursement by the Librarian of Congress
Federal Library Committee, various donors	Expenses of the committee
	Toward expenses of the Executive Workshop in Library Management and Information Services
Feinberg (Lenore B. and Charles E.) Fund	Purchase of books, manuscripts, and other materials by and about Walt Whitman and other American writers
Fellows of the Library of Congress, Various donors	Purchase of rare materials in American history
Finlandia Foundation, Inc.	Purchase of noncurrent materials in the Finnish field
Ford Foundation	Support of a revised and enlarged edition of Edmund C. Burnett's *Letters of Members of the Continental Congress*
Foreign Program, Various contributors	Support of the program for the purchase of material in foreign countries under Public Law 480 Fiscal year 1962 Fiscal year 1972 Fiscal year 1973

Cash in permanent loan [1]	Unobligated balance from previous year	Income or receipts, 1973	Total available for obligation	Obligated, 1973	Unobligated balance forwarded to 1974
$600.00			$600.00	$600.00	
264.84			264.84	264.75	$0.09
755.21			755.21		755.21
260.00			260.00		260.00
8,029.04			8,029.04	4,000.00	4,029.04
3,036.85			3,036.85	1,414.25	1,622.60
32,555.86	$36,821.91		69,377.77	45,580.31	23,797.46
16,997.23			16,997.23	16,997.23	
589,383.59	593,500.00		1,182,883.59	349,104.61	833,778.98
25.00			25.00		25.00
346.64	599.11		945.75	855.75	90.00
464.37	350.00		814.37	509.00	305.37
417.69	10,000.00		10,417.69	10,379.76	37.93
	24,046.28		24,046.28		24,046.28
299.25			299.25		299.25
22,813.36	37,500.00		60,313.36	51,917.96	8,395.40
4,363.18			4,363.18		4,363.18
42,950.00			42,950.00	42,950.00	
	50,700.00		50,700.00		50,700.00

Fund and donor	Purpose
Library of Congress Gift Fund–Continued	
Foreign Program, Various contributors–Continued	Support of the program for cataloging material purchased under Public Law 480 in Egypt India/Pakistan Indonesia Israel
	Support of the program for the purchase of material in Bangladesh under Public Law 480
	Support of the program for purchase of material in Indonesia under the terms of the Higher Education Act of 1965 as amended in 1968
	Acquisition of publications from Sri Lanka
Forest Press, Inc.	Toward the cost of a 4-year project to edit the 18th edition of the *Dewey Decimal Classification*
	Toward the cost of a 5-year project to edit the 19th edition of the *Dewey Decimal Classification*
Friends of Music, Various donors	Furtherance of music
George Washington University	Furtherance of the Library of Congress–George Washington University joint graduate program in American thought and culture
Gish (Lillian) Foundation	Furtherance of the Library's programs
Gulbenkian Foundation	Acquisition of Armenian books and periodicals published before 1967
Hall (G. K.) & Co.	Editing and preparation costs in connection with the publication of *Africa South of the Sahara; Index to Periodical Literature*
	Publication of a Far Eastern languages catalog
	Publication of a bibliography of cartography
Heineman Foundation	Purchase of Library material of special interest to the Music Division
Home State Production Company of Tulsa, Oklahoma	Acquisition of materials for the collections of the Library of Congress

Cash in permanent loan [1]	Unobligated balance from previous year	Income or receipts, 1973	Total available for obligation	Obligated, 1973	Unobligated balance forwarded to 1974
$47,279.19			$47,279.19	$30,000.00	$17,279.19
69,169.20			69,169.20	53,804.23	15,364.97
46,141.30			46,141.30	25,000.15	21,141.15
72,447.83			72,447.83	22,254.92	50,192.91
6,133.50		$20,700.00	26,833.50	4,934.40	21,899.10
15,567.03		107,000.00	122,567.03	120,539.68	2,027.35
		3,500.00	3,500.00		3,500.00
13,763.18		5 (12,119.10)	1,644.08	1,644.08	
		103,271.67	103,271.67	67,607.97	35,663.70
51.00			51.00		51.00
2,760.48		1,200.00	3,960.48	111.60	3,848.88
1,000.00		5,000.00	6,000.00		6,000.00
4,674.13			4,674.13	1,137.79	3,536.34
234.29			234.29		234.29
3,660.10			3,660.10		3,660.10
3,344.09		5,900.00	9,244.09	9,227.06	17.03
		5,000.00	5,000.00	4,012.02	987.98
345.60		631.96	977.56	977.56	

Fund and donor	Purpose
Library of Congress Gift Fund–Continued	
Jospey (Maxwell and Anne) Foundation	Furtherance of experimental work for the blind and physically handicapped
Knight, John	Furtherance of the Library's program for the blind
Library Resources, Inc.	For the use of the Librarian of Congress
Lindberg Foundation	Purchase of maps
Loeffler, Elise Fay, bequest	Purchase of music
Louchheim, Katie S.	Processing her papers in the Manuscript Division
Louchheim (Katie and Walter) Fund	Distribution of tape recordings of concerts to broadcasting stations
Louisiana Colonial Records Project, various contributors	To microfilm Louisiana colonial documents
Luce, Clare Boothe	Furtherance of the work of organizing her personal papers in the Library of Congress
Luce, Henry R.	Furtherance of the work of organizing the Clare Boothe Luce papers in the Library of Congress
Mearns, David Chambers	Purchase of manuscripts
Mellon, Paul	Purchase of a collection of Sigmund Freud letters
Modern Language Association of America	Editing the Journal of Henry David Thoreau
Moore, Ann Leslie	To facilitate the use of the Merrill Moore papers
National Carl Schurz Association, Inc.	Production costs of a bibliography of West German English-language titles in the social sciences
National Serials Data Program, Various donors	Toward expenses of the program
Naval Historical Foundation	Processing the Naval Historical Foundation collections deposited in the Library of Congress
	Publication of a catalog of the Naval Historical Foundation manuscript collection
Newberry Library, The	Purchase of maps
News and Observer Foundation	Organizing the Josephus Daniels papers

Cash in permanent loan [1]	Unobligated balance from previous year	Income or receipts, 1973	Total available for obligation	Obligated, 1973	Unobligated balance forwarded to 1974
$200.00			$200.00		$200.00
8,720.86			8,720.86	($288.31)	9,009.17
10.00		$3,910.00	3,920.00	3,920.00	
336.51			336.51		336.51
191.84		13.30	205.14		205.14
		1,200.00	1,200.00		1,200.00
27.00		[6] 2,554.77	2,581.77	2,581.77	
2,907.34		2,000.00	4,907.34		4,907.34
4,447.05			4,447.05		4,447.05
4,047.66			4,047.66		4,047.66
1,913.90		76.00	1,989.90		1,989.90
		90,000.00	90,000.00	90,000.00	
		2,650.00	2,650.00		2,650.00
1,262.48			1,262.48	984.96	277.52
962.57			962.57	(1,798.00)	2,760.57
		20,075.00	20,075.00	20,000.00	75.00
		5,140.00	5,140.00	183.20	4,956.80
		4,358.58	4,358.58		4,358.58
		200.00	200.00		200.00
		8,000.00	8,000.00	94.60	7,905.40

Fund and donor	Purpose
Library of Congress Gift Fund—Continued	
Oberlaender Trust	Foreign consultant program in Germany and other German-speaking countries
Program for the blind, various donors	Furtherance of the Library's program for the blind
Publications, various donors	Toward expenses of publications
Rizzuto, Angelo A., estate of	Arrangement, publication, and preservation of the photographs of New York known as the Anthony Angel Collection
Rockefeller Brothers Fund, Inc.	Organizing, indexing, and microfilming the Nelson W. Aldrich papers
Rosenwald (Lessing J.) Fund	Purchase of books to be added to the Rosenwald Collection
Seeing Eye, Inc., The	Purchase of 600 copies of a talking-book edition of *First Lady of the Seeing Eye*
Sobiloff, Hyman J.	Various poetry projects
Sonneck, Oscar G., bequest	Purchase of an original music manuscript or manuscripts
Surplus Book Disposal Project, various donors	Toward expenses of the project
Wilkins, Emily Howell, estate of	Purchase of antique stringed musical instruments
Zeta Phi Eta Foundation	Support of tape recordings for the blind and physically handicapped (in memory of Mrs. Louise Mead)
Total, Library of Congress Gift Fund	
Revolving fund service fees	
Cafritz Publication Fund	
Clapp (Verner W.) Publication Fund	
Council on Library Resources, Inc.	Facilitating the sale of machine-readable cataloging records and information
Engelhard (Jane) Fund	Production of facsimiles and other publications illustrative of the holdings and activities of the Library
Frissell (Toni) Fund	Maintenance of the Toni Frissell collection of photographs in the Library of Congress

Cash in permanent loan [1]	Unobligated balance from previous year	Income or receipts, 1973	Total available for obligation	Obligated, 1973	Unobligated balance forwarded to 1974
	$3.41		$3.41		$3.41
	302.96	$746.00	1,048.96	$175.77	873.19
	1,591.85		1,591.85		1,591.85
	40,961.24		40,961.24	5,829.64	35,131.60
	3,475.76		3,475.76	1,399.00	2,076.76
	13,817.33		13,817.33	4,593.64	9,223.69
	755.10		755.10		755.10
	557.83		557.83	557.83	
	4,156.91		4,156.91		4,156.91
	869.08	14,435.07	15,304.15	12,399.79	2,904.36
	5,000.00		5,000.00		5,000.00
	250.00		250.00		250.00
	1,225,794.48	2,165,146.55	3,390,941.03	2,042,575.63	1,348,365.40
		4,153.38	4,153.38		4,153.38
	17,599.23	5,403.72	23,002.95	12,444.50	10,558.45
	10,479.08		10,479.08		10,479.08
	10,150.00		10,150.00		10,150.00
	1,279.50	195.68	1,475.18	151.86	1,323.32

Fund and donor	Purpose
Revolving fund service fees–Continued	
Hispanic Foundation Publication Fund	
Kraus (Hans P.) Publication Fund	
Photoduplication Service	
Recording Laboratory, Music Division	
Sale of miscellaneous publications	
Traveling Exhibits Fund	
Various donors	Conversion of motion picture film to a safety base
Total service fees	
Total, all gift and trust funds	

1 Authorized under Public Law 541, 68th Congress, March 3, 1925, as amended, "An Act to create a Library of Congress Trust Fund Board and for other purposes."

2 Bequest of Gertrude M. Hubbard in the amount of $20,000 accepted by an act of Congress (Public Law 276, 62d Congress, approved August 20, 1912) and deposited with the U.S. Treasury, from which the Library of Congress receives an annual income of $800.

3 Investments held by the Bank of New York valued at approximately $1,255,000; half of the income accrues to the Library of Congress.

Cash in permanent loan 1	Unobligated balance from previous year	Income or receipts, 1973	Total available for obligation	Obligated, 1973	Unobligated balance forwarded to 1974
$6,001.51			$6,001.51	$1,565.54	$4,435.97
	1,000.00		1,000.00		1,000.00
	1,077,890.44	$2,191,689.12	3,269,579.56	2,152,329.65	1,117,249.91
	27,113.82	147,986.39	175,100.21	119,439.71	55,660.50
	18,594.40	15,280.10	33,874.50	15,316.10	18,558.40
	1,221.99	7,171.25	8,393.24	2,635.20	5,758.04
	10,981.39	12,666.78	23,648.17	13,263.11	10,385.06
	1,182,311.36	2,384,546.42	3,566,857.78	2,317,145.67	1,249,712.11
7 5,268,841.50	2,809,478.65	4,820,395.32	7,629,873.97	4,634,422.05	2,995,451.92

4 Bequest of Mrs. W. Duncan McKim, principally in the form of securities, valued at approximately $873,000, held by the American Security and Trust Company for the Trust Fund Board. All the income accrues to the Library of Congress. Income invested in short-term securities is valued at approximately $5,000.

5 Receipt of previous year, inadvertently shown for 18th edition, transferred to 19th edition.

6 Does not include securities, valued at approximately $30,000, held by the American Security and Trust Company for the Trust Fund Board. All of the income accrues to the Library of Congress.

7 Includes the principal of the Hubbard Account.

Appendix 12

EXHIBITS

RECENT MAJOR PHOTOGRAPHIC ACQUISI-
TIONS. A selection of early and recent examples
of the art of photography. October 18, 1972, to
March 18, 1973.

JAMES MADISON MEMORIAL BUILDING
EXHIBIT. Site plans, photographs, a model, and
architectural renderings of the Library's third
building, now under construction. Opened
December 14, 1972.

PHOTOGRAPHS BY ALFRED CHENEY
JOHNSTON. Portraits of Ziegfeld girls and leading personalities of the theater and cinema, made
between 1918 and 1939. Opened January 10,
1973.

TREASURES FROM THE LESSING J. ROSEN-
WALD COLLECTION. Eighty-two volumes illustrating the variety and scope of Mr. Rosenwald's
gifts to the Library, displayed on the occasion of
his 82d birthday. Opened February 11, 1973.

WHITE HOUSE NEWS PHOTOGRAPHERS
ASSOCIATION 30TH ANNUAL EXHIBIT.
Prizewinning photographs of 1972. Opened April
2, 1973.

CONTINUING MAJOR EXHIBITS

TREASURES OF EARLY PRINTING.

TRAVEL: THEN AND NOW. Closed August 31,
1972.

WHITE HOUSE NEWS PHOTOGRAPHERS
ASSOCIATION 29TH ANNUAL EXHIBIT.
Closed September 7, 1972.

140

SESQUICENTENNIAL OF MISSOURI'S
STATEHOOD. Closed December 31, 1972.

THE WIDE WORLD OF CHILDREN'S BOOKS.
Closed January 18, 1973.

PERMANENT EXHIBITS

THE GUTENBERG BIBLE AND THE GIANT
BIBLE OF MAINZ.

THE GETTYSBURG ADDRESS. First and second drafts.

THE DRAFT OF THE DECLARATION OF
INDEPENDENCE written by Thomas Jefferson,
with changes by Benjamin Franklin and John
Adams.

THE BILL OF RIGHTS. One of the original en-
grossed and certified copies.

THE VIRGINIA BILL OF RIGHTS. Autograph
draft by George Mason and Thomas Ludwell Lee.

THE MAGNA CARTA. Facsimile of the Lacock
Abbey version.

MANUSCRIPTS AND OTHER MATERIALS
associated with George Washington, Thomas Jefferson, Abraham Lincoln, Theodore Roosevelt,
and Woodrow Wilson.

LETTER OF JANUARY 26, 1863, from Abraham Lincoln to Maj. Gen. Joseph Hooker.

SHOWCASE EXHIBITS

CENTENNIAL OF THE BIRTH OF CALVIN
COOLIDGE (1872-1933). Photographs, political

cartoons, and other items relating to the career of the 30th President. July 3 to September 29, 1972.

THE HORSE IN MOTION: THE 100TH ANNIVERSARY OF EADWEARD MUYBRIDGE'S ACTION PHOTOGRAPHY. Books, photographic plates, and cardboard discs for Muybridge's Zoöpraxiscope. October 10, 1972, to February 5, 1973.

THE 200TH ANNIVERSARY OF THE BIRTH OF WILLIAM HENRY HARRISON (1773-1841). Selected items from the Harrison papers in the Manuscript Division, with additional materials from the Rare Book, Prints and Photographs, and Music Divisions. February 9 to May 31, 1973.

THREE HUNDREDTH ANNIVERSARY OF THE DISCOVERY OF THE MISSISSIPPI RIVER BY MARQUETTE AND JOLIET. Maps, prints, and journals relating to the French exploration of the Mississippi Valley in 1673. Opened June 1, 1973.

SPECIAL EXHIBITS

THE LIBRARY OF CONGRESS: 75 YEARS IN BLACK AND WHITE. A photographic display to mark the 75th anniversary of the Library's Main Building. Cosponsored by the Library of Congress Welfare and Recreation Association and the Library of Congress Professional Association. September 11 to 30, 1972.

TENTH ANNIVERSARY OF THE CHILDREN'S BOOK SECTION. A selection of works prepared by the section. March 5 and 6, 1973. .

DIVISIONAL EXHIBITS

Geography and Map Division

THE WORLD OF MAPS. Closed July 31, 1972.

U.S. NATIONAL PARKS: 1872-1972. Maps illustrating the development of national parks since the establishment of the National Park Service. September 5 to October 31, 1972.

Latin American, Portuguese, and Spanish Division

LUIZ DE CAMOES AND *THE LUSIADS*. Closed August 31, 1972.

150TH ANNIVERSARY OF BRAZILIAN INDEPENDENCE. Commentary, documentation, and illustrations relating to Brazil's achievement of independence on September 7, 1822. September 8 to December 31, 1972.

PUBLICATIONS OF THE LATIN AMERICAN, PORTUGUESE, AND SPANISH DIVISION. Opened February 5, 1973.

Law Library

THE LAW LIBRARY: 140 YEARS OF SERVICE AND GROWTH. An exhibit marking the anniversary of legislation enacted on July 14, 1832, establishing the Law Library as a separate department of the Library of Congress. Photographs, selected publications, and other items relating to the history of the Law Library. July 14 to September 29, 1972.

SCANDALS: AMERICAN AND ENGLISH. Publications concerning court trials involving, among others, Henry Ward Beecher, Caroline of Brunswick, and Evelyn Nesbit. October 2, 1972, to January 2, 1973.

THE PEOPLE'S REPUBLIC OF CHINA AND INTERNATIONAL LAW. Chinese-language materials highlighting critical points in the development of international law in China, with emphasis on the post-1949 period. January 3 to March 30, 1973.

LAW AND LEGAL MATERIAL IN THE NEAR EAST. Facsimiles of the law codes of Lipit-Ishtar and Hammurabi; Assyrian, neo-Babylonian, and Hittite legal documents; the Talmud and Old Testament; and a 17th-century manuscript copy of the Koran. Opened April 2, 1973.

Manuscript Division

MAHLON LOOMIS. Drawings, scientific notes, and letters of the pioneer in wireless telegraphy, commemorating the centenary of his July 1872 patent for an "improvement in telegraphing." Included patents, photographs, and several pieces of his electrical apparatus on loan from the Smithsonian Institution. July 1 to 31, 1972.

DIAMOND JUBILEE OF THE MANUSCRIPT DIVISION. Selected treasures from the Toner and Force collections, presidential papers, the Lincoln collection, and the papers of other eminent Americans. August 1 to December 30, 1972.

MATTHEW FONTAINE MAURY, "PATH-FINDER OF THE SEAS" (1806-1873). Manuscripts and correspondence of the first superintendent of the U.S. Naval Observatory, whose work on winds and sea currents revolutionized ocean transportation and aided in the laying of the first telegraph cable across the Atlantic. January 2 to March 31, 1973.

THE HARLEM RENAISSANCE. Correspondence, literary manuscripts, and photographs of Langston Hughes, Countee Cullen, and other writers associated with the Harlem Renaissance period in the 1920's. April 2 to June 30, 1973.

Music Division

THE MUSIC DIVISION: HIGHLIGHTS OF 75 YEARS. Closed March 31, 1973.

100TH ANNIVERSARY OF THE BIRTH OF SERGEI RACHMANINOFF, 1873-1943. Photographs, manuscripts, letters, and other memorabilia of the Russian composer. Opened April 1, 1973.

Prints and Photographs Division

RECENT ACQUISITIONS IN THE PRINTS AND PHOTOGRAPHS DIVISION. Closed July 31, 1972.

MEMORIAL TRIBUTE TO LUCIAN BERN-HARD. Fifteen posters, chiefly from the World War I period, illustrating Bernhard's excellence in the fields of typography and the graphic arts. August 1 to September 1, 1972.

THE RACE FOR THE WHITE HOUSE. Presidential campaign banners, songs, and political cartoons portraying candidates as participants in sporting events. September 5 to December 31, 1972.

WENCESLAUS HOLLAR. A group of 17th-century engravings, including maps, topographical views, costume pieces, and studies of plants, animals, ships, and buildings, by a native of Prague who spent much of his life in England. January 2 to April 1, 1973.

THE AMERICA OF CURRIER AND IVES. A selection of the most popular American prints of the 19th century. Opened April 2, 1973.

Rare Book Division

RECENT ACQUISITIONS IN THE RARE BOOK DIVISION. Closed December 20, 1972.

NINETEENTH-CENTURY AMERICAN LITERARY CLASSICS. First-edition copies of works by Poe, Melville, and others, many from the collections of Justice Oliver Wendell Holmes. Opened May 1, 1973.

Science and Technology Division

ACUPUNCTURE. Closed August 31, 1972.

AMERICAN ASSOCIATION FOR THE ADVANCEMENT OF SCIENCE EXHIBIT. Works in the Library's collections by present AAAS officers, special award winners, and invited convention speakers. December 22, 1972, to January 5, 1973.

500TH ANNIVERSARY OF THE BIRTH OF NICOLAUS COPERNICUS. Rare books, maps, globes, and pictorial materials relating to the life and theories of the founder of modern astronomy. December 22, 1972, to March 31, 1973.

MANNED UNDERSEA RESEARCH STATIONS. A variety of materials on underwater stations and submersibles, including books, journals, reports, and models. January 5 to April 30, 1973.

Serial Division

THE DECLARATION OF INDEPENDENCE IN THE DOMESTIC AND FOREIGN PRESS. Original Baltimore, Philadelphia, and London newspapers containing the text of the Declaration. Opened June 1, 1973.

Slavic and Central European Division

JAN AMOS KOMENSKÝ (COMENIUS): WORKS IN THE LIBRARY OF CONGRESS. A selection of studies by and about the 17th-century Moravian reform educator, philosopher, and religious leader. September 1 to December 31, 1972.

150TH ANNIVERSARY OF THE BIRTH OF ALEXANDRE PETÖFI. Books, manuscripts, and photographs covering the life and career of the 19th-century Hungarian poet and political leader. Opened May 1, 1973.

SPECIAL EXHIBITS OUTSIDE THE LIBRARY OF CONGRESS

Exhibits were presented by the Library of Congress in connection with the following professional meetings:

Society of American Archivists, Columbus, Ohio, October 31 to November 3, 1972.

American Library Association, Washington, D.C., January 28 to February 3, 1973.

American Library Association, Las Vegas, Nev., June 24 to 28, 1973.

TRAVELING EXHIBITS

Prepared and circulated by the Library of Congress

PRESERVATION THROUGH DOCUMENTATION: HISTORIC AMERICAN BUILDINGS SURVEY. Shown in Orono, Maine, Norton, Mass., Northfield, Minn., Boseman, Mont., Raleigh, N.C., and Alberta, Canada.

PAPERMAKING: ART & CRAFT. Shown in Pine Bluff, Ark., Lincoln, Nebr., Tuxedo Park, N.Y., Charleston, S.C., Georgetown, S.C., Manitowoc, Wis., and Milwaukee, Wis.

22D NATIONAL EXHIBITION OF PRINTS. Shown in Gainesville, Fla., Kalamazoo, Mich., Billings, Mont., Lincoln, Nebr., Oklahoma City, Okla., Allentown, Pa., and Chattanooga, Tenn.

CONTEMPORARY PHOTOGRAPHS FROM SWEDEN. Shown in Moscow, Idaho, Mankato, Minn., Billings, Mont., Charleston, S.C., and Manitowoc, Wis.

BORN OF THE HOPS. Shown in Little Rock, Ark., San Bernardino, Calif., Pensacola, Fla., Charleston, S.C., Manitowoc, Wis., and Milwaukee, Wis.

THE PERFORMING ARTS IN 19TH-CENTURY AMERICA. Shown in Hartford, Conn., Elmira, N.Y., Charlotte, N.C., Williamsburg, Va., and Manitowoc, Wis.

Prepared by the Library of Congress and circulated by the Smithsonian Institution Traveling Exhibition Service:

CONTEMPORARY AFRICAN PRINTMAKERS. Shown in Stamford, Conn., South Bend, Ind., Boston, Mass., Worcester, Mass., and Wilberforce, Ohio.

Prepared by the Library of Congress and circulated by the International Exhibitions Foundation:

HAIR: A PICTORIAL TRIBUTE. Shown in Tempe, Ariz., Davenport, Iowa, Baton Rouge, La., Cambridge, Mass., Elmira, N.Y., Abilene, Tex., and Beloit, Wis.

Prepared by others and incorporating materials lent by the Library of Congress:

CLARENCE H. WHITE. Circulated by the Museum of Modern Art and shown in Worcester, Mass., Cleveland, Ohio, and Richmond, Va.

JUST BEFORE THE WAR. Circulated by the Smithsonian Institution Traveling Exhibition Service and shown in San Bernardino, Calif., Decatur, Ill., Grayslake, Ill., Columbia, Mo., Jamestown, N.Y., and Troy, N.Y.

THE ART OF THE COMIC STRIP. Circulated by the Smithsonian Institution Traveling Exhibition Service and shown in San Francisco, Calif., Fort Wayne, Ind., Bloomfield Hills, Mich., Kansas City, Mo., Hempstead, N.Y., Austin, Tex., and Toronto, Canada.

THE DÜSSELDORF ACADEMY AND THE AMERICANS. Circulated by the High Museum of Art, Atlanta, Ga., and shown in Washington, D.C., and Utica, N.Y.

Appendix 13

CONCERTS, LECTURES, AND
OTHER PROGRAMS

CONCERTS

The Elizabeth Sprague Coolidge Foundation

1972

OCTOBER 30. The Deller Consort.

NOVEMBER 17. The New York Chamber Soloists.

DECEMBER 1. The Yuval Trio.

1973

JANUARY 5. Musical Arts Studio.

FEBRUARY 16. New York Pro Musica.

MARCH 23. The Contemporary Chamber Ensemble.

MAY 11. The Academy Trio.

The Gertrude Clarke Whittall Foundation

1972

OCTOBER 12, 13. The Juilliard String Quartet.

OCTOBER 19, 20. The Juilliard String Quartet.

OCTOBER 26, 27. The Juilliard String Quartet.

NOVEMBER 2, 3. The Juilliard String Quartet and Richard Goode, piano.

NOVEMBER 10. Quartetto di Roma.

NOVEMBER 24. The New York Woodwind Quintet.

DECEMBER 18, 19. The Juilliard String Quartet and John Graham, viola.

1973

JANUARY 26. The Beaux Arts Trio of New York.

FEBRUARY 23. Angelicum Orchestra of Milan.

FEBRUARY 26. The French String Trio.

MARCH 16. Lynn Harrell, violoncello, and Richard Goode, piano.

MARCH 29, 30. The Juilliard String Quartet.

APRIL 5, 6. The Juilliard String Quartet and Claude Frank, piano.

APRIL 12, 13. The Juilliard String Quartet and Beveridge Webster, piano.

APRIL 19, 20. The Juilliard String Quartet.

APRIL 26, 27. The Juilliard String Quartet.

The McKim Fund in the Library of Congress

1972

DECEMBER 8. Charles Treger, violin, and Samuel Sanders, piano.

1973

JANUARY 12. Earl Carlyss, violin, and Ann Schein, piano.

145

146

REPORT OF THE LIBRARIAN OF CONGRESS, 1973

FEBRUARY 9. Jaime Laredo, violin, and Ruth Laredo, piano.

MARCH 2. Joseph Fuchs, violin, and Joseph Villa, piano.

MARCH 9. Szymon Goldberg, violin, and Artur Balsam, piano.

MAY 4. Raphael Druian, violin, and Ilse von Alpenheim, piano.

POETRY READINGS, LECTURES, AND DRAMATIC PERFORMANCES

Sponsored by the Library of Congress

1972

OCTOBER 2. Josephine Jacobsen, 1971-73 Consultant in Poetry in English, poetry reading.

1973

MAY 7. Josephine Jacobsen, "The Instant of Knowing," lecture.

Sponsored by the Gertrude Clarke Whittall Poetry and Literature Fund

1972

OCTOBER 16. X. J. Kennedy and Anne Sexton, poetry reading and discussion; Josephine Jacobsen, moderator.

NOVEMBER 13. Arnold Moss, "John Donne: 'A World in Himself,' " honoring the 400th anniversary of Donne's birth; assisted by Annette Hunt, soprano, with Russell Woollen at the piano.

NOVEMBER 20. Samuel Allen (Paul Vesey) and Ned O'Gorman, poetry reading and discussion; Josephine Jacobsen, moderator.

NOVEMBER 27. Ian Hamilton, lecture on recent poetry in Great Britain.

1973

MARCH 5. Erik Haugaard, lecture on Hans Christian Andersen, in observance of the 10th anniversary of the Children's Book Section.

MARCH 26. Lucille Clifton and Owen Dodson, poetry reading and discussion; Josephine Jacobsen, moderator. Mr. Dodson was assisted by David Bryant, who chanted and danced in accompaniment to Mr. Dodson's reading.

APRIL 16. Donald Justice and Carolyn Kizer, poetry reading and discussion; Josephine Jacobsen, moderator.

Sponsored by the Norman P. Scala Memorial Fund

1972

OCTOBER 6. Frederick Fennell, "American Band Music 100 Years Ago," lecture, with illustrative examples played on contemporary instruments by a group of some 20 musicians.

CONFERENCE

Sponsored by the Gertrude Clarke Whittall Poetry and Literature Fund

1973

JANUARY 29, 30. Conference on Teaching Creative Writing.

"A Perspective of Academic Programs in Creative Writing," chairman, Elliott Coleman; panelists: John Ciardi, Paul Engle, George Garrett, Theodore Morrison, and Wallace Stegner. "The Writing of Poetry," chairman, Paul Engle; panelists: Michael Dennis Browne, John Ciardi, Elliott

Coleman, Josephine Jacobsen, Anthony McNeill, N. Scott Momaday, and Miller Williams.

Evening readings, Margaret Walker, Miller Williams, William J. Lederer, and John Barth.

"The Writing of Fiction," chairman, Wallace Stegner; panelists: John Barth, Ralph Ellison, Ernest J. Gaines, George Garrett, Robie Macau-

ley, and Margaret Walker. "The Writing of Nonfiction Prose," chairman, John Ciardi; panelists: William J. Lederer, Ralph Ellison, Josephine Jacobsen, N. Scott Momaday, Louis D. Rubin, Jr., and Wallace Stegner.

Evening readings, Anthony McNeill, N. Scott Momaday, Michael Dennis Browne, and Ernest J. Gaines.

Appendix 14

LIBRARY OF CONGRESS
PUBLICATIONS [1]

ACCESSIONS LISTS. Subscriptions available to libraries from the Field Director, Library of Congress Office, at the addresses indicated.

BANGLADESH. American Embassy, New Delhi, India. 1 issue.

CEYLON. American Embassy, New Delhi, India. 3 issues, including cumulative list of serials and annual author and subject indexes. Title changed to *Accessions List: Sri Lanka* in February 1973.

EASTERN AFRICA. P.O. Box 30598, Nairobi, Kenya. 4 issues, including annual serial supplement.

INDIA. American Embassy, New Delhi, India. 11 issues and annual list of serials.

INDONESIA, MALAYSIA, SINGAPORE, AND BRUNEI. American Embassy, APO San Francisco 96356. 11 issues, including annual author index.

ISRAEL. American Embassy, Tel Aviv, Israel. 15 issues, including supplement of serial titles deleted through June 1970 and annual index and list of serials. Publication ceased with April 1973 issue.

MIDDLE EAST. United States of America Interests Section, Spanish Embassy, Cairo, Egypt. 11 issues, including annual list of serials and annual index to monographic titles.

NEPAL. American Embassy, New Delhi, India. 3 issues, including cumulative list of serials and annual author and subject indexes.

PAKISTAN. American Consulate General, Karachi, Pakistan. 15 issues, including cumulative lists of serials for 1971 and 1972 and quinquennial index, 1967-71.

SRI LANKA. American Embassy, New Delhi, India. 1 issue. Formerly *Accessions List: Ceylon.*

ANGELO RIZZUTO'S NEW YORK: "IN LITTLE OLD NEW YORK, BY ANTHONY ANGEL." 1972. [55 p.] Paper. Free to libraries, patriotic and charitable organizations, and other such tax-exempt institutions from the Central Services Division.

ANNUAL REPORT OF THE LIBRARIAN OF CONGRESS FOR THE FISCAL YEAR ENDING JUNE 30, 1972. 1973. 147 p. Cloth. $3.85. Free to libraries from the Central Services Division.

ANNUAL REPORT OF THE REGISTER OF COPYRIGHTS FOR THE FISCAL YEAR END-

[1] This is a list of publications issued during the fiscal year. For a full list of publications see *Library of Congress Publications in Print March 1973.* Unless otherwise indicated, priced publications are for sale by the Superintendent of Documents, U.S. Government Printing Office, Washington, D.C. 20402. When Card Division is specified as the distributor, orders should be addressed: Card Division, Library of Congress, Building 159, Navy Yard Annex, Washington, D.C. 20541. Other requests should be addressed to the division or office listed, Library of Congress, Washington, D.C. 20540.

Payment must accompany all orders for priced publications. For foreign mailing of publications available from the Superintendent of Documents, one-fourth of the publication price should be added unless otherwise stated. Card Division and Information Office publication prices include the cost of foreign and domestic mailing.

148

ING JUNE 30, 1972. 1973. 26 p. Paper. Free from the Copyright Office.

ANTARCTIC BIBLIOGRAPHY. Edited by Geza T. Thuronyi. Vol. 5. 1972. 499 p. Cloth. $5.75.

ARMS CONTROL & DISARMAMENT; A QUARTERLY BIBLIOGRAPHY WITH ABSTRACTS AND ANNOTATIONS. Paper. $1 a copy for summer 1972 and fall 1972 issues; $1.75 a copy for winter 1973 and spring 1973 issues. Ceased publication with Spring 1973 issue.

BOOKS: A MARC FORMAT. 5th ed. 1972. Addenda 2-7. Free from the Card Division.

CALENDAR OF EVENTS IN THE LIBRARY OF CONGRESS. Paper. Free from the Central Services Division. 12 issues.

CATALOG OF COPYRIGHT ENTRIES. THIRD SERIES. Paper. Complete yearly catalog, $50 domestic, $62.50 foreign.

Part 1. BOOKS AND PAMPHLETS, INCLUDING SERIALS AND CONTRIBUTIONS TO PERIODICALS. Section 1, Current and Renewal Registrations. Section 2, Title Index. $15 a year. Vols. 24 and 25.

Part 2. PERIODICALS. $5 a year. Vols. 24 and 25.

Parts 3-4. DRAMAS AND WORKS PREPARED FOR ORAL DELIVERY. $5 a year. Vol. 25, no. 2, and vol. 26.

Part 5. MUSIC. Section 1, Current and Renewal Registrations. Section 2, Name Index. $15 a year. Vol. 25 and vol. 26, no. 1.

Part 6. MAPS AND ATLASES. $5 a year. Vol. 25, no. 2, and vol. 26.

Parts 7-11A. WORKS OF ART, REPRODUCTIONS OF WORKS OF ART, SCIENTIFIC AND TECHNICAL DRAWINGS, PHOTOGRAPHIC WORKS, PRINTS AND PICTO-

RIAL ILLUSTRATIONS. $5 a year. Vol. 25, no. 2, and vol. 26.

Part 11B. COMMERCIAL PRINTS AND LABELS. $5 a year. Vols. 25 and 26.

Parts 12-13. MOTION PICTURES AND FILMSTRIPS. $5 a year. Vol. 25, no. 2, and vol. 26.

CATALOGING SERVICE. Bulletin. Paper. Free to subscribers to the Card Distribution Service. No. 105.

CHILDREN'S BOOKS 1972; A LIST OF BOOKS FOR PRESCHOOL THROUGH JUNIOR HIGH SCHOOL AGE. Compiled by Virginia Haviland and Lois B. Watt. 1973. 16 p. Paper. 25 cents.

CHILDREN'S LITERATURE: A GUIDE TO REFERENCE SOURCES. FIRST SUPPLEMENT. Compiled by Virginia Haviland with the assistance of Margaret N. Coughlan. 1972. 316 p. Cloth. $3.

CLASSIFICATION [schedules].
   Class Q. SCIENCE. 6th ed. 1973. 415 p. Paper. Card Division, $9.

CREATING INDEPENDENCE, 1763-1789. 1972. 62 p. Paper. 75 cents.

THE DEVELOPMENT OF A REVOLUTIONARY MENTALITY. Papers presented at the first Library of Congress Symposium on the American Revolution. 1972. 157 p. Cloth. $3.50.

DEWEY DECIMAL CLASSIFICATION: ADDITIONS, NOTES, AND DECISIONS. Vol. 3, no. 2. September 1972. Free from the Decimal Classification Division.

DIGEST OF PUBLIC GENERAL BILLS AND RESOLUTIONS. Paper. Single copy prices vary. $50 a session, $62.50 foreign.
   92d Congress, 2d session. 3 cumulative issues, 5 supplements, and final issue.
   93d Congress, 1st session. First issue, 1 cumulative issue, 4 supplements.

150

A DIRECTORY OF INFORMATION RE-SOURCES IN THE UNITED STATES: BIOLOGICAL SCIENCES. Compiled by the National Referral Center, Science and Technology Division. 1972. 577 p. Paper. $5.

FILMS: A MARC FORMAT. 1970. Addenda 1-3. Free from the Card Division.

FOREIGN NEWSPAPER REPORT. Free to libraries and institutions from the Central Services Division. 1 issue.

FRENCH-SPEAKING CENTRAL AFRICA; A GUIDE TO OFFICIAL PUBLICATIONS IN AMERICAN LIBRARIES. 1973. 314 p. Paper. $3.25 GPO Bookstore, $3.70 domestic postpaid.

THE GUTENBERG BIBLE: FIRST PAGE OF GENESIS FROM THE LIBRARY OF CONGRESS COPY. Facsimile No. 2a. 1972. Single leaf with folder. Information Office, $1.75.

HANDBOOK OF LATIN AMERICAN STUDIES. NO. 34, HUMANITIES. 1973. Edited by Donald E. J. Stewart. 683 p. Cloth. For sale by the University of Florida Press, 15 West 15th Street, Gainesville, Fla. 32603. $25.

INDEX TO THE WILLIAM HOWARD TAFT PAPERS. Vols. 1-6. 1972. Paper. $24.

INFORMATION FOR READERS IN THE LIBRARY OF CONGRESS. 1972. 12 p. Paper. Free from the Central Services Division.

INFORMATION ON THE MARC SYSTEM. 3d ed. 1973. 44 p. Paper. Free from the Central Services Division.

LC CLASSIFICATION–ADDITIONS AND CHANGES. Paper. Card Division, $20 a year. Lists 166-169.

LC SCIENCE TRACER BULLET. Paper. Free from the Reference Section, Science and Technology Division. TB 72-5 through TB 73-10.

LIBRARY OF CONGRESS CATALOG– BOOKS: SUBJECTS. A cumulative list of works represented by Library of Congress printed cards. Paper. Card Division, $470 a year. 3 quarterly issues and annual cumulation.

LIBRARY OF CONGRESS CATALOG– MOTION PICTURES AND FILMSTRIPS. A cumulative list of works represented by Library of Congress printed cards. Paper. Card Division, $25 a year. Free to subscribers to the National Union Catalog. 2 quarterly issues.

LIBRARY OF CONGRESS CATALOG–MUSIC AND PHONORECORDS. A cumulative list of works represented by Library of Congress printed cards. Paper. Card Division, $20 a year. Free to subscribers to the National Union Catalog. 1 semiannual issue.

LIBRARY OF CONGRESS INFORMATION BULLETIN. Paper. Card Division, $5 a year. Free to publicly supported libraries from the Information Office. 52 issues.

LIBRARY OF CONGRESS PUBLICATIONS IN PRINT. March 1973. 41 p. Paper. Free from the Central Services Division.

LIBROS PARLANTES; TALKING BOOKS. Compiled by the Division for the Blind and Physically Handicapped. 1972. 10 p. Paper. Free from the Division for the Blind and Physically Handicapped.

MANUSCRIPTS: A MARC FORMAT. Specifications for magnetic tapes containing catalog records for single manuscripts or manuscript collections. 1973. 47 p. Paper. 80 cents.

MAPS: A MARC FORMAT. 1970. Addenda 1-2. Free from the Card Division.

MARC USER SURVEY. 1972. 58 p. Paper. Free from the Central Services Division.

MONTHLY CHECKLIST OF STATE PUBLICATIONS. Paper. $6.50 a year domestic, $8.25 foreign. 12 issues and index.

THE MUSIC DIVISION: A GUIDE TO ITS COLLECTIONS AND SERVICES. 1972. 22 p. Paper. 45 cents.

MUSIC OF MOROCCO. Edited by Paul Bowles. Recording Laboratory AFS L63-L64, 4 s., 12″ phonorecords, 33-1/3 rpm microgroove. With 9-page descriptive pamphlet. Music Division. $7.95.

NATIONAL REGISTER OF MICROFORM MASTERS, 1971. 1972. 1,076 p. Paper. Card Division, $25. Free to subscribers to the *National Union Catalog.*

NATIONAL UNION CATALOG. A cumulative author list representing Library of Congress printed cards and titles reported by other American libraries. Compiled by the Library of Congress with the cooperation of the Resources Committee of the Resources and Technical Services Division, American Library Association. In addition to all issues of the *National Union Catalog,* subscribers receive at no extra charge the separately issued *Motion Pictures and Filmstrips* and *Music and Phonorecords* catalogs, the *National Union Catalog–Register of Additional Locations,* and the *National Register of Microform Masters.* Card Division, $730 a year. Annual issue, 1971, cloth; 9 monthly issues and 3 quarterly cumulations, paper.

NATIONAL UNION CATALOG OF MANUSCRIPT COLLECTIONS, 1971, AND INDEX, 1970-1971. Compiled from reports provided by American repositories. 1973. 722 p. Cloth. Card Division, $50.

NATIONAL UNION CATALOG: REFERENCE AND RELATED SERVICES. Compiled by John W. Kimball, Jr. 1973. 33 p. Paper. Free from the Union Catalog Reference Unit.

NEW BRAILLE MUSICIAN. Supplement (in print). Summer 1972. 61 p. Paper. Free from the Division for the Blind and Physically Handicapped.

NEW SERIAL TITLES. A union list of serials commencing publication after December 31, 1949. Supplement to the *Union List of Serials,* 3d edition. Card Division, $160 a year. Annual cumulation, 8 monthly issues, and 3 quarterly cumulations.

NEW SERIAL TITLES–CLASSED SUBJECT ARRANGEMENT. Paper. Card Division, $25 a year. 12 issues.

NON-GPO IMPRINTS RECEIVED IN THE LIBRARY OF CONGRESS IN 1971; A SELECTIVE CHECKLIST. Compiled by the Exchange and Gift Division. 1972. 27 p. Paper. Card Division, $1.25.

ORDER DIVISION AUTOMATED SYSTEM. 1972. 74 p. Paper. Free from the Central Services Division.

THE PEOPLE'S REPUBLIC OF CHINA AND INTERNATIONAL LAW: A SELECTIVE BIBLIOGRAPHY OF CHINESE SOURCES. Compiled by Paul Ho. 1973. 45 p. Paper. Free from the Far Eastern Law Division, Law Library.

QUARTERLY JOURNAL OF THE LIBRARY OF CONGRESS. Published as a supplement to the *Annual Report of the Librarian of Congress.* Paper. $1.25 a copy. $4.50 a year, $5.25 foreign. 4 issues.

QUESTIONS TO AN ARTIST WHO IS ALSO AN AUTHOR. A conversation between Maurice Sendak and Virginia Haviland. 1972. 18 p. Paper. 30 cents.

RECON.PILOT PROJECT. Final report on a project sponsored by the Library of Congress, the Council on Library Resources, Inc., and the U.S. Department of Health, Education, and Welfare, Office of Education. 1972. 49 p. Cloth. $1.50.

REGISTERS OF PAPERS IN THE LIBRARY OF CONGRESS. Free from the Manuscript Division.

MERRILL MOORE. 1972. 99 p. Paper.

THE NATIONAL ASSOCIATION FOR THE ADVANCEMENT OF COLORED PEOPLE, 1909-1939. 1972. 99 p. Paper.

OWEN WISTER. 1972. 32 p. Paper.

SUBJECT HEADINGS USED IN THE DICTIONARY CATALOGS OF THE LIBRARY OF

CONGRESS. Supplement to the 7th edition. Paper. Card Division, $15 a year. 3 issues.

TWO LECTURES: LEFTOVERS AND FROM ANNE TO MARIANNE. Lectures delivered at the Library of Congress on May 3, 1971, by William Stafford and on May 1, 1972, by Josephine Jacobsen. 1973. 31 p. Paper. 35 cents.

THE WIDE WORLD OF CHILDREN'S BOOKS. Compiled by Virginia Haviland. 1972. 84 p. Paper. 50 cents.

INDEX

153

INDEX

162

INDEX

CPSIA information can be obtained
at www.ICGtesting.com
Printed in the USA
BVHW04*1103170918
527708BV00014B/1575/P

9 780260 053497